Texas
ORGANIC
VEGETABLE
GARDENING

LONE STAR BOOKS

Lanham • New York • Oxford

Texas

ORGANIC VEGETABLE GARDENING

THE TOTAL GUIDE TO GROWING VEGETABLES, FRUITS, HERBS, AND OTHER EDIBLE PLANTS THE NATURAL WAY

J. HOWARD GARRETT

C. MALCOLM BECK

Texas ORGANIC VEGETABLE GARDENING

PUBLISHED BY LONE STAR BOOKS
An Imprint of the Rowman & Littlefield Publishing Group
450l Forbes Boulevard – Suite 200
Lanham, MD 20706
Distributed by National Book Network

Library of Congress Cataloging-in-Publication Data

Garrett, Howard, 1947–
  Texas organic vegetable gardening: the total guide to growing
  vegetables, fruits, herbs, and other edible plants the natural way/
  J. Howard Garrett and C. Malcolm Beck.
     p.   cm.
  Includes index.
  ISBN 0-88415-855-1 (alk. paper)
  1. Vegetable Gardening—Texas. 2. Fruit–culture—Texas. 3. Herb
gardening—Texas. 4. Organic gardening—Texas. I. Beck, Malcolm,
1936– . II. Title.
SB324.3.G385 1998
635′.0484—dc21
                                           98-36701
                                              CIP

Printed in the United States of America

Photos provided by Howard Garrett and Malcolm Beck.

Cover and book design by Roxann L. Combs.

Photos, unless otherwise noted, provided by the authors.

Text entered into the computer for editing and typesetting by Tracy Fields, because Howard and Malcolm cannot type.

Seed for photos provided by Marshall Grain and Garden-Ville.

To my *Dallas Morning News* column readers and my WBAP radio listeners. A very large group of friends who have not only been supportive and responsible for my success, you have been my research staff (the largest in the world) and have provided much valuable gardening information. The tips, arguments, debates, recommendations, and anecdotes have been interesting, helpful, and productive. We don't have a university, at this writing, to give us research data, advice, and recommendations. Why not? Well, because university researchers don't yet believe in organic gardening. Malcolm and I do, and my research staff does, and together we have discovered the most productive and cost-effective program on earth for managing the land and growing ornamental and food crops.

J. Howard Garrett

I probably would never have persisted in becoming an organic grower if it wasn't for the many people who told me I was foolish, a nut, old-fashioned, and that organic gardening wouldn't work on a large acreage. Some called my wife and business partner Dell and me hippies, and some even called me a quack. The more I heard from the critics, the more the determination grew to study every aspect of nature to learn and grow, by nature's own methods, the biggest and best.

To them I dedicate my share of this book. From them I got the energy and never-ending quest for more truth and knowledge of nature.

C. Malcolm Beck

CONTENTS

CHAPTER 3

When to Plant in Texas, 21

CHAPTER 4

Improving the Soil the Natural Way, 28

CHAPTER 5

Controlling Pests the Natural Way, 40

CHAPTER 6

Texas Vegetables and Other Food Crops, 61

APPENDIX, 203

INDEX, 215

PREFACE

Some of the information in this book comes from the Texas A&M Extension Service, research stations, and specific people within the system. Surprised? Yes, the data they provide on planting the dates, dates from planting to emergence, soil temperature requirements, and a fair amount of the recommended varieties information come from extension service people and their publications. What gardeners should ignore is their usual advice on soil preparation, fertilizers, and pest control because they still recommend artificial fertilizers and synthetic toxic pesticides. We feel very strongly that these products pollute the environment, don't work, and are unnecessary.

Our love/hate relationship with A&M and other universities is gradually moving toward "like" because their thinking is moving in our direction. On the other hand, some individuals and specific research locations within the system have gone all-the-way organic. The research station at Stephenville is one example. Dr. Joe McFarland and staff have gone organic in their peanut-growing research and are the source of the cornmeal fungi treatment recommendations. Dr. Joe Novack at A&M University is teaching organic vegetable growing with the blessing of his boss, Dr. Sam Cotner. Dr. Novack has always been organic in his home garden. Dr. Nancy Roe at Tarleton State College also teaches organic growing. Dr. Jerry Parsons and Dr. Calvin Finch, both with the extension service at San Antonio, give organic advice and recommendations. And there are other A&M PhDs and teachers who no longer criticize organic growing but even promote and look for organic answers to problems. On the other hand, there are still many who do not have a clue.

All universities are talking more and more about the importance of organic matter, biological controls, and the use of beneficial insects and low-impact pesticides. It's a start. The problem for A&M or any other land-grant university is that research has to be funded by someone. Unfortunately, the organic contractors, manufacturers, and distributors don't have a lot of extra money lying around to spend on research. But that's all changing. Hopefully this book will help move that change along.

Understanding organic gardening helps more people understand how to achieve good health. Many studies have documented the anticancer properties of vegetables, whole grains, fruits, and nuts. Their benefits for a healthy heart and for prevention of many other degenerative illnesses is also well-documented. Broccoli, cauliflower, garlic, cabbage, kale, radishes, turnips, carrots, and green onions have well-documented health benefits. Vegetables and fruits high in beta-carotene that have shown strong effects against lung and other cancers include carrots, spinach, broccoli, kale, squash, and apricots. Foods high in vitamin C that help reduce the risk of stomach, esophageal cancers, and heart disease include tomatoes, broccoli, and brussels sprouts. The vegetables known as crucifers, such as broccoli, cabbage, cauliflower, turnips, and brussels sprouts, have been shown to reduce the risk of cancer. Fiber from beans, broccoli, brussels sprouts, and whole grains helps protect against colon cancer. Selenium and vitamin E, found in whole grains, are also anticancer agents. Studies have also shown that organically grown fruits are much higher in food value than conventionally grown produce. Because of more available minerals in healthy soil, organically grown foods have more minerals, thus more sugar. That's right: Taste and food value go hand in hand.

The goal of this book is to serve as a tool to help convert the world to organics. The result of that conversion will be productive soil and nutritious and delicious vegetables, herbs, and fruit. The result of that will be healthy animals and healthy people with sound bodies and stable minds.

THE BASIC ORGANIC PROGRAM

Organic gardening is much more than merely a method of growing tomatoes and other food crops. It's a way of life. It's about paying attention to nature. It's about understanding how everything in nature is related. It's about working within nature's perfectly designed system. Here are the basics.

BASIC ORGANIC PROGRAM

ORGANIC APPROACH	ORGANIPHOBIC APPROACH
❧ Lawn height higher and cut less often.	❧ Lawn height low and cut often.
❧ Grass clippings left on the ground.	❧ Grass clippings caught and removed.
❧ Low-analysis fertilizer 2–3 times per year.	❧ High-analysis fertilizer 4–7 times per year.
❧ Low-nitrogen natural organic fertilizers.	❧ High-nitrogen artificial fertilizers— no organic matter.
❧ Fertilizer based on soil needs.	❧ Fertilizer based on plant needs.
❧ Fertilizers loaded with trace minerals.	❧ Fertilizers with few or no trace minerals.
❧ Works within nature's laws and systems.	❧ Attempts to control nature.
❧ Treats soil and actual problems—the reasons for the pests.	❧ Treats symptoms (insects, diseases, and leaf color).
❧ Improves soil and plants for natural pest resistance.	❧ Uses toxic synthetic pesticides.
❧ Only preventative used is food-grade repellants and soil improvement.	❧ Uses the sprays as preventatives.
❧ Uses beneficial insects as a major tool.	❧ Discourages the use of beneficial insects.
❧ Uses teas, homemade mixtures and labeled products.	❧ Uses only EPA labeled products.

Testing the soil. Have soil tested to determine available levels of organic matter, nitrogen, sulfur, phosphorus, calcium, magnesium, potassium, sodium, chloride, boron, iron, manganese, copper and zinc. A Texas lab that offers organic recommendations is Texas Plant and Soil Lab in Edinburg, 956-383-0739. They also offer tissue sample tests which may be even more helpful.

Planting. Prepare new planting beds by scraping away existing grass and weeds, adding a 4- to 6-inch layer of compost and lava sand at 40–80 pounds, organic fertilizer at 20 pounds and sugar at 5

pounds per 1,000 square feet and tilling to a depth of 3 inches into the native soil. Excavation and additional ingredients such as concrete sand, topsoil and pine bark are unnecessary and can even cause problems. More compost is needed for shrubs and flowers than for ground cover. Add Texas greensand to black and white soils and high calcium lime to acid soils.

Fertilizing. Apply an organic fertilizer two to three times per year. During the growing season, spray turf, trees and shrub foliage, trunks, limbs, and soil monthly with compost tea, molasses, natural apple cider vinegar, and seaweed mix (Garrett Juice). Add lava sand annually at 40–80 pounds per 1,000 square feet.

Mulching. Mulch all shrubs, trees and ground cover with 1–3 inches of compost, shredded tree trimmings or shredded hardwood bark to protect the soil, inhibit weed germination, decrease watering needs and mediate soil temperature. Mulch vegetable gardens with 8 inches of alfalfa hay, rough textured compost, or shredded native tree trimmings. Avoid Bermuda hay, unless you are sure of no broadleaf herbicides.

Watering. Adjust schedule seasonally to allow for deep, infrequent watering in order to maintain an even moisture level. Start by applying about 1 inch of water per week in the summer and adjust from there. Water needs will vary from site to site.

Mowing. Mow weekly, leaving the clippings on the lawn to return nutrients and organic matter to the soil. General mowing height should be 2½ inches or taller. Put occasional excess clippings in compost pile. Do not bag clippings. Do not let clippings leave the site. Do not use line trimmers around trees. Mulching mowers are best if the budget allows.

Weeding. Hand-pull large weeds and work on soil health for overall control. Mulch all bare soil in beds. Avoid synthetic herbicides, especially preemergents, broadleaf treatments and soil sterilants. These are unnecessary toxic pollutants. Spray broadleaf weeds with full strength vinegar, molasses, and citrus mix or remove mechanically.

Pruning. Remove dead, diseased and conflicting limbs. Do not over prune. Do not make flush cuts. Leave the branch collars intact. Do not paint cuts except on oaks in oak-wilt areas when spring pruning can't be avoided.

Making Compost. Compost is nature's own living fertilizer that can be made at home or purchased ready-to-use. A compost pile can be started any time of the year and can be in sun or shade. Good ingredients include leaves, clean hay, grass clippings, tree trimmings, food scraps, bark, sawdust, rice hulls, weeds, nut hulls, and animal manure. Mix the ingredients together in a container of wood, hay bales, hog wire, concrete blocks or simply pile the material on the ground. The best mixture is 80 percent vegetative matter and 20 percent animal waste, although any mix will compost. Since oxygen is a critical component, the ingredients should be a mix of coarse and fine-textured material to promote air circulation through the pile. Turn the pile once a month if possible, more often speeds up the process but releases nitrogen to the air. Another critical component is water. A compost pile should have roughly the moisture of a squeezed-out sponge to help the living microorganisms thrive and work their magic. Compost is ready to use as a soil amendment when the ingredients are no longer identifiable. The color will be dark brown, the texture soft and crumbly, and it will smell like the forest floor. Rough, unfinished compost can be used as a topdressing mulch around all plantings.

Manure Compost Tea. Manure compost tea is effective on many pests because of certain naturally occurring microorganisms. Use any container, but a plastic bucket is easy for the homeowner. Fill the bucket or barrel half full of compost and finish filling with water. Let the mix sit for 10–14 days, then dilute and spray on the foliage of any and all plants including fruit trees, perennials, annuals, vegetables, roses, and other plants that are regularly attacked by insect and disease pests. Compost tea is very effective

(table continued on page 4)

BASIC ORGANIC PROGRAM

on blackspot on roses and Southern blight on tomatoes. How much to dilute the dark compost tea before using depends on the compost used. A rule of thumb is to dilute the leachate down to one part compost liquid to four to ten parts water. It should look like iced tea. Be sure to strain the solids out with old pantyhose, cheese cloth, or row cover material. Full strength tea makes an excellent fire ant mound drench when mixed with molasses and citrus oil.

Controlling Insects. Aphids, spider mites, whiteflies and lacebugs: Release ladybugs and green lacewings regularly until natural populations exist. Garrett Juice and/or garlic-pepper tea (recipes below) are effective controls. Use strong water blasts for heavy infestations. Caterpillars, bagworms: Release trichogramma wasps. Use *Bacillus thuringiensis* (Bt). Spray at dusk per label. Fire ants: Use Garrett Juice plus citrus oil or beneficial nematodes. Grubworms: Beneficial nematodes and sugar help, but maintaining soil health is the primary control. Mosquitoes: Use *Bacillus thuringiensis* 'Israelensis' for larvae in standing water. Spray citrus oil and garlic-pepper tea for adults. Lavender and eucalyptus also repel mosquito adults. Slugs, snails, fleas, ticks, chinch bugs, roaches, and crickets: Spray or dust diatomaceous earth products and crushed red pepper. Citrus oil and molasses also kills these pests.

Controlling Diseases. Black spot, brown patch, powdery mildew, and other fungal problems: The best control is prevention through soil improvement, avoidance of high-nitrogen fertilizers, and proper watering. Spray Garrett Juice plus garlic and neem. Baking soda or potassium bicarbonate sprays are also effective. Treat soil with cornmeal. Alfalfa meal and mixes containing alfalfa are also good disease fighters.

Garlic-Pepper-Seaweed Tea Insect Repellent. In a blender with water, liquefy 2 bulbs of garlic and 2 cayenne or habañero peppers. Strain away the solids. Pour the garlic-pepper juice into a 1-gallon container. Fill the remaining volume with water to make 1 gallon of concentrate. Shake well before using and add ¼ cup of the concentrate to each gallon of water in the sprayer. To make garlic tea, simply omit the pepper and add another bulb of garlic. Add 1 tablespoon of seaweed and molasses to each gallon.

GARRETT JUICE
(PER GALLON OF WATER)

Compost tea—label directions or, if homemade, use 1–2 cups
Seaweed—1 tablespoon
Molasses—1 tablespoon
Natural apple cider vinegar—1 tablespoon
To make an insect control product, add 1 ounce citrus oil.

DIRT DOCTOR POTTING SOIL

5 parts compost	1 part earthworm castings
4 parts lava sand	½ part sugar
3 parts peat moss	½ part organic fertilizer
2 parts aged	¼ part sul-po-mag
pecan shells or	¼ part Texas greensand
cedar flakes	¼ part cornmeal
1 part soft rock	
phosphate	

Biodiverse garden.

Organic gardening is about the health of the soil, health of plants, health of animals, health of people, and health of the world. Organic living is good health, good business, and good economics. It is not antibusiness, or antitechnology, or antiscience. It is, however, against bad business, bad technology, bad science, and bad economics. Organic gardening is about growing vegetables, herbs, fruits, and nuts, but it's also about our future.

Most common food crops are harder to grow in Texas than landscape plants because there are very few native vegetables in Texas. Squash, corn, beans, tomatoes, asparagus—none of these are native here. Neither are any pears, peaches, or apricots. Some introduced fruits and vegetables are somewhat adapted if planted in healthy soil and pampered, but none of them are native. There are a few native food crops, but not many. The edible natives are primarily fruit and berry plants.

There are those who say vegetables and other food crops cannot be grown without the use of toxic chemical pesticides. We

strongly disagree. Many vegetables, fruits, nuts, and herbs can be grown without any pesticides at all and, under no circumstances, are the toxic-chemical choices needed.

The secret to growing successful and delicious food crops in Texas is to plant adapted plants in healthy soil at the right time of the year. Because many vegetables and fruits are not native to Texas, an organic program is even more important for them. Also important is tender, loving care, common sense, and careful attention to the pesky little troubles that pop up along the way.

Biodiverse planting is important because plants can and do help each other. Biodiversity is a fancy word given to the concept of having everything in place as nature designed. Improving biodiversity is done by introducing many plant types (trees, shrubs, ground cover, vines, perennials, and annuals) and allowing insects, frogs, toads, lizards, snakes, birds, and microorganisms to repopulate and flourish. Encouraging life and biodiversity by introducing beneficial insects and

protecting those that exist is an important part of a successful gardening program. Gardeners can purchase and release ladybugs, green lacewings, and trichogramma wasps in the beginning, but the need to release every year will diminish because natural populations will establish.

Nature doesn't allow monocultures of single plant species. Gardeners shouldn't either. By using a basic organic program, biodiversity will materialize as if by magic. Birds and other garden friends such as bats, lizards, toads, and beneficial insects will take up permanent residency if they are simply allowed to do so.

Man is part of nature, not in control of it. Understanding natural balances and using common sense is what we hope to encourage. No garden program is perfect except one: nature's. We suggest that you start with our recommended programs and techniques. Then massage them through trial and error until the best formula for you and your property becomes evident. One of the benefits of organic gardening is its forgiving tolerance. Healthy soil and adapted plants have tremendous buffering powers to help us feeble gardeners.

If we establish the right conditions, nature will perfect our gardens and food crops by bringing all the elements into balance. In the natural environment, physics, biology, and chemistry all are related. In gardening, physics relates to the structure, aeration, and drainage of the soil. Biology relates to the living organisms in the soil, and chemistry relates to the mineral nutrients in the soil and in plants. Organic gardening brings all these elements into their proper relationships.

◀ Animals in the garden—anole on patrol.

GROWING VEGETABLES AND OTHER FOOD CROPS IN TEXAS

All plants, including food crops, basically need the same conditions and materials: sunlight, air, rock minerals, organic matter, soil life, organic fertilizer and water.

TESTING YOUR SOIL

The first thing you should do before you begin planting is have your soil tested by a lab that gives organic recommendations to learn the total and available levels of organic matter, nitrogen, calcium, magnesium, sulfur, phosphate, potassium, sodium, chloride, boron, iron, manganese, copper, and zinc. The Texas Plant and Soil Lab in Edinburg, 956-383-0739, is recommended. You should also check for life by counting the earthworms in a cubic foot of soil. There should be at least ten worms.

PREPARING VEGETABLE BEDS

One of the most important aspects of new bed preparation for food crops is well-tilled or hand-worked beds. Aeration is critical to proper root development and root development is critical to plant health. After the beds have been tilled up to a depth of at least 8–10 inches, you should never walk on those rows again. Wide seed beds (15–16 inches or more) are the best for vegetables. They can be as wide as 4 feet so that 2 feet of bed can be worked from both sides without having to step into the bed. Footsteps around growing plants can severely damage the health of the soil and the roots of plants. If compaction is carefully avoided, year-after-year tilling is unnecessary. It is in fact detrimental to healthy soil.

Bed preparation—tilling compost, volcanic rock, and organic fertilizer into the native soil.

Smoothing the bed prior to planting.

When you work the soil deeply in the spring, thousands of tiny seeds from weeds are brought to the surface or the germination zone. If the soil sits for two or three days before planting, many of the tiny weeds will germinate and become a problem. It's best not to work the soil until the day before or the day of planting. This last-minute stirring of the soil turns up hundreds of weed seedlings. They are so tender at this point that the slightest disturbance kills them.

When the surface of the soil gets dry, lightly till the top inch or two of soil between rows and near the plants. This cultivation wipes out hundreds of weeds before they come to the surface.

After four or five shallow cultivations, most of the annual weed seeds in the top layer of soil have germinated. You won't have to do much weeding after that. If you mulch all the bare soil properly, this technique is rarely needed. Also, the application of corn gluten meal at 20 pounds per 1,000 square feet serves as a powerful natural fertilizer and preemergent. However, it will also restrict the germination of vegetable seeds. Use only when transplants are planned or on your seeded plants after they are well-rooted and growing.

ADDING NUTRIENTS TO THE SOIL

Compost is the best fertilizer available. It is nature's own living fertilizer and can be made at home or purchased ready-to-use. A compost pile can be started any time of the year and can be placed in sun or shade. Good ingredients include leaves, hay, grass clippings, tree trimmings, food scraps, bark, sawdust, rice hulls, weeds, nut hulls, and animal manure. Mix the ingredients together in a container of wood, hay bales, hog wire, concrete blocks, or simply pile the material on the ground. The best mixture is 80 percent vegetative matter and 20 percent animal waste, although any mix will compost. Since oxygen is a critical component, the ingredients should be a mix of coarse and fine-textured material to promote air circulation through the pile. Turn the pile once a month if possible, more often speeds up the process but releases nitrogen to the air.

Another critical component is water. A compost pile should have roughly the moisture of a squeezed-out sponge to help the living microorganisms thrive and work their magic. Compost is ready to use as a soil amendment when the ingredients are no longer identifiable. The color will be dark brown, the texture soft and crumbly, and it will smell like the forest floor. Rough, unfinished compost can be used as a topdressing mulch around all plantings.

The following amendments should be added to the bed and tilled into the native soil prior to planting a seed or a transplant in high-calcium soil, or what we call black and white soils:

- Compost at the rate of 4–6 inches
- Organic fertilizer at 20 pounds per 1,000 square feet
- Lava sand or other volcanic rock at 40–80 pounds per 1,000 square feet
- Texas greensand at 40–80 pounds per 1,000 square feet
- Sugar such as dry molasses at 5–10 pounds per 1,000 square feet
- Soft rock phosphate at 20–40 pounds per 1,000 square feet
- Sulfur at 5 pounds per 1,000 square feet

The following amendments should be added to sandy, acid soils:

- Compost at the rate of 4–6 inches
- Organic fertilizer at 20 pounds per 1,000 square feet
- Lava sand at 40–80 pounds per 1,000 square feet
- High-calcium lime (calcium carbonate) at 50–100 pounds per 1,000 square feet

Hairy vetch on the edges of wide rows.

🍂 Sugar at 5 pounds per 1,000 square feet

🍂 Soft rock phosphate at 20–40 pounds per 1,000 square feet

The soil in all beds can be sprayed with a liquid foliar feeding material or biostimulant. Garrett Juice can be sprayed or poured on the soil. Other choices include Bioform, Maestro Gro, Sea Source, Medina, Agrispon, and Agri Gro. Other natural soil stimulants include natural vinegar, liquid humate, and sugar solutions. See Chapter 5 for the formula for making Garrett Juice.

Planting rows should be raked to a smooth surface with the back of a rake prior to planting.

PLANTING SEEDS OUTDOORS

Seeds should be broadcast at the proper spacing and the soil should be firmed by using the back of a hoe or a board, giving the seeds good soil-seed contact. Seeds can then be covered with a very thin layer of earthworm castings or screened compost. Exceptions to this rule are covered in Chapter 6 in each plant entry.

The seedbed should be watered gently and kept moist until the small seedlings are up. The watering should then be cut back to the proper watering schedule and amount for each particular plant species. For small gardens, an effective technique to improve germination is to cover the seeded area with moist burlap, which serves to shade and keep the seedbed evenly moist. Remove the burlap to save and reuse after the seeds have sprouted.

Thinning is a controversial subject. Ruth Stout, gardening author and mulching proponent, says that thinning is unnecessary. The small plants she leaves always have good production. Many other gardeners believe in removing some of the seedlings so the remaining seedlings have plenty of space for the root systems and top to grow. With wide spacing, the roots will go deeper. Thinning can be done by pulling a rake through the seedbed when the seedlings are about an inch tall. Thinning can also be done by hand by clipping the seedlings with scissors. These cuttings can be used in salads. Crops that can be thinned with a rake include parsley, chard, collards, kale, Chinese cabbage, radishes, lettuce, kohlrabi, spinach, turnips, rutabagas, mustard, beets, and carrots. It is not a good idea to thin beans or peas with a rake because this may damage tender stems. Most crops need only one pass with the rake. Try both methods and see what works best for you.

STARTING SEEDS INDOORS

Most vegetable seeds need a constant warm temperature, about room temperature, to germinate. Most seeds don't need light to germinate, and can be put on top of the refrigerator or other out-of-the-way places. Newspaper and/or plastic sheets or lids can be put over the flats or pots to help maintain the constant temperature and moisture level. The window sill is a poor place to germinate seeds because of temperature fluctuations. Window sills are hot places on sunny days and often too cold at night.

Seed flats should be checked daily. After sprouts emerge, remove the covering. To prevent seedlings from leaning toward the light, turn the pots or flats around at least every two days. If the seedlings don't get enough light, they'll stretch and get weak and spindly. Tomatoes and onions are about the only plants that can recover from legginess. You can help tomatoes by planting them deeply and burying most of the leggy stems. Almost all other plants do not respond well to this deep planting technique.

Water the seedlings gently. If you cover your flats and trays, the soil will stay moist until you remove the covering. After that, check the soil several times a day with your fingers. If it is dry, add water. Plants on a table near heaters, vents, or on top of the refrigerator will dry out quickly and may need water more than once a day. Seedlings are delicate and shouldn't be over or harshly watered. They can easily collapse under the weight of the water. Water gently around the edge of the container or at the base of each plant.

Planting seed in pots.

Bottom watering is preferred by some gardeners. Fill a sink or other container with 2 inches of water and put your flats or pots in water until it seeps up into the surface of the soil. Some gardeners oppose this method because it tends to keep the soil too wet and pushes out the oxygen. We prefer watering from above.

Organic fertilizer can be added to the soil after seedlings are about an inch tall. Earthworm castings and compost are very gentle and may be the best choices for young plants. Garrett Juice can be added to the watering at 2 ounces per gallon. Even though it is primarily a foliar feeding material, it is also an excellent mild fertilizer for the soil.

Seedlings need to be hardened off for a week or so outdoors before being transplanted into their final place in the garden. Introducing young plants to an outdoor environment should be done gradually on a mild day. Plants should be left in partial shade and protected from wind for a few hours the first day, then given a little more exposure time each day. It normally takes three or four days to accustom young plants started indoors to direct sunlight outdoors. In a week or so the plants can stay out all day in the full sun. Seedlings can be moved back indoors during the transition period if the weather changes abruptly. If all this sounds like a lot of trouble, it is, but it's worth it for your ultimate vegetable or herb production.

PLANTING TRANSPLANTS

Flats or pots always need to have a good soaking before they are taken outdoors. We like to soak the plants in a bucket of water with seaweed until they are saturated before planting time. Using Garrett Juice in the water is also a good technique. Plant roots should be sopping wet and planted into a moist bed.

Pinching the lower leaves off of lettuce, cabbage family plants, and tomato transplants is normally a good idea. Do not pinch the leaves off eggplant, peppers, or any vine

Onion bulbs being planted in the fall.

crops. To protect young plants from cutworms, slugs, and snails, sprinkle a healthy amount of diatomaceous earth around the plants after planting. Crushed hot pepper also works. Cedar flakes are also helpful. Garden-Ville Fire Ant Control formula will also kill the pests.

MULCHING TO PROTECT PLANTS

After planting vegetables, cover all bare soil with at least 3 inches of mulch. Mulch is not a soil amendment to be mixed into the soil—it's a covering placed on top of the soil after the plants have been installed. It helps conserve moisture, buffers the soil from temperature extremes, shades out weeds, looks good, increases the tilth of the soil, and supplies food for the microorganisms and nutrients for the soil. There's only one exception. Wait to mulch spring-seeded plants until after the soil has warmed.

Pecan shell mulch with oregano.

ORGANIC MULCHES	RATING	APPLICATION	REMARKS
Cedar, shredded	A+	Use 2–5 inches thick.	The very best mulch.
Compost	A	Use partially decomposed material 3–5 inches thick.	Save the decomposed compost to till directly in the soil.
Cottonseed hulls	B	Apply 3–4 inches deep; best for ornamentals.	Has fertilizer value. Similar to cottonseed meal. Very light and tends to blow around. Watch for chemical contamination.
Cypress chips	C	Apply 2–3 inches deep.	Can seal off oxygen; expensive; harvested and shipped from Florida.
Lava gravel	C	Apply 1–2 inches deep.	
Lawn clippings	D	Better to mix into compost pile.	Good source of nitrogen, but the flat pieces plate and seal off oxygen.
Leaves	A	Best if run through a chipper before applying around small plants.	Leave around large plants just like the forest floor.
Manure	C	Apply only after composting.	Fresh manure has lots of nitrogen and can burn plants. Weed seed can also be a problem.
Pecan shells	B+	Apply 2–3 inches deep. Best to compost or let age first.	Becoming more available; high in nutrients and growth stimulators.
Peat moss	F	Don't use; the worst mulch choice.	Expensive; blows and washes away.
Pine bark (Large size)	C	3 inches deep in ornamental beds.	Very coarse texture; doesn't provide many nutrients and is slow to break down.
Pine bark (Small to medium)	D	Use as a last resort only.	Washes and blows around. Flat pieces tend to seal off oxygen from the soil and it leaches phenols and other toxins into the soil.
Pine needles	A	Apply 3–5 inches thick on vegetable gardens and ornamental beds.	Looks best when used in association with pine trees.
Sawdust	D-	Use in the compost pile, but not as a mulch.	Will wash and blow away.
Straw, hay	C	Apply 4–5 inches in ornamental beds; 8–10 inches in vegetable garden.	Use for winter protection. Alfalfa is best. Bermudagrass is the worst because of possible broadleaf, herbicide contamination.
Shredded hardwood bark	A	3–4 inches deep in all beds.	Excellent on sloped areas.
Shredded native tree trimmings	A	Apply 3–4 inches deep around all plants.	Better than hardwood and cheaper.

(table continued on page 16)

ORGANIC MULCHES	RATING	APPLICATION	REMARKS
Gravel	D	Best used at 3–6 inches in utility areas—not around plants.	Large, decorative stones are good for use in shady landscape areas.
Lava rock	D	Apply 3–5 inches deep in limited areas.	Avoid using in large areas; too harsh; no organic matter or nutrients.
Shredded rubber	D	1–2 inches around ornamental plants only.	Artificial-looking and may contain contaminants.

In general, the best mulch is coarse-textured recycled dead organic matter from plant material that grew on your property. Fine-textured mulch looks better to some people, but the coarse-textured mulches are much better for the soil and plant roots.

Shredded native cedar mulch—
the best choice.

Shredded hardwood bark—
the second best choice.

PLANTING VETCH

There are several ways to increase productivity of food crops. One method that works well for tomatoes and many other vegetables is to plant a green manure cover crop such as hairy vetch.

In late summer or early fall, make a bed or beds for your tomatoes about 4 feet wide and as long as you like. Seed the ground with hairy vetch, *Vicia villosa,* a very hardy annual legume. The first time you plant, use a legume inoculant for vetch. Once you've added those microbes to the soil, you won't have to do it again.

Vetch needs to grow for about a month before a very hard freeze (about 22°F) shuts

Hairy vetch.

down everything in the garden. You should plant the vetch one to three weeks before the first fall frost. You want the plants to get

Tomatoes planted into hairy vetch.

at least 4 inches tall before they stop growing for the season, though in warmer regions the vetch can keep growing all winter.

In spring, kill the vetch by simply cutting it close to the ground and laying it in place on the beds. In the garden, it is probably best to use a scythe, hedge shears, or a hand sickle. You should end up with a dense mulch that is 4 to 5 inches thick. It is important to cut all the vetch and cover the stubble. Plant the tomatoes down the middle of the bed by parting the mulch, setting the plants in, and then tucking the mulch back around them. Any vegetable that is grown from transplants or has large seeds will work well in this system. Cucumbers, squash, melons, peppers, eggplant, sweet corn, and even green beans are candidates. Small-seeded closely-spaced vegetables such as beets, carrots, and lettuce would have trouble growing through the thick mulch.

Tomatoes without vetch on chemical fertilizer.

This system has performed phenomenally well in USDA tests in Beltsville, Maryland. The tomato-vetch trial plots using no nitrogen fertilizer and without any weeding have consistently outyielded plastic mulch and fertilizer plots by about 2.5 percent and fertilized bare soil by 100 percent.

17

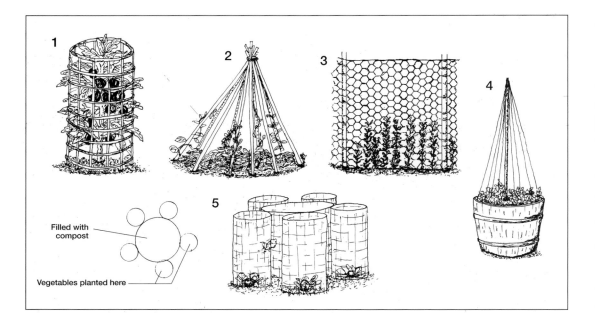

Filled with
compost

Vegetables planted here

STRUCTURES FOR CLIMBING VEGETABLE PLANTS

Another trick to increase productivity is to use structures for climbing vegetables. These structures are easy to make yourself. 1) Concrete-reinforcing wire mesh is the best material for making tomato cages. Many other vegetables can also be grown vertically in these structures. 2) Teepee trellises can be made from bamboo poles or metal rods. This structure is particularly good for growing beans, peas, cucumbers, and other climbing vegetables. 3) Chicken wire, chainlink fence, or welded wire fabric mounted vertically and attached to metal or wooden stakes is another good structure for climbing peas and beans. 4) A barrel trellis can be made using a single metal rod or bamboo pole in the center with string or wire connecting the top of the pole to the inside edge of the barrel.

5) The Japanese Ring is another unique planting device. The ring can be made of welded wire or reinforcing wire. The ring should be placed on well-prepared and raised soil, should be 3 to 5 feet tall, and filled with compost. Tomato, squash, pepper,

or other plants should be planted in additional rings attached to the outside of the big ring and spaced approximately 24 inches on center. The diameter of the ring can range from 2 feet to 4 feet. The plants can be staked, wired to the Japanese ring, or have their own individual rings. The plants are irrigated by watering the compost in the center ring. The water traveling through the compost carries natural fertilizer to the plants at each watering. The ring can also be recessed into the soil and filled with compost.

Vegetables are heavy feeders and do best when extra amounts of humus are available. High-quality compost, which is at least 20 percent manure, and earthworm castings are the best sources of humus in this case. Raise the planting area by building flat-topped hills or rows. The raised bed created by either technique improves drainage and soil aeration. Don't forget how important oxygen is to the root system.

HAND POLLINATION

There are gardeners who recommend hand pollination when the flowers of food crops aren't setting. The procedure is simple. Break off a male flower and dab the pollen on the female flowers (those with the swollen short stems.) You can also use a small paintbrush to do the work. Personally, if you have time to do this, you need to get a life. The real answer to better pollination is to go organic, encourage biodiversity, and have plenty of bees, wasps, lacewings, and other beneficial insects so the pollen will be moved around the natural way. First step: stop spraying pesticides.

ROW COVERS

Increased production also comes from the use of row covers. Row covers are made from plastic or synthetic fabrics and are used to protect plants and promote growth. They can be divided into two broad categories: 1) heavy plastic covers, supported on frames or hoops to form a tunnel over the plants, and 2) very light synthetic fabrics that "float" or rest directly on the crop. Plastic row covers are generally cheaper, but more labor-inten-sive because of the frames and the need for more frequent removal. Plastic row covers create higher daytime temperatures, which is desirable, if you need to maximize soil warmth. Floating row covers are more versa-tile in that they allow not only light and heat but also water, sprays, and air to penetrate. They can be left on longer than plastic cov-ers. For this reason they also tend to provide better protection against flying insects than plastics. Gardeners can plant earlier and can keep crops producing through the fall by using row covers. Brand names include Gro Web, Easy Grow, Fast Start, and Garden-Ville Plant Shield. If handled carefully, these fab-rics can be saved and used for several years.

Row covers have been found to provide the following benefits:

Stop diseases. Tomatoes, peppers, and other vegetables are highly susceptible to viruses that are transmitted by insects. Floating row cover stretched over plants soon after emerg-ing or transplanting will keep the disease-car-rying insect away from the plant.

Floating row cover on tomato cages in early spring.

Slow down wind and moisture loss. Plant scientists tell us wind over 15 miles an hour stresses plants and stops growth.

Frost protection. On frosty mornings floating row covers can make a two degree difference in temperature and offer some frost protection. They do not overheat plants as plastic does in the heat of the day.

Hail storm protection. Plants in cages covered with row cover sustained only slight damage, while plants in cages nearby without row cover were completely destroyed.

Eliminate the need for insecticides. Row covers screen out troublesome insects.

Promote plant growth and fruit set. Years of research have shown that tomato plants double, and in some years triple, in growth and fruit set when planted under row cover protection compared to unprotected plants. This is because photosynthesis is increased and plants suffer less stress from the wind, insects, and diseases.

Increase photosynthesis. Row covers defuse and reflect sunlight all over the plant in moderate amounts instead of being too hot and intense from one angle.

Stop bird damage to fruits and vegetables. Row covers are much better than bird netting because plants do not grow through them, as vines do with bird netting, making it difficult to remove.

As soon as plants emerge from the soil, prop row cover up in tent fashion so as not to hinder plant growth. Seal the edges with soil so the wind can't blow it away and insects can't crawl under it.

For large plants such as peppers and tomatoes, place large cages (20 to 30 inches high and wide) around each plant immediately after transplanting, cover with floating row cover, and carefully pin it tight with clothespins so there are no gaps or holes for insects to enter. Cover the floating row cover bottom with soil to anchor the fabric and cage against high winds and insects crawling under.

On tomatoes, peppers, and other self-pollinating plants, floating row cover need not be removed until the plant is too large for the cage used. If the plant is shaded or cloudy weather persists, causing low-light conditions, floating row cover should be removed. On plants such as melons or squash that need insects to pollinate, remove the row cover when the first female blooms appear; however, it may be reapplied at night.

For fruit trees and grape vines, floating row cover need not be applied until a few days before the fruit is ripe. Clothespins are excellent to anchor it securely.

SAVING SEED

Saving the seed of open-pollinated seed (non-hybrids) is simple. Clean the seed from healthy, mature fruit and dry naturally on butcher paper. Butcher paper is better than newspaper only because it has no ink with chemical ingredients. When the seeds are dry, put them in glass containers, toss in a pinch of natural diatomaceous earth, and seal with a lid. Put the containers in the refrigerator until you need to plant the next season.

Plant variety selection is the most important of all gardening rules. When the best-adapted variety is found, it pays further dividends to upgrade that species to your locality by saving the seed from the best fruit each year. It is a little more trouble than just putting away dried corn or beans.

For sticky-gooey seed such as tomatoes, use a screen wire basket strainer. Blast the seeds clean using a water hose with a nozzle and a strong force of water. After the seeds are thoroughly clean, let them dry on more screen wire or a slick material to which the seeds won't stick. Cover the seed with natural diatomaceous earth, and once they are completely dry, put them in glass containers. Label with a variety and date and store in a refrigerator.

WHEN TO PLANT IN TEXAS

There are two planting seasons. Texas gardeners can plant in the spring and the fall, and certain vegetable varieties are best adapted for one or the other season. Plants of the mustard and cabbage families, for example, definitely do best in the fall garden. If they mature as the days get shorter and cooler, they will taste better and be more nutritious. If they are planted a little late in the spring, or if the weather warms up very quickly, these plants will bolt (which means flowering or seed stem formation will be premature), become bitter, and go to seed sooner than they should. You're also almost guaranteed that a strong army of harlequin bugs will attack those stressed plants.

There are many vegetables adapted for planting in both spring and fall in Texas; these are varieties that mature in 30–70 days. One such crop is spinach, which can be planted spring or fall as long as the soil temperature is below 76°. The seed won't sprout in hot soils. If you wait until late fall to plant in order to harvest on cool days, you will find that the spinach tastes much better than when it is harvested during long, warm days. Summer squash is another plant that matures fast, but it prefers warm soils for germination. You must plant it much earlier in the fall and later in the spring than spinach. All seeds have a preferred soil temperature for sprouting, but the range is usually about 10° in either direction, which gives us some leeway in planting days. Usually, it is the late spring or early fall freezes that cause problems.

The long-maturing (90–120 days) varieties are planted in the spring only, and usually as early as possible. There are other varieties that prefer very warm soil and growing conditions—for example, okra, eggplant, and peppers. If you plant these vegetables too early and are able to get their seed to sprout in the cool spring soil, the plants will probably just sit there and wait until the soil and weather warms up. During that waiting period, the plants will be stressed and more susceptible to insects and diseases.

The varieties of vegetables that mature in 30–70 days are best for fall planting. The long-maturing crops that need 90–120 days do best if planted as early in the spring as possible.

The agricultural extension service usually publishes a gardening bulletin that lists the

(text continued on page 27)

AVERAGE FIRST FREEZE DATES IN THE FALL

City	Date	City	Date
Amarillo	October 24	Kerrville	November 6
Austin	November 22	Lubbock	November 3
Corpus Christi	December 15	McAllen	December 8
Dallas	November 13	Port Arthur	November 16
El Paso	November 12	San Antonio	November 26
Galveston	December 25	Texarkana	November 11
Houston	December 11	Wichita Falls	November 11

AVERAGE LAST FREEZE DATES IN THE SPRING

City	Date	City	Date
Amarillo	April 17	Kerrville	April 6
Austin	March 18	Lubbock	April 9
Corpus Christi	February 9	McAllen	February 9
Dallas	March 23	Port Arthur	March 11
El Paso	March 9	San Antonio	March 15
Galveston	January 24	Texarkana	March 21
Houston	February 14	Wichita Falls	March 27

AVERAGE DATE OF LAST FROST

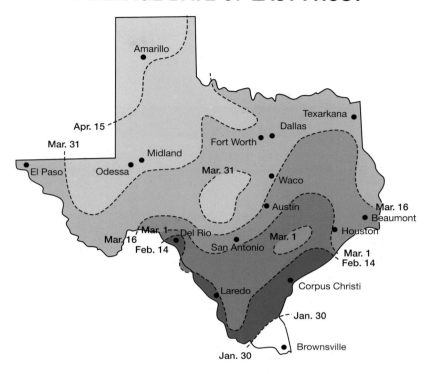

AVERAGE DATE OF FIRST FROST

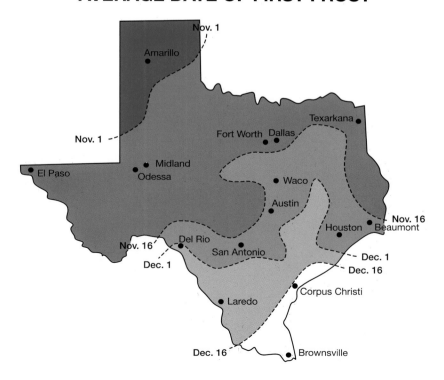

VEGETABLE	REGION I	REGION II
Asparagus	After March 1	After February 15
Beans, snap bush	April 15–May 15	April 1–May 5
Beans, snap pole	April 15–May 1	April 1–May 1
Beans, lima bush	May 1–May 15	April 15–May 15
Beans, lima pole	May 1–May 15	April 15–May 15
Beets	March 1–June 1	February 15–May 20
Broccoli	March 1–June 15	February 15–March 20
Brussels sprouts	February 15–April 1	February 15–March 10
Cabbage	March 10–April 15	February 15–March 10
Carrots	March 10–April 15	February 15–March 10
Cauliflower	March 1–April 15	February 15–March 10
Chard, Swiss	March 1–June 1	February 15–May 1
Collards (kale)	March 1–May 1	February 15–April 10
Corn (sweet)	April 1–May 20	March 15–May 1
Cucumber	April 15–June 1	April 1–May 15
Eggplant (transplants)	May 10–June 1	April 10–May 1
Garlic (cloves)	January 1–January 15	Not rec.
Kohlrabi	March 1–April 15	February 15–March 1
Lettuce	March 1–May 15	February 15–May 1
Muskmelon (cantaloupe)	May 1–June 1	April 10–May 1
Mustard	March 1–May 15	February 15–May 1
Okra	May 15–June 15·	April 25–July 1
Onion (plants)	March 1–April 15	February 15–March 10
Parsley	March 1–April 15	February 15–March 10
Peas, English	February 15–March 15	February 15–March 1
Peas, southern	May 1–June 15	April 20–May 15
Pepper (transplants)	May 10–June 1	April 10–May 1
Potato	March 15–April 7	March 10–April 1
Potato, sweet (slips)	May 15–June 15	April 25–May 15
Pumpkin	May 15–June 1	April 25–May 20
Radish	March 1–June 1	February 15–May 20
Spinach	March 1–April 1	February 1–March 1
Squash, summer	May 1–June 1	April 10–May 1
Squash, winter	May 1–May 15	April 1–April 25
Tomato (transplants)	May 10–June 1	April 10–May 1
Turnip	March 1–June 1	February 15–May 20
Watermelon	May 10–May 15	April 10–May 1

Gardening Regions

I

II

III

IV

V

Amarillo

Texarkana

Fort Worth Dallas

El Paso

Midland

Odessa

Waco

Austin

Houston Beaumont

Del Rio

San Antonio

Corpus Christi

Laredo

Brownsville

SPRING VEGETABLE CROPS

REGION III	REGION IV	REGION V
After February 1	After January 15	Not rec.
March 5–May 1	February 10–April 15	February 1–March 15
March 5–April 15	February 10–March 15	February 1–March 15
March 15–April 15	March 1–April 1	February 15–April 1
March 15–April 15	March 1–April 1	February 15–April 1
February 1–March 1	January 15–April 15	January 1–March 5
February 1–March 1	February 15–February 25	January 1–February 15
Not rec.	Not rec.	Not rec.
February 1–March 1	January 15–February 10	January 1–February 1
January 15–March 1	January 15–February 10	January 1–February 1
February 1–March 1	January 15–February 15	January 15–February 15
February 1–March 10	January 15–April 1	January 1–April 1
February 1–March 25	January 15–March 15	January 1–March 15
February 25–May 1	February 15–March 15	February 1–March 15
March 5–May 1	February 10–April 10	February 1–April 1
March 15–May 1	February 20–April 1	February 1–March 15
Not rec.	Not rec.	Not rec.
February 1–March 1	January 15–February 15	January 1–February 15
February 1–March 15	January 15–March 15	January 1–March 1
March 15–May 1	February 20–April 15	February 1–April 1
February 1–April 1	January 15–March 15	January 1–March 1
April 1–June 1	March 15–June 15	March 1–June 1
February 1–March 1	January 15–February 10	January 1–February 1
February 1–March 1	January 15–February 10	January 1–February 1
February 1–March 1	January 15–February 1	Not rec.
March 25–May 20	March 15–April 15	March 1–April 15
March 15–May 1	February 20–March 10	February 1–March 10
February 15–March 1	January 15–February 15	January 1–February 1
April 10–May 15	March 15–May 10	March 1–April 15
April 1–April 20	March 10–May 1	March 1–April 1
February 1–May 1	January 15–April 15	January 1–April 1
January 1–February 15	January 1–February 15	January 1–February 1
March 5–May 1	February 10–April 10	February 1–April 1
March 5–May 1	February 10–April 10	February 1–April 1
March 15–April 10	February 20–March 10	February 10–March 10
February 1–March 10	January 15–April 15	January 1–March 1
March 15–May 1	February 20–April 1	February 1–April 1

FALL DIRECT SEEDING GUIDE

VEGETABLES	REGION I	REGION II	REGION III	REGION IV	REGION V
Beans, snap bush	July 15	August 1	September 1	September 10	October 1
Beans, lima bush	July 15	July 25	August 20	September 1	September 15
Beets	August 15	September 1	October 15	November 1	December 15
Broccoli	July 15	August 1	September 1	October 1	November 1
Brussels sprouts	July 15	August 1	September 1	October 1	November 1
Cabbage	July 15	August 1	September 1	October 1	November 1
Carrots	July 15	August 15	September 1	November 20	December 15
Cauliflower	July 15	August 1	September 1	October 1	November 1
Chard, Swiss	August 1	August 15	October 1	October 20	December 15
Collards	August 1	August 15	October 10	October 20	December 15
Corn, sweet	July 1	August 10	August 20	September 10	September 20
Cucumber	July 15	August 1	September 1	September 10	October 1
Eggplant	July 1	July 1	July 1	July 10	August 1
Garlic (cloves)	July 1	August 1	October 1	November 1	December 1
Kohlrabi	August 15	September 1	September 10	October 1	November 1
Lettuce, leaf	September 1	September 15	October 10	November 1	December 1
Mustard	September 1	October 1	November 1	December 1	December 15
Onion (seed)	not rec.	not rec.	November 1	December 1	December 15
Parsley	September 15	October 1	October 10	November 1	December 1
Peas, southern	June 15	July 1	August 1	August 15	September 1
Pepper	June 1	June 15	July 1	July 15	August 1
Potato	not rec.	August 1	September 1	October 1	not rec.
Pumpkin	June 1	July 1	August 1	August 10	September 1
Radish	September 1	October 1	November 25	December 1	December 15
Spinach	August 15	September 1	November 15	December 1	December 15
Squash, summer	August 1	August 15	September 10	October 1	October 10
Squash, winter	June 15	July 1	August 10	September 1	September 10
Tomato	June 1	June 15	July 1	July 10	August 1
Turnip	September 1	October 15	November 1	December 1	December 15

(text continued from page 22)

best-adapted food crop varieties for spring and fall planting. They also list the best planting dates for each crop. Many seed packages contain planting instructions; usually they suggest planting a certain number of days before or after the last freeze of the spring. The problem with that is no one knows when the last freeze will occur.

Selecting a planting date is just one more of the gambles farmers and gardeners must take. A few days can mean the difference between success or failure, and having to replant is a big expense on large acreage.

GARDENING BY THE MOON

Because of the unpredictable weather, some gardeners and even farmers of large acreage are fairly successful by letting the moon phases dictate when to plant. For example, if soil conditions permit, they always plant potatoes in the period between the third and seventh day after the full moon in February.

Even though some scientists still reject the notion of moon-sign planting, moon gardening makes the hobby still more fun. There is a good lunar gardening guide on the market, *Llewellyn's Moon Sign Book,* published annually. This book is useful for deciding planting dates, but it doesn't tell you about variety, seasons, soil types, and the many other things you need to know about vegetable growing. Maybe, just maybe, moon-sign planting can stack the odds in our favor in the when-to-plant gamble!

Here are the most common general recommendations.

New moon to first quarter. Plant the seeds of above-ground crops that have external seed. Plants in this category include asparagus, broccoli, brussels sprouts, cabbage, cauliflower, strawberries, celery, grains, leeks, lettuce, parsley, and spinach. Pick the most appropriate sign for the specific crop: Cancer, Scorpio, Taurus, Libra, or Pisces.

First quarter to full moon. Plant above-ground food crops and flowers that contain seed within a fruit or pod. This is the quarter for planting beans, melons, squash, cucumbers, tomatoes, grapes, and peppers. The best signs are Cancer, Scorpio, and Pisces, followed by Taurus, Capricorn, and Libra.

Full moon to last quarter. Plant bulbs and root crops, along with biennials and perennials that need strong roots. Plants in this category include beets, carrots, turnips, garlic, onions, and radishes, and they do well when planted in Pisces, Taurus, Capricorn, or Libra.

Last quarter to new moon. If you must plant, do so in a fruitful sign. It's better to spend time weeding, cultivating, and controlling pests in a barren sign.

THE LUNAR MONTH

New   **Waxing (Increasing Light) Phase**

Age	0	1	2	3	4	5	6	7	8	9	10	11	12	13	14

Full   **Waning (Decreasing Light) Phase**

Age	15	16	17	18	19	20	21	22	23	24	25	26	27	28	29

CHAPTER 4

IMPROVING
THE SOIL THE
NATURAL WAY

There is only one way to fertilize food crops—organically. Not only are the natural fertilizers safer and more environmentally friendly (there's an overused term), they are important for the proper nutrition of the soil and of the plants grown in that soil. The best true natural fertilizers include microbe, earthworm, and insect excrement. Therefore, using soil amendments that cause the fungi, bacteria, other microorganisms, and earthworms to flourish is critical.

Organic fertilizers nourish and improve the life in the soil with every application. Unlike synthetic fertilizers, they help the soil because they do not create high unnatural levels of nitrates and other salts in the soil that kill or repel beneficial soil organisms. Organic fertilizers release nutrients slowly and naturally. All components in an organic fertilizer are usable by the soil and the plants because there are no useless and sometimes dangerous fillers as there are in artificial fertilizers. Organic fertilizers add organic matter to the soil; synthetic fertilizers do not. Organic fertilizers also provide many trace minerals that aren't in artificial fertilizers. Artificial fertilizers don't have the energy source (carbon) that microbes need to convert fertilizer elements to plant food. Artificial fertilizers are unbalanced and unhealthy plant foods. Plus, they don't do anything good for the soil.

gen. The standard recommendation is a ratio of 3-1-2 or 4-1-2, such as 15-5-10 or 16-4-8. These recommendations are based on forced crop production instead of on soil needs. They are irresponsible recommendations for several reasons. These artificial fertilizers don't have any organic matter and few trace minerals, but they often do have industrial waste contaminates.

Studies at the Department of Agronomy at Alabama Polytechnic University many years ago showed that as much as 50 percent of all synthetic nitrogen applied to the soil will be leached out, and the half that does reach the plant may be hurting the plant because of its unnatural concentration. Other studies show that an excess of artificial fertilizer slows or even stops the activity of microflora and microfauna such as beneficial bacteria, algae, fungi, and other microorganisms. Harsh fertilizers also cause damage to macroorganisms such as earthworms, millipedes, springtails, and centipedes, which are all extremely important to the natural processes in the soil.

Many landscaping businesses are still recommending high nitrogen fertilizers such as 24-8-16, 15-5-10 (or even higher). We've made the same recommendations in the past, but now know that those amounts of nitrogen, phosphorus, and potassium are unnecessary and even damaging to soil health.

THE NITROGEN-PHOSPHORUS-POTASSIUM STORY

The nitrogen-phosphorus-potassium analysis (N-P-K), which federal law requires to be printed on bags of fertilizer, is basically irrelevant in an organic program. Feeding the soil and plants with nothing but nitrogen, phosphorus, and potassium is like feeding your kids nothing but white bread. Soil, like plants, animals, and people, needs a balance of nutrients. For some unknown reason, fertilizer recommendations continue to emphasize these three so-called major nutrients, with special emphasis on high levels of nitro-

ORGANIC FERTILIZERS

Organic fertilizers are derived from once-living plant and/or animal life, which means all the nutrients are in correct proportions to sustain new plants. Also, organic fertilizers contain carbon, which is the energy source that all life needs. Only plants have the ability to take energy from the sun. All other living things must get their energy from the plants. Humans, animals, and underground life such as microbes and earthworms must have this energy source.

Artificial fertilizers contain no carbon and no energy. They aren't complete even though it may say so on the bag. Organic fertilizers will always have low numbers such as 6-2-2 or 3-1-5. The three numbers will rarely total over 14. The rest of the organic fertilizer is the organic matter or energy source that the soil life must have. Organic fertilizers break down into soil conditioners that create the necessary crumb structure that keeps the soil aerated so oxygen and water can penetrate and gases can escape from the soil. When using high-analysis synthetic fertilizers in soil that is low in organic matter, the microbes have to take their carbon from the soil. Without replenishing it, the carbon is eventually used up. The result is loss of soil health and stressed, unhealthy plants. Then nature sends in pests to destroy the plant. They are the cleanup crew. To make matters worse, toxic poisons are still used to artificially keep sick plants alive. People then get to eat unwholesome fruits and vegetables.

Organic fertilizers are naturally slow-release and provide major and minor nutrients to plants and they do it when the conditions are right. Synthetic fertilizers tend to glut plants with nutrients and often at the wrong time. Organic fertilizers work within nature's laws and systems, while synthetic fertilizers try to control nature. It can't, however, be done.

NUTRIENTS

The soil's most plentiful major component is mineral matter. In the top 6 inches of healthy soil, the mineral portion will be approximately 45 percent. The mineral composition is the principal determinant of the soil's property. Minerals occur as a result of the physical or chemical action of the parent rock near the surface of the soil. There are 92 naturally occurring mineral elements.

Minerals are responsible for the growth of a plant's cells. Plants depend on three essential nutrients derived from the air and water: carbon, hydrogen, and oxygen. Plants also depend on essential nutrients derived from the minerals in the soil as inorganic salts: iron, potassium, calcium, magnesium, nitrogen, phosphorus, sulfur, manganese, chlorine, boron, zinc, copper, and molybdenum.

The other 70 or so trace minerals are not fully understood but are important to the soil, to plants, and to Nature's whole.

But organic fertilizers do not have very high amounts of nitrogen, phosphorus, and potassium. Aren't these amounts important? When fertilizing or adding mineral nutrients, it's important to think about balance. Healthy soils and plants have a balance of elements and ingredients. A proper fertilization program will help keep that balance intact. That's why it's important to avoid an overkill of the well-known elements nitrogen, phosphorus, and potassium.

When buying fertilizer, remember how relatively unimportant nitrogen, phosphorus, and potassium are. They are important but not as important as balance. Think in terms of providing to the soil those products and elements that will help maintain the natural balance. If the soil is in a healthy, balanced condition (which includes organic matter and air), nitrogen, potassium, and phosphorus will be released naturally by the feeding of microorganisms and relatively little will need to be added.

ORGANIC FERTILIZERS AND SOIL AMENDMENTS

Alfalfa Meal

Approximate analysis is 3-1-2. Alfalfa meal and hay used for mulch contain vitamin A, folic acid, trace minerals, and the growth hormone "tricontanol." Use at 25 pounds per 1,000 square feet or 400–800 pounds per acre. Alfalfa helps plants create larger flowers and increases the tolerance to cold. Make alfalfa tea by soaking 1 cup of alfalfa meal per 5 gallons of water. It's good for all flowering plants.

Bat Guano

Approximate analysis is 10-3-1. Bat guano is a very powerful organic fertilizer that is high in nitrogen, phosphorus, and trace minerals and has natural disease-fighting capabilities. In its natural form, it is very dusty and hard to use on a large scale unless mixed with other more moist materials. Use at 15 pounds per 1,000 square feet or about 300 pounds per acre.

Biostimulants

These are liquid or dry formulations that either contain microorganisms or contain materials that stimulate the native microbes in the soil. Included in this category are Agri-Gro, Bioform, F-68, BioInnoculant, Medina, and Garrett Juice.

Blood Meal

Approximate analysis is 12-1-1. This is a good nitrogen source but smelly and expensive. This natural meal has a low pH and many trace minerals, including iron. Use at 20 pounds per 1,000 square feet or 300–400 pounds per acre. A good blend is made by mixing 80 percent cottonseed meal with 20 percent blood meal.

Bonemeal

Approximate analysis is 2-12-0. Bonemeal is a good calcium and phosphorus source but slower-acting and more expensive than soft rock phosphate. Analysis of bonemeal will vary from about 2-12-0 to 4-12-0, with 2–5 percent calcium. Young bones usually have less phosphorus and more nitrogen than older bones. Commonly available steamed bonemeal is made from bones that have been boiled or steamed at high pressure to remove fats and proteins. This process reduces nitrogen but increases phosphorus. Bonemeal works more quickly on well-aerated soils. Use at 20–40 pounds per 1,000 square feet or 400–500 pounds per acre.

Bioform

These are liquid products that contain fish, seaweed, molasses, and dry products that contain poultry manure and other natural ingredients.

Use Bioform 4-2-4 with 3 percent sulfur for lawns at 2 to 4 quarts per acre, diluted in 20 gallons water. Water well.

For all other uses, mix 4 tablespoons per gallon of water and mist.

A 40-pound bag of dry Bioform 5-3-4 with 1 percent sulfur covers approximately 2,000 square feet. Water well.

Bradfield Fertilizer

Approximate analysis is 3-1-5. Bradfield's natural fertilizers are alfalfa-based fertilizers blended with animal protein, natural potassium sulfate potash, and molasses. They should be used at the rate of 20–30 pounds per 1,000 square feet. Most broadcast spreaders, set fully open, will dispense this fertilizer at approximately 10 pounds per 1,000 square feet per pass.

Chicken Manure

Approximate analysis is 6-4-2. Chicken manure is a good natural fertilizer high in nitrogen. Pelletized forms are better because they are not as dusty. Unfortunately, commercial chickens are still being fed lots of unnatural or toxic natural things. It is best to compost before using.

Coffee Grounds

Approximate analysis is 2-3-6. Coffee grounds are an excellent natural fertilizer with an acid pH and up to 2 percent nitrogen. Collect grounds at home and from your local restaurant or coffee shop and use in the compost pile or apply directly to the soil at 20–80 pounds per 1,000 square feet.

Compost

Approximate analysis is 1-1-1. This is the best all-around organic fertilizer—after all, it's nature's. Apply at a minimum of 50–100 pounds per 1,000 square feet or 800–4,500 pounds per acre. Use in all potting soil mixes and to prepare all new beds. Compost is far superior to any other form of organic matter for use in building the soil.

Compost Tea

This tea is made from the leachate of compost and may be the best foliar feeding tool of all. It is not only an effective foliar fertilizer, it has powerful insect- and disease-control properties. The humic materials and microorganisms in compost tea are effective on many pests. German researchers studied the effects of compost tea, but gardeners have known its beneficial properties for years. Common fungal problems like black spot on roses and early blight on tomatoes can be controlled with compost tea. How much to dilute the dark compost tea before using depends on the compost used. A rule of thumb is to dilute the leachate down to one part compost liquid to 4–10 parts water. Applying compost tea at late evening, just about dusk, works best.

Cornmeal

Use cornmeal at 20 pounds per 1,000 square feet or 200–800 pounds per acre to add cellulose and stimulate the beneficial microorganisms that control several disease pathogens such as *Rhizoctonia, Pythium, Fusarium, Phytophthora,* and others. It can also be used in pools and water features to control algae at 2 cups of cornmeal per 100 square feet or 150 pounds per acre.

Corn Gluten Meal

Approximate analysis is 9.5-0.5-0.5. Corn gluten meal is a natural pre-emergent fertilizer that reduces the germination and establishment of troublesome annual weeds. It is available as a powder or in granular form. It is 60 percent protein and approximately 10 percent nitrogen by weight. It is a by-product of the wet milling process and is commonly used in pet and livestock feed. It can be used in vegetable gardens as a fertilizer and can help with weed control, but be careful. It can

damage the germination of your food crops. Use it only after your vegetable seeds are up and young plant roots are well-established. It is a powerful fertilizer and will create large healthy weeds if applied after they germinate. This unique use of corn gluten meal was discovered by Dr. Nick Christians and his research staff at Iowa State University.

Cottonseed Meal

Approximate analysis is 7-2-2. This is an acid pH fertilizer with lots of trace minerals. It has possible pesticide residue because so many toxic poisons are used in the cotton industry. Use at 20–25 pounds per 1,000 square feet or 700–800 pounds per acre.

Cow Manure

Approximate analysis is 2-1-1. Trace mineral content varies widely depending on raw materials used in the cow feed. Cow manure is loaded with beneficial living organisms. Manure is one of our greatest natural resources, if not overused. It is best to use cow manure in composted form to avoid weed seed and odor. It can be used at the rate of 1–4 tons per acre. Organiphobes often use the high salt content of cow manure as a common scare tactic. Contamination from broadleaf herbicides is a more serious concern.

Desert Peat *(also sold as DinoSoil)*

A natural humic material that comes from the Big Bend area, desert peat looks like soil but is a very powerful soil amendment that contains humic and other natural acids as well as many trace minerals.

Diatomaceous Earth

Normally used as a pest control product, diatomaceous earth is also a good soil amendment because it contains a long list of trace minerals. It can be used from 1–100 pounds per 1,000 square feet. See Organic Pesticides.

DinoSoil—*See Desert Peat*

Earthworm Castings

Approximate analysis is 1-.1-.1. Earthworm castings contain beneficial bacteria, many trace minerals, humus, and earthworm eggs. Use at 20–40 pounds per 1,000 square feet for all plants. They are one of the best fertilizer choices for interior potted plants but also good for all outdoor beds and plants.

Epsom Salts

Epsom salt is made by treating magnesium, hydroxide, or carbonate with sulfuric acid. Epsom salts is the common name for magnesium sulfate. Magnesium is a vital element in the production of chlorophyll in plants. A deficiency shows in the discoloration of the leaves between the veins, which develops into dead areas if the condition is allowed to persist. Epsom salts is a fast-acting source of magnesium and sulfur normally used as a foliar feed, but it can also be applied to soil. Use 1 tablespoon per gallon and spray monthly if needed on flowering plants. Broadcast at the rate of 5–10 pounds per 1,000 square feet. It can also be applied by putting a small amount in transplant holes for vegetables and flowers. Epsom salt is not a natural organic product, but is acceptable to us.

Fireplace Ashes

Ashes have a bad reputation but are an excellent ingredient for the compost pile and good as a soil amendment if not overused. Organiphobes will cry that fireplace ashes are alkaline and should never be used in the black and white soils. Well, what are fireplace ashes? They are basically trees with the carbon burned away. Ashes are a concentration of mineral salts, including nitrogen, potassium, sodium, calcium, magnesium, along with many trace minerals. Mix fireplace ashes into the compost pile up to 20 percent of the pile or apply directly on the soil at 20–40 pounds per 1,000 square feet. They are most effective for acid soils.

Fish Emulsion

Approximate analysis is from 4-1-1 to 5-2-2. Fish emulsion is a foliar plant food that helps with insect control, but it stinks! It is a concentrated liquid fish fertilizer for use directly in the soil or as a foliar feed. It is reported also to be an effective insecticide and a great all-purpose spray when mixed with liquid seaweed. It has an odor for about 24 hours—a pretty strong one, in fact. Fish hydrolosates are better because they use the whole fish. Foliar feed plants per label instructions.

Fish Meal

Approximate analysis is 12-1-1. Fish meal has lots of vitamins and minerals, but is smelly. It is a natural fertilizer originally used in this country by Native Americans growing corn. Fish meal is a powerful natural fertilizer, but it's expensive and stinky, so use with caution. Use at 20–30 pounds per 1,000 square feet.

Garden-Ville Soil Food

Approximate analysis is 6-2-2. This is an organic fertilizer for gardens and lawns containing bat guano, brewer's yeast, desert humate, Norwegian kelp, compost, fish meal, meat and bone meal, molasses and langbeinite, cottonseed meal, blood meal, and alfalfa meal. Use at 20–30 pounds per 1,000 square feet.

It is also a 9-1-1 organic fertilizer for lawns containing cottonseed meal, leather meal, alfalfa meal, fish meal, bat guano, and other natural ingredients, for those who want higher nitrogen.

Garrett Juice

Garrett Juice is a high quality, subtly powerful foliar feeding spray. It can be used as a liquid soil fertilizer as well. For foliar feeding, use it with water at 2–3 ounces per gallon and use on herbs, vegetables, ground cover, shrubs, vines, trees, turf grasses, and greenhouse plants. Garrett Juice is a blend of manure, compost tea, seaweed, natural apple cider vinegar, and molasses. It can be used on any age plants, but it's always best to spray any liquid materials during the cooler parts of the day. For soil treatment, the application rate can be doubled. Garrett Juice provides major nutrients, trace minerals, and other beneficial components. See Chapter 5 for recipe.

Granite Sand

Approximate analysis is 0-0-5. Granite is a low-cost source of minerals, especially potash. It is a sand-like residue from granite quarries or natural deposits. Granite dust or granite stone meal is a natural energy and potash source. Its potash content varies between 3 and 5 percent and it contains valuable trace mineral elements. Granite dust can be used as a topdressing or worked directly into the soil. In the garden, suggested rates of application are 10–100 pounds per 1,000 square feet and on the farm, 1 to 2 tons per acre.

Greensand

Approximate analysis is 0-2-5. This is a natural source of phosphorus, potash, and trace minerals. Texas greensand is different than the glauconite from the New Jersey area. The natural Texas product contains about 19 percent iron and about 2 percent magnesium. Its pH is 8.3, but don't let that fool you. Use it on all plants for an effective green-up.

GreenSense

Approximate analysis is 5-2-4. GreenSense, all-purpose lawn and garden fertilizer, is an odor-free fertilizer made from composted dairy manure, cottonseed meal, corn gluten meal, molasses, sul-po-mag and yeast. Apply 10–20 pounds per 1,000 square feet.

GreenSense lawn and garden fertilizer has an analysis of 6-2-4. It is a granular fertilizer rich from composted poultry manure, blood meal, bonemeal, and more. Apply 10–20 pounds per 1,000 square feet.

Gypsum

This natural material is calcium sulfate and is an excellent source of calcium and sulfur. Gypsum helps neutralize plant toxins, removes sodium from the soil, and opens the soil structure to promote aeration and drainage. Gypsum is approximately 23 percent calcium and 17 percent sulfate and should not be used in high-calcium soils.

Horse Manure

Horse manure is higher in nitrogen than most other farm animal manures and is an excellent material to use for the manufacture of compost. Fresh manures should not be tilled directly into the soil unless they are applied a month before planting.

Hou-Actinite

Approximate analysis is 6-3-0 with 2 percent iron. Hou-Actinite is a granular organic fertilizer manufactured from sludge. Its nutrients are derived from activated sludge from the Department of Public Utilities–Wastewater Operations, Houston, TX. It is a low-priced fertilizer that is acceptable in an organic program if the heavy metals are monitored and kept at low levels.

Humate

Leonardite shale is basically low-grade lignite coal and is a good carbon source. Percentages of humic acid will vary. It may be mixed into liquid form or used in the dry form and is an excellent source of humic acid and trace minerals. Approximately 70 million years ago there were swamps, deltas, and streams covering most of the West. Some were salt water and some fresh water. In all cases organic material was deposited and covered by either clay or sand. Over the years these layers of organic material were slowly compressed in the earth to form oil, coal, and humate. As mountains lifted, the lower areas were exposed to the air. This exposure increased oxidation, thereby, freeing and concentrating the humic acids.

Humate is a generic name for a salt form of humic acid. Humates regulate water-holding capacity, have extremely high ion exchange capacities, and reduce soil erosion by increasing the cohesive forces of the very fine soil particles. Very low concentrations of humates have been shown to stimulate seed germination and root growth. They have also been shown to stimulate desirable soil microorganisms.

The percentage of humic acid in a humate will vary from product to product. Humates may be made into liquid form or used in the dry form.

Hydrogen Peroxide

H_2O_2 is water with an extra oxygen molecule. It is a good product for oxygenating the soil. At 3 percent it is used medicinally, at 20 percent it is lethal, and at 35 percent it is explosive.

It is a liquid source of oxygen for use in diluted amounts on soil. Hydrogen peroxide can be added to foliar feeding, fertilization, and irrigation to improve oxygen levels. Higher oxygen levels improve the plant's ability to take up available nutrients. Rates to use vary widely but start at 4 ounces of 35 percent hydrogen peroxide per 100 gallons of treated water. Severe problems require up to 32 ounces. Concentrated hydrogen peroxide mixed with organic liquids should not be transported, jostled, or left in the sprayer. It will explode! It should be handled with extreme caution. Concentrated hydrogen peroxide is very dangerous. It will burn skin, start fires, and blind animals and humans.

K-Mag—See Sul-Po-Mag

Kelp

Kelp and seaweed are the same. Large brown seaweed, especially the families *Laminariaceae* and *Fucaceae,* have been found valuable as soil conditioners. *Ascophyllum nodosum* has been given the most university research. Kelp is available in liquid or dry meal form.

Kelp Meal

Approximate analysis is from 1-0-2 to 1-2-8 with lots of trace minerals. Seaweed is a source of enzymes, nutrients, and hormones. Kelp meal is a dry fertilizer made from seaweed. It is an excellent source of plant hormones that stimulate root growth and regulate plant growth. Seaweed also provides soil-conditioning substances that improve the crumb structure or tilth. It is a good natural source of copper and boron. Use at 20–40 pounds per 1,000 square feet or 300–500 pounds per acre.

Lava Sand

The sand-sized and smaller waste material left from lava gravel is an excellent, high-energy soil amendment material. It can be used in potting soils, germination media, and bed preparation.

Lava sand, or lava in any size, increases the water-holding capacity of the soil and increases the paramagnetism. The result is increased production of any plant crop. Broadcast at 40–80 pounds per 1,000 square feet (1 ton per acre) or till into new beds at 80–150 pounds per 1,000 square feet. Lava sand works in potting soil, propagation flats, and in any container plants.

Leather Tankage

Leather tankage is a high-nitrogen slaughter house by-product. Several organic fertilizers are derived from leather tankage. Some tankage contains chemicals used in the tanning process.

Lime

Chemically, lime is the oxide of calcium, with the formula CaO. It occurs in limestone, marble, and chalk as calcium carbonate. Finely ground limestone is the best form to use because it will be more available to plants. There are two kinds of limestone available: calcic and dolomitic. Low-calcium soils usually have ample magnesium, so high calcium or calcic lime is the best calcium source. Dolomitic lime contains 30–35 percent magnesium. High-calcium lime contains only 10 percent magnesium and is preferred because most low-calcium soils have enough or too much magnesium.

Maestro-Gro

Maestro-Gro is a line of organic fertilizers that has a bonemeal base. Products include a wide variety of ingredients such as bonemeal, fish meal, feather meal, rock phosphates, kelp meal, greensand, and microorganisms. Texas T is a general-purpose product within this line. It was one of the first organic fertilizers formulated.

Medina Hasta Gro

Approximate analysis is 6-12-6. Hasta Gro is a Medina product that combines organic materials such as seaweed with urea.

Milorganite

This is sewer sludge fertilizer from Milwaukee that has been widely used on golf courses. There was a scare for a while that the product caused Lou Gehrig's disease, but this was proved to be false. It's best not to use any sewer sludge product on edible plants unless the manufacturer offers proof of no heavy metal contamination.

Molasses

Approximate analysis is 1-0-5. Molasses provides food for microorganisms and is a source of carbon, sulfur, and potash. It is a good, quick source of energy for the soil life and microbes in a compost pile, and will chase fire ants.

Pig Manure

Approximate analysis is .5-.3-.5. It is a good source of humus, microorganisms, major nutrients, and trace minerals.

Potassium Sulfate

Natural sulfate of potash is made from minerals extracted from the Great Salt Lake. A unique process combines solar energy in a solar evaporation pond system as a first step, and water and natural gas in the final step. The potash and sulfate ions dissolved in the lake water are concentrated and crystallized with solar energy in the large solar evaporation pond system. Some organic fertilizers contain this material as a natural potash source. Use potassium sulfate by itself, when needed, up to the rate of 10 pounds per 1,000 square feet or 200–300 pounds per acre.

Rabbit Manure

Approximate analysis is from 2-1-5 to 3-2-1. Rabbit manure is not used enough; it is an excellent source of natural nutrition. Mixed with leaves, sawdust, straw, grass, and other vegetative materials, it makes an excellent compost. Rabbit manure is rich in nitrogen, is good for heating a compost pile, and can be applied directly to the garden soil. It can be used on lawns, vegetable gardens, and around trees and shrubs all through the year.

Sawdust, straw, dry leaves, grass, cedar flakes, and similar dry materials can be used for litter in the hutch, producing an excellent compost when the droppings and urine are caught and absorbed by these materials. Earthworms love rabbit manure. Rabbit manure compost is an excellent soil builder.

Sheep Manure

Approximate analysis is .55-.31-.15. Sheep manure is a good natural fertilizer and a good ingredient for the compost pile.

Sludge Compost

Approximate analysis is 3-2-0. Sludge compost is made from city sewage and a high-carbon source such as wood chips or tree trimmings. Most cities should produce this product. Heavy metal contamination is a concern, especially for food crops. As long as the heavy metal levels are kept under control, this is an excellent organic soil amendment.

Soft Phosphate Rock (Colloidal)

Soft rock phosphate is a clay material that is surface mined from the old settling basins of former hard phosphate rock mining operations in Florida. It contains about 20 percent P_2O_5 as well as over 25 percent lime and other trace minerals. It is a very fine material, but can be applied with all common fertilizer spreaders. Natural phosphate stays where it's put when applied and does not move or dissolve into the soil solution. It needs to be plowed under or tilled into the soil.

Phosphate, indicated by the middle letter of N-P-K, is a major element used in abundance. A plant must have it for root development when the seed sprouts or a seedling is transplanted. The availability is very low in strongly acid and high-alkaline soils. The availability is also low in cool soils, when the microbes are not very active.

An annual plant takes up to 60 percent of its total phosphates needs the first few weeks of its life. If it doesn't get phosphate, it is always behind and never catches up. Soft rock phosphate used directly under the seed or transplant at planting time is the very best

method of application, especially in low-acid or high-alkaline soils. It is not as critical, but still beneficial, in slightly acid to neutral soils. It is almost impossible to overuse soft rock phosphate. You can grow beautiful plants directly in it without any harmful effects.

Plants need a boost of phosphate again for blooming, but in organically rich soils, microbes are active enough and root mass is large enough to supply plenty.

The old style super phosphate 0-18-0 or 0-20-0, made by treating rock phosphate with an equal amount of sulfuric acid, was also a good source of phosphate in low-acid or high-alkaline soils because it became calcium sulfate and calcium phosphate, which are two natural products found in nature. However, little, if any, is still made.

The phosphate source more commonly used now is triple super phosphate 0-46-0. It is used in most fertilizers. It is made by treating rock phosphate with phosphoric acid. The end product is considered "naked" and tends to bond with iron, zinc, manganese, and other trace minerals and renders them unavailable.

Soft phosphate rock should be applied at a rate approximately double that of hard phosphate rock, about two tons per acre with other organic amendments. This phosphorus source will soon be gone. It is the by-product of the making of 0-18-0, and only one company still bags it. In alkaline soils, apply the phosphate directly under the seed or transplants so the small roots don't have to search for it. Tests at Garden-Ville have shown that this technique can double production.

Sugar

Sugar is a helpful soil amendment used to stimulate microorganisms and to initiate the metabolic processes in the soil. White sugar, when used with other trace minerals in organic fertilizers, is an excellent carbohydrate source. Molasses is even better. For more on the benefits of sugar, read Dr. Arden Anderson's *Science in Agriculture*. Sugar should be used on gardens or fields at about 5–10 pounds per 1,000 square feet or less.

Some farmers are using small amounts per acre of sugar, humate, and urea. A starting formula for transition to an organic program could be 50 pounds of sugar, 100 pounds of humate, and 100 pounds of urea per acre.

Sulfur

Sulfur is a basic mineral often lacking in alkaline soils. Applying granulated sulfur at 5 pounds per 1,000 square feet twice annually can bring base saturation of calcium down and raise magnesium. Be careful not to breathe dust, over apply, or use when planting seed. It can also act as a preemergent. Mix with corn gluten meal and humate for even better results. Sulfur dust is also used as a pesticide in some situations.

Sul-Po-Mag

Approximate analysis is 0-0-22. It is also called Langbeinite and K-Mag. Sul-Po-Mag is a mined source of sulfur, potassium, and magnesium. It is a naturally occurring mineral containing 22 percent sulfur, 22 percent potash, and 11.1 percent magnesium that is naturally granulated. Apply at 20 pounds per acre as needed.

Sustane

Approximate analysis is 5-2-4. A granulated fertilizer made from composted turkey manure, sustane has some odor for 24 to 36 hours but has shown excellent soil improvement and reduction of diseases. It is one of the fastest working organic fertilizers. Apply at 20 pounds per 1,000 square feet or 400–800 pounds per acre.

Turkey Manure

Turkey manure is a high-nitrogen manure that is an excellent ingredient for compost. It is best to compost before using.

Urea

Urea is a synthetic protein and the best choice of all the synthetic fertilizers. Microbes accept urea as they do urine. It contains 45 percent nitrogen. Natural urea is a waste product from animals. Synthetic urea is the only manmade fertilizer that contains carbon. However, sugar or molasses and humic acid needs to be applied with it to maximize its efficiency. It is made synthetically by reacting ammonia and carbon dioxide under high pressure and temperature. Urea, when used in conjunction with organic matter and sugar, is an effective and organically acceptable fertilizer. Humates are a good organic-matter choice for this use. Large amounts of urea can damage seeds, and vegetation can be toxic to aquatic life because of ammonia buildup. Not acceptable in organic gardening.

Urine

This is a natural source of urea. Livestock urine is high in nitrogen and potassium, containing two-thirds of the nitrogen and four-fifths of the potassium voided by an animal. Use plenty of bedding to capture the urine. Soaked bedding or liquid can be applied at will to garden or field crops and pastures. Because urine is relatively concentrated, it should be applied sparingly and only in damp weather for best results.

Fertilization with urine alone can produce extra-fine growth of grasses and clover much earlier in the spring than other types of feeding. The elements in urine are more quickly available because they are in solution. Urine is also a good activator for converting crop residues to humus.

Vinegar

Vinegar is a wonderful organic tool that was discovered by accident ten thousand years ago when wine was accidentally allowed to ferment too long and turned sour. It can be made from many products including beer, apples, berries, beets, corn, fruits, grains, honey, malt, maple syrup, melons, molasses, potatoes, rice, sorghum, and other foods containing sugar. Natural sugars from these food products are fermented into alcohol, which is then fermented into vinegar.

Fruit vinegar is made from the fermentation of a variety of fruits. Apples are most commonly used, but grapes, peaches, berries, and other fruits also work. The product label will identify the starting ingredients, such as "apple cider vinegar" or "wine vinegar." Malt vinegar is made from the fermentation of barley malt or other cereal grains. Sugar vinegar is made from sugar, syrup, or molasses. White, spirit, or distilled vinegar is made by fermenting distilled alcohol. Distilled white vinegar is made from 190-proof alcohol that is fermented by adding sugar and living bacteria. Natural vinegar contains at least 50 trace minerals.

The strongest vinegar available for general use is 20 percent or 200-grain, meaning that about 20 percent of the liquid is acetic acid. At this strength, which is corrosive enough to eat metal and must be handled carefully in plastic containers, it will obviously kill weeds, making it an effective nonselective organic herbicide. It works best when sprayed full strength during the heat of the day and in full sunlight. While 200-grain (20 percent) material is the best strength for killing weeds, 100-grain (10 percent), which is made by doubling the amount of water in the 200-grain vinegar, seems to work just about as well if used consistently. Moreover, since this diluting process cuts the cost in half, it's usually advisable to use the weaker solution.

The other horticultural use for vinegar is the watering can. If your water is alkaline, add 1 tablespoon of 50-grain (5 percent) natural apple cider vinegar to each gallon of water to improve the quality of the water for potted plants and bedding. This doesn't have to be done with every watering, though it wouldn't hurt. This technique is especially helpful when trying to grow acid-loving plants such as gardenias, azaleas, and dogwoods. A tablespoon of vinegar per gallon added to the sprayer when foliar feeding lawns, shrubs, flowers, and trees is also highly beneficial, especially where soil or water is alkaline.

Zeolite

A natural ore used to absorb odors, gases, liquids, and as an amendment to most soils, zeolites originates from volcanic minerals with unique characteristics. Their chemical structure classifies them as hydrated aluminosilicates comprised of hydrogen, oxygen, aluminum, and silicon arranged in an interconnecting lattice structure. Zeolites have the ability to absorb certain harmful or unwanted elements from soil, water, and air. An example of this is the removal of calcium from hard water. Zeolite has a strong affinity for certain heavy metals such as lead and chromium. Zeolite works as a soil amendment by absorbing nutrients, especially ammonia, and then releasing them at a rate more beneficial to plant root development.

Zeolite can also be used for air and water purification, cat litter material, shoe deodorizers, animal feed supplements, garage floor spill removers, cooler and refrigerator odor and moisture removers, animal stall odor and moisture removers, and soil amendments. Mix raw zeolite (powder or granular) into the soil for new bed preparation. Broadcast onto contaminated soil to detoxify. Rates can vary from 10 to 50 pounds per 1,000 square feet. More than 50 pounds won't hurt anything but is probably a waste of money. Zeolite has a very high cation exchange capacity (CEC). It helps fertilizer to be more efficient.

CHAPTER 5

CONTROLLING PESTS THE NATURAL WAY

Ever wonder how insects were kept under control or why plants weren't devoured by destructive insects before man started to "control" the environment? The answer lies in the fact that nature has a balanced, natural order.

With the proliferation of chemicals during the twentieth century, many beneficial insects have been killed along with harmful insects. Generally, the harmful ones will re-establish themselves more quickly than will the beneficial ones, and plant loss accelerates. Encouraging beneficial insects to establish again is a primary goal of an organic program. However, there are many safe or low-toxic products available to transition from a chemical program to an organic program that will reduce the harmful effects to beneficial insect population.

A report by the scientific journal *Bioscience* says that a mere one percent of the pesticides applied to plants ever reaches its ultimate destination—the insects. The other 99 percent pollutes and poisons the air, soil, water, good bugs, animals, and man.

Releasing lady beetles.

BENEFICIAL INSECTS

It would be impossible to cover all the beneficial insects because approximately 98 percent of the world's insects are beneficial. It could be argued that even the destructive bugs are good because they eliminate weak plants.

Friendly bugs are being used more and more to help control destructive insects in vegetable gardens, stored grain, greenhouses, and orchards. Parasitic mites and wasps are being used to control houseflies, barnyard flies, and fire ants.

Earthworms, centipedes, and millipedes are not technically insects, but they are beneficial. Centipedes and millipedes are helpful because they aerate the soil, produce nutrients, and help break down organic material.

Biodiversity is a critical part of successful organic gardening. The vegetable garden and landscape should have a healthy and dynamic mix of insects, plants, animals, and birds.

Man must fit into that puzzle as well. Here's some information on the insects that can help you maintain your gardens. The best way to control troublesome insects is to allow them to control themselves. Nature provides beautiful checks and balances if we allow them to function.

Ground Beetles

One-third of all living creatures and 40 percent of all insects are beetles. All beetles have hard, opaque wing covers that meet in a straight line down the middle of their backs. Ground beetles are important predators of plant-eating insects. They usually feed at night on soft-bodied larvae including cankerworms and tent caterpillars. They also eat many kinds of slugs and snails. Soldier beetles, which are ground beetles, feed on aphids, grasshopper eggs, cucumber beetles, and various caterpillars.

Ladybugs

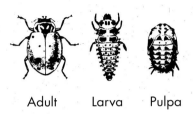

Adult   Larva   Pulpa

Lady bird beetle is the proper term for these insects, but these little friends are best known as ladybugs. The ladybug is the most popular and most universally known beneficial insect. There are several hundred different kinds in North America, and all are beneficial. The most common native varieties are black with red spots or gray with black spots. They are all very helpful and should be protected. Orange ladybugs with black spots are the most available commercially.

Yellow ladybug eggs are visible in the late winter and early spring in clusters on the backs of leaves and on the trunks of trees. The adult ladybug can eat 200 aphids per day, the larvae 70– 100 per day. The larvae and the adult beetles eat large quantities of aphids and other small, soft-bodied insects such as scale, thrips, and mealy bugs. They should be released after aphids are visible and at night (or at least the cool part of the day) after the foliage has been wet down. Let a few out at a time to see if they are hungry. If they fly away, put the remaining ones in the refrigerator for a day or two and try again later after they have used up their stored food. Ladybugs will store in the refrigerator for a few days (35°–45° is best for storage). They will remain dormant and alive under these cool temperatures, although storage tends to dry them out and a few will die. They will naturalize if chemical sprays are eliminated.

For ladybugs to mature and lay eggs, they need a nectar and pollen source, such as flowering plants. Legumes such as peas, beans, clover, and alfalfa are especially good. To make an artificial food, dilute a little honey with a small amount of water and mix in a little brewer's yeast or bee pollen. Streak tiny amounts of this mixture on small pieces of waxed paper, and fasten these to plants. Replace these every five to six days, or when they become moldy. Keep any extra food refrigerated between feedings. The ladybug's favorite real food is the aphid.

If ladybugs are released indoors or in a greenhouse, you might want to screen off any openings to prevent their escape.

Fireflies (Lightning Bugs)

Adult

The firefly is a fascinating insect that produces a light by releasing luciferin from its abdomen to combine with oxygen. When conditions are right, the male flashes his light every six seconds to be answered by the female two seconds later. Firefly larvae feed on snails, slugs, cutworms, and mites.

Green Lacewings

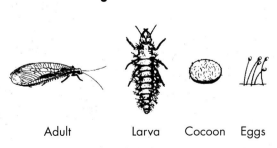

Adult   Larva   Cocoon   Eggs

The green lacewing is a beautiful, fragile, light green or brown insect with lustrous, yellow eyes. The adult is approximately one-half inch long, holds its wings up tent-like when at rest, and feeds on honeydew, nectar, and pollen. The adults really aren't terribly beneficial. They just fly around, look pretty, and mate. The larvae, on the other hand, are voracious eaters of aphids, red spider mites, thrips, mealybugs, cottony cushion scale, and many worms.

The lacewing larvae (also known as "aphid lions") emerge from eggs that look like tiny cotton swabs on the end of thin, white filaments attached to leaves or stems. The larva pupates by spinning a cocoon with silken thread. The adult emerges in about five days by cutting a hole in the cocoon.

If it is inconvenient to release the lacewing immediately after purchase, the eggs or larvae may be refrigerated for a few days, but be careful not to freeze. Temperatures of 38° to 45°F will delay development but not hurt the eggs.

Eggs and larvae can be sprinkled by hand wherever harmful insects exist or are suspected. Even if you put them in the wrong place, they will search almost 100 feet for their first meal. One of the best ways to distribute lacewing eggs and larvae is with a pill bottle with a small hole in the cap. A salt shaker will work but you have to increase the size of the holes. A thimble will hold about 10,000 eggs. Releasing the green lacewing from a card or cup mounted in a tree will keep fire ants from getting them before they do their work. It helps to put some Tree Trunk Goop on the tree (see page 59) to help block the ants' access.

Lacewing larvae are gray in color. They look like tiny alligators and mature in two to three weeks. Biweekly releases are ideal. Flowering plants attract green lacewings; buckwheat, vetch, mints, and other fragrant plants are especially good.

Nematodes

Beneficial nematodes are microscopic roundworms used to control cutworms, armyworms, corn rootworms, cabbage loopers, Colorado potato beetles, grubworms, termites, and other soil pests. They will even help with fire ants and fleas. Nematodes enter the insect pest through the mouth or

other body openings. Once inside the host, the nematodes feed and reproduce until the food supply is gone. Then hordes of nematodes emerge in search of new victims. Early applications prior to heavy pest infestations, followed by monthly or quarterly applications, is the ideal solution.

Heterorhabditis (Heteros) nematode species are the best for controlling grubs. *Steinernema* (Steiners) work for grubs but are better for moths.

Predatory Mites

The adult predatory mite is orange in color. The immature stages are a pale salmon color. Predatory mites can be differentiated from the "red" two-spotted spider mite by the lack of spots on either side. The body is pear-shaped, and the front legs are longer than those of pest mites. Predatory mites move about quickly when disturbed or exposed to bright light, and they multiply twice as quickly as pest mites do, with the females laying about 50 eggs. They eat from five to twenty eggs and adults of troublesome mites per day.

Release predatory mites at the first sign of spider mite damage. For heavy infestations, you will probably need to reduce the populations of pest mites with organic sprays such as citrus sprays or garlic-pepper tea and seaweed. Seaweed alone or Garrett Juice are the best choices because they don't hurt the beneficial insects.

Praying Mantis

These fierce-looking but friendly critters will eat almost any insect, especially caterpillars, grasshoppers, beetles, and other damaging pests. Be careful not to confuse the egg cases with the asp, which is a soft, hairy insect with a powerful sting. The praying mantis egg case looks very similar to an asp or puss caterpillar but is hard like papier-mâché. The only negative characteristics about praying mantis is that they are known to eat beneficial insects.

Spiders

Most spiders are beneficial and harmless, with the exceptions of the black widow and brown recluse. You'll rarely see a brown recluse because they seek out dark corners in closets, etc., and move about at night. The female black widow is easy to identify by the red hourglass under her abdomen. Beware of her because her venomous sting is very powerful and can cause illness and even death. The puny little male isn't much trouble. In fact, the female devours him after mating. Control dangerous spiders with thorough vacuuming and citrus sprays.

Trichogramma Wasps

Trichogramma wasps, or "moth egg parasites," are used to control pecan casebearer, cabbage worms, tomato horn worms, corn earworms, and other caterpillars. They are

tiny parasitic wasps that attack over 200 types of worm pests. Trichogramma wasps sting the pest worm eggs and deposit eggs inside. The eggs hatch and the larvae feed on and kill the pests.

Early release of trichogramma before a problem has been diagnosed is the ideal way to begin a pest control program. The first releases of the year should be about the time of leaf emergence in the spring. Weekly or biweekly releases throughout the early growing season are ideal.

Wasps

All wasps and mud daubers are beneficial. One of their favorite foods is the webworm that often disfigures pecan trees. The tiny trichogramma wasp is very effective for controlling cutworms, moths, and the pecan casebearer by laying its eggs on the eggs of the pests. When the wasp's eggs hatch, the larvae feed on the pest's eggs. Wasps will sting only if you threaten them, and the mud dauber only if you grab it! Trichogramma and other friendly wasps don't sting at all. Mud daubers help eliminate black widow spiders and flies in horse stables and barns. Braconid wasps kill pests by laying their eggs in hosts like hornworms, codling moths, and aphids. Wasps are very beneficial in the vegetable garden and orchard.

Whitefly Parasites

The whitefly parasite can help to deter serious damage to tomatoes, cucumbers, and ornamental plants. *Encarsia formosa* is a small, efficient parasite of the whitefly. It is about the size of a spider mite. It attacks the whitefly in the immature stages, laying eggs in the third and fourth stages, while feeding off the first and second stages. Early application of *Encarsia formosa* prior to heavy infestations is recommended. Parasites should be released at the first sign of whitefly.

HARMFUL INSECTS

Aphids—the most famous insect pest—
or are they?

Aphids

Aphids are sucking insects that can destroy the tender growth of plants, causing stunted and curled leaf growth and leaving a honeydew deposit. They can be controlled by spraying citrus oil or molasses or just strong blasts of water and then releasing green lacewings and ladybugs. Protecting ladybugs and lacewings and promoting soil health and biodiversity is the best control for these indicator pests. Regular releases of beneficial insects give excellent control, but adapted plants and healthy soil are the best permanent control.

Ants

There are many different ants, including carpenter ants, cut ants, fire ants, and pharaoh ants. Solutions for ants indoors include diatomaceous earth, boric acid, and baking soda. Soapy water poured into individual mounds is a safe and effective technique for getting rid of ants. The best tool is a mix of manure compost tea, citrus oil, and molasses. Fertilizers that contain molasses are helpful long-term.

Bagworms

Bagworms are a common pest of ornamental trees and some shrubs. They prey on many different species of plants such as cedar, juniper, and cypress. In the larval stage they can defoliate trees. They look like tiny Christmas trees walking and eating across the leaf surface. They can be controlled by *Bacillus thuringiensis* (Bt). Hand picking the bags is also beneficial for control. Trichogramma wasps can help to control problem infestations. Garden-Ville Fire Ant Control formula also works.

Bees

Bees are beneficial and should be protected. For the proper environmental control, contact the beekeeper club or society in your area. Someone from the club will usually come to get the bees or give you advice on control. Problem bees can be killed with soapy water or citrus-based sprays.

Beetles

Many adult beetles eat plant foliage and can destroy plants completely. An effective solution for destructive beetles is dry diatomaceous earth and/or citrus oil. Garlic tea is an even less toxic control. It's important to remember that many beetles are beneficial and only eat problem insects.

Borers

Borers attack softwood trees and trees in stress. Adult beetles will eat tender terminal growth and then deposit their eggs in the base of the tree. Eggs hatch into larvae and

bore into trees and tunnel through the wood until the tree is weakened. Active, tunneling larvae can be killed with a stiff wire run into the holes. Beneficial nematodes put directly in holes will usually kill active larvae, but keeping trees healthy and out of stress is the best prevention. A generous amount of diatomaceous earth at the base of susceptible trees will also help. Tree Trunk Goop (see end of this chapter) applied to borer damage on trunks is possibly the best tool for existing borer attacks.

Cabbage Loopers

Cabbage loopers are the larvae of moths and are brown with silver spots in the middle of each wing. They can be killed with Bt spray when in the larval stage. Use soap as a surfactant and spray late in the day because these guys feed at night. Trichogramma wasps will also help control these critters. Chemical insecticides are ineffective at controlling loopers. Citrus-based products will also control them.

Cankerworms

The cankerworm hangs on a silk thread from trees. It doesn't do a lot of damage. Wasps will usually control them. If not, use Bt for heavy infestations. Spray infestations with Bt products or citrus-based products.

Caterpillars

Caterpillars are best known for their ability to defoliate trees and vegetables. *Bacillus thuringiensis* (Bt) is an excellent biological control. Wasps are also a great help in controlling caterpillars of all kinds. Remember that caterpillars grow up to be beautiful butterflies, so don't kill them all.

Chiggers

Chiggers are known for their very annoying bite. The itching usually starts the day after you are bitten and lasts two to four days. Vinegar rubbed on bites will eliminate the itching. Diatomaceous earth and sulfur will help prevent bites and control the critters. Treat infested sites with 5 pounds of sulfur per 1,000 square feet.

Chinch Bugs

Chinch bugs are tiny, black, pinhead size or larger. During hot, dry weather, chinch bugs can destroy unhealthy turf and other crops. Lawns will look yellow, turn brown, and then die. This insect hardly ever attacks healthy, well-maintained grass. Diatomaceous earth will easily control them. Dust at 2 pounds per 1,000 square feet.

Crickets

Crickets live in and out of doors, destroy fabrics such as wool, cotton, synthetics, and

silk, and also attack plants. Their irritating sound is the primary objection from most people; however, they will eat tender sprouts of wildflowers and vegetables. Solutions include diatomaceous earth for outdoors, and boric acid for indoor use. *Nosema locustae,* a biological control for grasshoppers and crickets, sold under the brand names Nolo Bait, Grasshopper Attack, and Semisphore, is the best overall control available. Citrus-based products also work.

Elm Leaf Beetles

Wherever there is an American, Siberian, or cedar elm tree, the elm leaf beetle can be found. The elm leaf beetle will eat and damage lots of foliage and then move to the next tree. Trees can die from defoliation but only unhealthy trees are seriously attacked by elm leaf beetles. Solutions include Bt and citrus sprays. Strong populations of beneficial insects will also help.

Fire Ants

Individual mounds can be killed out on dry days by stirring dry diatomaceous earth into the hills. The D-E treatment is not effective on humid days. Dry instant grits and other cereals poured on top of mounds also seem to work. The best tool is a drench of manure compost tea, citrus oil, and molasses. Applying beneficial nematodes to the site is another effective treatment for fire ants. Once the heavy infestations have been knocked back, the ants can be kept away with a regular spraying of any organic spray product that contains molasses, such as Garrett Juice. I do not recommend any synthetic product any longer because the toxic products simply aren't necessary. Establishing biodiversity of frogs, toads, snakes, lizards, birds, insects, and native microorganisms is the best long-term control of the imported pests.

Fleas

Fleas can live for many months without food. They generally invade a house on a pet or on people. While not destructive to plants, they are a nuisance for pets and their owners. Control with diatomaceous earth and citrus sprayed around pets' favorite resting spots. Plant rue, wormwood, and pennyroyal mint. Spray with Garden-Ville Fire Ant Control and use beneficial nematodes outdoors. Dust pet sleeping quarters with natural diatomaceous earth and bathe animals in citrus (d-limonene based) shampoos.

Flies

Flies can be repelled with fresh, crushed tansy or garlic. Fly parasites are the most economical and most effective control.

Fleahoppers

This is a common vegetable garden pest. It sucks juices from the foliage and causes a loss of leaf color, which stresses plants. Sulfur and

diatomaceous earth will usually get rid of it. Citrus oil spray is an effective tool. Garrett Juice plus neem, citrus, and garlic is even better.

Forest Tent Caterpillars

These caterpillars will sometimes do some damage in early spring, but if pesticides are avoided, the beneficial wasps will usually keep these guys under control. Bt products can be used if the caterpillars get out of hand. At worst, they are only a temporary problem.

Fungus Gnats

Fungus gnats are present when the soil surface is too wet. They do little, if any, damage but are annoying. They can be eliminated by drying out the soil. Baking soda sprayed lightly on soil will quickly solve the problem. Drenches of citrus or neem or Bt will also work. Add 00-sandblasting sand to surface of soil in pots.

Grasshoppers

Grasshoppers feed on numerous plants. They are usually kept in check by natural predators such as birds, but on occasion the conditions can be right for them to increase to numbers significant enough to be devastating. Use strong citrus-based sprays. Garlic-pepper tea spray will discourage them. *Nosema locustae* is an effective, long-term, biological control.

Grubworms

Adult June beetles will chew leaves, and subterranean grubs will eat roots of grass and garden plants. Broadcast sugar at 5 pounds per 1,000 square feet and release beneficial nematodes. Grubs are rarely a problem in healthy, biologically active, well-drained soil.

Lacebugs

Lacebugs attack various deciduous trees and broadleafed evergreens. The lacebug is flat and oval and sucks the sap from the underside of the leaf. A quick solution for this pest is garlic-pepper tea and diatomaceous earth. Healthy biodiversity in the garden will eliminate a destructive population of this pest.

Leafhoppers

Leafhoppers excrete honeydew and damage leaves causing stunted, dwarfed, and yellow foliage. They can be controlled with citrus spray or simply by the encouragement of diverse populations of beneficial insects.

Leaf Miners

Leaf miners will cause brown foliage on tips that often continues over the entire leaf. Neem products or a mix of compost tea, citrus, and molasses are effective. Leaf miners cause minor damage only, so treatment is rarely needed.

Leaf Skeletonizers

These insects are the same as the sawfly caterpillar. They cause cosmetic damage to red oak and other tree leaves. Usually it is not necessary to treat these pests because damage is usually confined to isolated spots in the foliage.

Mealybugs

Mealybugs are sucking insects that look like cotton on plant stems. Mealybugs suck sap from the foliage and stems and can destroy plants. Mealybugs like warm weather and will also infest houseplants. Helpful controls include citrus sprays, neem, natural diatomaceous earth, predator insects, and lizards. For houseplant problems, dab alcohol on the bugs with a cotton swab.

Mosquitoes

Drain all stagnant water. Other controls include citrus sprays, purple martins, frogs, toads, and bats. *Bacillus thuringiensis* 'Israelensis' will kill mosquito larvae in decorative ponds without harming fish or aquatic plants. Encouraging birds, especially purple martins, is extremely helpful. Bats are also great friends in controlling mosquitoes. Garlic-pepper tea can be sprayed before a party or outdoor event to lessen the problem. Citronella candles will also help to repel these pests. Garrett Juice plus citrus and hot pepper is the best control.

Nematodes

Many nematodes are beneficial, but there are those that will attack trees, garden plants,

Phylloxera

This is a microscopic louse that feeds on grape vines and other food crops by attaching itself to and sucking the life from roots. It is a big problem in California, but can happen here too in unhealthy soil. Use of cover crops and a strong buildup of humus and tilth will help retard the movement of this pest. Orange peeling pulp will help, and strong microbial biodiversity will end the problem.

annuals, and perennials. Controls include increasing the organic level in soil, using organic fertilizers, and applying products that increase microbial activity. Cedar flakes applied to the soil surface will also help. Citrus pulp or liquid will completely control root knot nematodes.

Red Spider Mites

Pill Bugs

Red spider mites are very small and feed on garden plants and ornamental trees. You probably will not see the mites but you will notice the webbing that accompanies them. The best control is beneficial insects such as green lacewings. Controls also include spraying seaweed or garlic-pepper tea. Predatory mites are also effective.

Pill bugs and sow bugs are crustaceans and related to shrimp, crabs, and crawfish. They are found in damp places and feed on organic matter but, when abundant, will also eat plants. Beer in a trap is still one solutions, but it is too much trouble. Banana peels attract them so you can scoop them up and drop them into a soapy water solution. Hot pepper sprays or dry crushed red pepper and diatomaceous earth are effective.

Roaches

Plum Curculios

Garrett Juice plus garlic applied at pink bud, then again after the flower petals have fallen, and then at least once a month is the recommended spray program. Thick mulch, at least 4 inches of compost, rough bark, or tree chips is important. Regular spraying of garlic tea is also effective. Biodiversity is critical for control of this pest.

There are numerous cockroaches, but only a few really pose a problem. Cockroaches usually live out of doors and are nocturnal by nature. They will enter a home or building through any crack or crevice. They will chew on cloth or books. Some solutions are a shoe, newspaper, diatomaceous earth, keeping your house clean, eliminating standing water, and sealing all openings. Boric acid indoors gives effective control. Eliminating the food and water sources is a great help. They are not much trouble outdoors for gardeners.

Scale

Scale insects attach to stems, branches, and trunks and suck sap from the plants. Controls include horticultural oil and Garden-Ville with cedar resin. Use citrus spray with seaweed on interior plants. The black, scale-eating ladybug is very helpful. Neem products are also effective.

Slugs

Slugs and snails must be kept moist at all times and will go anywhere there is moisture. Effective controls include garlic-pepper tea and diatomaceous earth, crushed red pepper, beer traps, and wood ashes.

Squash Bugs

Squash bugs are difficult to control and attack squash, cucumbers, pumpkins, and other cucurbits. Control by smashing the eggs, dusting the adults with all-purpose flour, and planting lemon balm or petunias in between plants. Citrus oil sprays will kill them. Even better is Garrett Juice plus citrus and garlic.

Squash Vine Borers

The squash vine borer is an insect whose larva is a worm that bores into the base stem

of squash, cucumber, melon, gourd, and pumpkin. Control includes cutting the stem open, removing the worms, and covering the wounded area with soil. Another way is to inject Bt into the base of the stem with a syringe. Spraying with Bt will also help. Best control is to spray regularly with Garrett Juice plus citrus and garlic or neem and apply beneficial nematodes to the soil.

Stink Bugs

Stink bugs sting fruit and cause rotted spots. They can be controlled with citrus-based sprays. Some stink bugs are beneficial.

Termites

Use a boric acid, wood-treatment product. Using 00-sandblasting sand or 16-grit sand barrier on the inside and outside of grade beams works well. New construction can use the sand under the slab with the engineer's approval. Citrus products will kill the pests on contact. Sulfur on top of the soil will also help. Apply beneficial nematodes to the soil around buildings. Termites are little trouble to food crops.

Thrips

Thrips attack buds and tight-petaled flowers such as roses. Thrips are barely visible to the naked eye but will rasp the plant tissue and drain the sap. Heavy infestations can kill plants. Thrips are general eaters and will attack flowers or field crops. Controls include seaweed and green lacewings. For more power, use a mix of Garrett Juice, citrus, garlic, and neem.

Ticks

Ticks are difficult to control, but spraying with citrus, garlic, and neem works quite well. Bathing pets regularly will help considerably. Beneficial nematodes applied to the site will also help.

Whiteflies

Whiteflies are very small and resemble little white moths. They are extremely hard to control with chemicals and will suck the juices from several kinds of plants. They will attack vegetables and ornamental plants outdoors and indoors. Seaweed, citrus, and garlic-pepper tea spray work well. However, beneficial insect populations will prevent the pest. Whiteflies have many natural enemies. (To make garlic-pepper tea, see page 57.)

ORGANIC DISEASE CONTROL

Increased disease resistance for plants results as a nice side benefit from the use of organic products and healthy soil.

When soil is healthy, there is a never-ending microscopic war being waged between the good guys and bad microorganisms, and the good guys usually win. Disease problems are simply situations in which the harmful

Damping off disease on young seedlings.

microscopic plants and animals have gotten out of balance. If allowed to do so, nature will *usually* control the disease problems.

Drainage is also a key ingredient for the prevention of diseases. Beds or tree pits that hold water and don't drain properly are the ideal breeding place for many disease organisms.

As with insects, spraying for diseases treats the symptoms only, not the major problems. The primary cause of problems is usually related to the soil and the root system. Therefore, it is critical to improve drainage, increase air circulation, add organic material, and stimulate and protect the living organisms in the soil.

Occasional soil fungi problems can be controlled with cornmeal at 20 pounds per 1,000 square feet. Foliage pathogens in general can be controlled with Garrett Juice plus garlic and neem.

Other diseases can be addressed as explained below.

Anthracnose

This is a serious fungal problem in some trees, beans, and other food crops in which the foliage turns a tan color overnight. Control is difficult other than by avoiding susceptible plants. Bordeaux mix, baking soda, garlic, or neem sprayed as leaves emerge in the spring will sometimes help. The best cure is soil improvement.

Bacterial Blight

This bacterial disease causes dark-green water spots that turn brown and may leave a hole in the leaves of tomatoes, plums, and other crops. Control includes healthy soil, baking soda spray, potassium bicarbonate spray, garlic tea, neem, Bordeaux mix, or Garrett Juice, plus one of the above.

Black Spot

This is the more common name of fungal leaf spot. Black spot attacks the foliage of plants such as roses. There is usually a yellow halo around the dark spot. Entire leaves then turn yellow and ultimately die. Best controls include selection of resistant plants, sprays of Garrett Juice plus one of the following: neem, garlic, or potassium bicarbonate. Garrett Juice plus garlic is usually all that's needed long-term.

Canker

This is a stress-related disease of trees and shrubs that causes decay of the bark and wood. Healthy soil and plants are the best solution. Use Tree Trunk Goop for problem areas.

Cotton Root Rot

A fungal disease common in alkaline soils, cotton root rot attacks poorly adapted plants. The best preventative is healthy soil with a balance of nutrients and soil biology. Solutions include adding sulfur and sometimes sodium to the soil at 5–10 pounds per 1,000 square feet. Products that contain sodium will sometimes help. Cornmeal and biological products such as Actinovate and BioInnoculant will also help.

Damping Off

This is a disease of emerging seedlings in which tiny plants fall over as if severed at the ground line. Avoid damping off by using living (not sterilized) soil and by placing colloidal phosphate on the surface of planting media. Treatment with cornmeal is also effective.

Entomosporium

A disease of photinia, hawthorns, and other related plants. This fungal leaf spot can be controlled by improving soil conditions and avoiding susceptible plants. Aerate the root zone and apply compost, Texas greensand, sugar, cornmeal, and one of the biostimulants.

Fireblight

This is a disease of plants in the rose family in which twigs and limbs die back as though they have been burned. Leaves usually remain attached but often turn black or dark brown. Prune back into healthy tissue and disinfect pruning tools with a 3 percent solution of hydrogen peroxide. Spray plants at first sign of disease with Garrett Juice plus garlic and neem. Consan 20 and agricultural streptomycin are also effective controls.

Powdery Mildew

This is a white or gray, powdery, fungal growth on the leaf surface and flower buds of zinnias, crape myrtles, and many vegetables. Controls include baking soda spray, potassium bicarbonate spray, neem, garlic, and horticultural oil.

Phytophthora

This is a genus of fungi that is a root, crown, or stem pathogen and a common disease of ornamental and food crops. Beneficial microbes in healthy soil will keep this disease organism under control. Cover crops and lots of humus in the soil will also help.

Sooty Mold

This is black fungal growth on the foliage of food crops infested with aphids, scale, or whiteflies. It is caused by the honeydew (excrement) of the insect pests. Best control is to release beneficial insects to control the pest bugs. Also spray Garrett Juice plus garlic.

WEEDS

Weeds are nature's greatest and most diverse group of plants. Even though many members of the weed families are beautiful, man has been convinced by the herbicide fraternity to condemn weeds and consider them his enemy. Mention weeds and most people think in terms of control through spraying chemicals. They rarely think of the reasons weeds grow or of their value.

Weeds are here on Earth for very specific purposes. Different weeds have different jobs to do. Some are here to ensure that the soil always has the protection of a green blanket to shade and cool the ground. Others are here to prevent the erosion of bare soil. Others are here to help balance the minerals in the soil. Many weeds provide all these important functions.

Weeds take no chances. They germinate and spread to protect any soil left bare by man's mismanagement of the land. In every cubic foot of soil lie millions of weed seeds waiting to germinate when needed. When man strips the green growth from the land, weeds are needed. When hard winters freeze the ornamental lawn grasses, weeds are needed. When we mow too low and apply harsh chemicals to the soil, weeds are needed.

If it weren't for weeds, the topsoil of the Earth would have eroded away years ago. Much of the topsoil has already gone forever from our farms to muddy our rivers and fill our lakes and eventually end up in the ocean.

It's a common misunderstanding that weeds rob our crops of moisture, sunlight, and nutrients. Weeds only borrow water and nutrients and eventually return it all to the soil for future crop use.

Weeds are tough. Rarely do you find weeds destroyed by insects or disease. Some weeds are pioneer plants as they are able to grow in soil unsuited for edible or domesticated plants. Weeds are able to build the soil with their strong and powerful roots that go deep, penetrating and loosening hard-packed soil. The deep roots bring minerals, especially trace elements, from the subsoil to the topsoil.

Weeds are indicators of certain soil deficiencies and actually collect or manufacture certain mineral elements that are lacking in the soil. This is nature's wonderful way of buffering and balancing the chemistry of soil.

Some weeds are good companion plants. Some have insect-repelling abilities, while others with deep roots help surface-feeding plants obtain moisture during dry spells. Weeds act as straws to bring water up from the deep, moist soil so that shallow-rooted plants can get some of the moisture.

Control becomes necessary when vigorous weeds become too numerous in fields and gardens. However, not understanding the dangers of spraying chemicals into the environment, many farmers, gardeners, and landscape people have primarily used powerful, toxic herbicides. Most herbicides upset or unbalance the harmony of soil organisms, and some herbicides can persist in the soil for months. Even though microbes can repopulate after chemical-treatment damage, they are slow to reestablish the complicated, natural balance.

There are safe and nonpolluting weed control methods such as mechanically aerating, mulching with organic materials, and using organic fertilizers to stimulate the growth of more desirable plants. The old, reliable methods of hand weeding, hoeing, and timely cultivating are not yet against the law and are good exercise.

Easy and effective weed control in the ornamental and vegetable beds is done by keeping a thick blanket of mulch on the bare soil at all times. Remember that clover, wild violets, and other herbs and wildflowers should sometimes be encouraged. Many plants that start out looking like noxious weeds end up presenting beautiful flower displays, wonderful fragrances, and healthy food.

ORGANIC PESTICIDES

Antidesiccants

Also called antitranspirants, these products are made from pine oil and are nontoxic and biodegradable. They are sometimes used for the prevention of powdery mildew. They work by spreading a clear film over the leaves. They are not highly recommended for use as fungicides. Cedar resin appears to be a possible tool in this category.

Bacillus Thuringiensis (Bt)

This organic pesticide is sold under a variety of names including Thuricide, Dipel, and Bio-Worm. Use *Bacillus thuringiensis* 'Israelensis' (Bti) in water for mosquitoes. Use molasses with Bt for extra effect. Sugar in the molasses provides carbohydrates and keeps insect-killing bacteria alive on the foliage longer, even during rain.

Baking Soda

Baking soda is composed of sodium and bicarbonate. Both are necessary in the soil, but only in very small amounts. Mixed at the rate of 4 teaspoons per gallon of water, baking soda makes an excellent fungicide for black spot, powdery mildew, brown patch, and other fungal problems. Add 1 teaspoon of liquid soap or vegetable oil to the mix. Potassium bicarbonate is also effective and better for the soil.

Bordeaux Mix

This is a fungicide and insecticide usually made from copper sulfate and lime. It is good for most foliar problems and is an effective organic treatment for disease control on fruits, vegetables, shrubs, trees, and flowers such as anthracnose, botrytis blight, peach tree curl, and twig blight. Wet down decks and other hard surfaces before spraying. Some staining is possible.

Bug Juice Spray

Slugs and pill bugs can be effectively controlled by using a spray made from the bodies of the pest species. To control pill bugs, for example, mix 1 ounce of ground pill bugs with 2 ounces of water to make a paste and then dilute 1 ounce of the bug concentrate in 1 gallon of water. Spray a heavy amount of the bug juice on problem areas. This same technique works for slugs, squash bugs, cucumber beetles, and other hard-to-kill insect pests such as Mexican bean beetles, armyworms, stink bugs, and cutworms. Always use the juice from the bug you want to control.

Another technique that sounds gross but seems to work is "sick bug spray." It's literally a spray made out of the juice of pureed sick pests. That's the way Bt was discovered. Scientists found a dead caterpillar in the wild, and made a concoction of its dead body. The disease organisms in the body were isolated and then reproduced and have become our most popular caterpillar control.

The use of plants with genetically implanted Bt threatens to destroy the effectiveness of this excellent organic tool. That mad science should be stopped.

Note: Keep insecticides, even the mild organic choices, away from children and pets and don't breathe the dust of any dusty product. Remember, anything can injure or kill if mishandled.

Citrus Oil Spray

Fill a container ½ full with any citrus peelings or pulp. Orange is best. Fill the remainder of the container with water. Let it sit in a cool place for a week or so. Strain. Use 1 cup of the homemade concentrate per gallon of spray.

Note: Commercial orange oil is more powerful than homemade orange oil. It is a powerful solvent and can burn plants. We recommend using it at a rate of less than 2 ounces per gallon of water as a spray and always mix with molasses and compost tea.

Compost Tea, Manure

Manure compost tea is effective on many pests because of certain naturally occurring microorganisms. Use any container but a plastic bucket is easy for the homeowner. Fill the bucket or barrel half full of compost and finish filling with water. Let the mix sit for

10–14 days, then dilute, and spray on the foliage of any and all plants including fruit trees, perennials, annuals, vegetables, roses, and other plants that are regularly attacked by insect and disease pests. How much to dilute the dark compost tea before using depends on the compost used. A rule of thumb is to dilute the leachate down to 1 part compost liquid to 4 to 10 parts water. It should look like iced tea. Be sure to strain the solids out with old pantyhose, cheese cloth, or row cover material. Full-strength tea makes an excellent fire ant mound drench when mixed with molasses and citrus oil.

Corn Gluten Meal

Corn gluten meal has university research and data, has EPA registration, and is available from garden centers and feed stores that sell organic products. It is available under such brand names as GreenSense, Garden-Ville, and Garden's Alive. Because the names are so similar, corn gluten meal is often confused with cornmeal.

Corn gluten meal is a natural preemergent herbicide and organic fertilizer with an analysis of about 9.5-0.5-0.5. Corn gluten meal reduces the establishment of troublesome annual weeds such as henbit, dandelions, crabgrass, and grass burrs. It is available as a powder or in granular form now. It is 60 percent protein, approximately 10 percent nitrogen by weight. It is a by-product of the wet corn milling process and commonly used in pet and livestock feed. Its primary use is for lawns, but it can also be used in vegetable gardens as a fertilizer and as help with weed control, if you are very careful. It can damage the establishment of your food crops started from seed. Use it only after your vegetable seeds are up and young plant roots are well-established. It is also a powerful natural fertilizer and will create large healthy weeds if applied after they germinate. This unique use of corn gluten meal was discovered by Dr. Nick Christians and his research staff at Iowa

State University. You can get more information from them at 515-294-0036. It should be used at 20 pounds per 1,000 square feet for the control of summer weeds such as grass burrs and crabgrass. Cool season weeds such as dandelions and henbit require the same treatment around October 1st.

Diatomaceous Earth (DE)

Natural diatomaceous earth is approximately 5 percent aluminum, 5 percent sodium, 86 percent silicon. It is the skeletal remains of microscopic organisms (one-celled aquatic plants called diatoms) that lived in sea water or freshwater lakes millions of years ago in the western United States. The broken skeletons have razor sharp edges that scratch the exoskeleton of insects causing them to desiccate and die. Apply using a dusting machine (manual or electrostatic) and cover plants or treatment area entirely. Be sure to use a dust mask when applying! DE is nonselective, so use sparingly. Breathing any dusty material can cause lung problems. As a food supplement, use at 1 to 2 percent of the food volume for feeding pets or livestock. Swimming pool DE has been partially melted and is much more dangerous to breathe. Use only natural diatomaceous earth that contains less than 1 percent crystalline silica dioxide.

Never use swimming pool DE for anything other than pool filters.

Floating Row Cover

Gardening fabrics are designed to cover plants in a moist greenhouse warmth while allowing water, light, and ventilation for proper plant respiration. These row-cover materials protect foliage from wind, hail, chewing insects; prevent harmful insects from laying eggs; and reduce diseases carried by pests. They also discourage birds, rabbits, and other animals from feeding on plants.

Garden-Ville Fire Ant Control

This is the most effective product on the market for controlling fire ants and other hard-to-control pests such as squash bugs. It is available commercially or can be made in three ways:

- Mix 2 parts Garrett Juice commercial concentrate with 1 part citrus oil. Mix to spray at 2–6 ounces per gallon of water.
- Mix 2 ounces of citrus oil into your homemade Garrett Juice.
- Make your own fire ant control concentrate by mixing 1 part compost tea, 1 part molasses, 1 part citrus oil. Use in the spray at 2–6 ounces per gallon of water.

Experiment with the strength that works for various insect pests without burning foliage of plants. Never store homemade mixes in glass. Use plastic only with loose fitting lids. It's best to use the entire mixture each time and avoid having to store the mix.

Garden-Ville Organic Weed Control

This is a commercial organic weed-control product that contains acetic acid, molasses, and a surfactant. It works very well on hot days as a non-selective contact herbicide.

Garlic-Pepper Tea

This is an organic insect- and disease-control material made from the juice of garlic and hot peppers such as jalapeño, habañero, cayenne, or any other hot pepper. However, its use should be limited because it will kill small beneficial insects. For a homemade brew, mix the juice of 2 garlic bulbs and 2 hot peppers into a gallon of water. Use ¼ cup of the concentrate per gallon of water. For added strength, add 2 tablespoons of vegetable oil or horticultural oil to each gallon of water in the sprayer. To make garlic tea, simply omit the pepper and add another bulb of garlic.

Garrett Juice is available commercially or can be homemade.

Garrett Juice

Mix the following ingredients in a gallon of water to make the ready-to-use spray.

1 cup manure-based compost tea
1 ounce molasses
1 ounce natural apple cider vinegar
1 ounce liquid seaweed

For added insect and disease control add:

¼ cup garlic tea or garlic-pepper tea per gallon of spray.

For tougher-to-kill insects, such as fire ants and squash bugs, add:

2 ounces of citrus oil or d-limonene per gallon of ready-to-use spray.

Liquid Seaweed

Use from 1–2 ounces per gallon of water for red spider mites and whiteflies. Apply late in the afternoon, around dusk. Saturate the foliage thoroughly.

Neem

This botanical insecticide is extracted from the seed of the tropical neem tree from India. Neem has been used for centuries for a wide variety of pests. The active ingredient is azadirachtin, which works by preventing molting, suppressing feeding, or repelling, depending on the insect. It does not harm humans, birds, plants, earthworms, or beneficial insects. This product is registered for use on ornamentals (registration is pending on food crops) against aphids, whiteflies, thrips, hornworms, mealybugs, leaf miners, gypsy moths, weevils, webworms, loopers, psyllids, and sawflies. Tests conducted by USDA showed neem extracts repel cucumber beetles for up to 6 weeks. It is most effective against insects that pass through all stages of metamorphosis.

Nosema Locustae

A biological control for crickets and grasshoppers, *Nosema locustae* works the same way Bt works on caterpillars. Applied as a dry bait, the insects eat the material, get sick and are cannibalized by their friends. Brand names include Nolo Bait, Grasshopper Attack, and Semispore.

Oils

There are now four types of spray oils: dormant, summer, horticultural, and vegetable. Dormant oils are petroleum-based, relatively free of impurities, and have been used as far back as 1880. Dormant oils have lower volatility and more insect-killing power than the other oils, but they can be more toxic to plants. These oils should only be used during the winter months when plants are dormant. Summer oils, also petroleum-based, are lighter, less poisonous to plants, more volatile, and less effective on insects. They can be used during the heat of summer on some hard-to-kill bugs. Horticultural oils are the lightest and most pure petroleum oils. They can be used for spraying pecan trees and fruit trees, but they are also effective on shrubs and flowers that have scale or other insect infestations. Vegetable oils are plant extracts. They are environmentally safe, degrade quickly by evaporation, fit into organic or integrated pest-management programs, are nonpoisonous to the applicator, are noncorrosive to the spray equipment, and kill a wide range of insects. All of the oils kill beneficial as well as pest insects, so use only as a last resort.

Pepper Products

Commercial hot pepper products are available that contain pepper and other repellent ingredients like castor oil. Some have wax that helps keep the spray on plant leaves. Garlic-pepper tea is the best choice, but it is not yet available commercially. Find the homemade recipe earlier in this chapter.

Trombone sprayer is the best tool for the home gardener.

Potassium Bicarbonate

Works in a similar fashion to baking soda to help control plant disease but contains potassium instead of sodium, so it is more beneficial to most of our Texas soils.

Row Cover. *See Floating Row Cover*

Soap

Nonphosphate liquid soaps and water mixed together into a spray are used to control aphids and other small insects. Strong solutions can damage plant foliage, and even weak solutions can kill many of the microscopic beneficial insects. We really don't recommend soap products for insect control any longer.

Sulfur

Finely ground sulfur is used by mixing with water or dusting on dry to control black spot, leaf spot, brown canker, rust, peach leaf curl, powdery mildew, and apple scab. Mix with liquid seaweed to enhance fungicidal properties. Sulfur will also control fleas, mites, thrips, and chiggers. To avoid leaf burn, do not use when temperature is 90° or above.

Tree Trunk Goop

Slop on tree wounds. Mix ⅓ of each of the following in water: soft rock phosphate, natural diatomaceous earth, and manure-based compost. Manure-based compost is essential. Fully composted manure is not

Tree Trunk Goop

harmful or odiferous. It is available commercially in bags or bulk. Always use fine-screened compost.

Vinegar Herbicide

Full-strength vinegar is an effective herbicide on a hot, sunny day, especially the 20 percent food grade concentration. It's a nonselective herbicide, so be careful to keep it off your plants. It is even more powerful when mixed with citrus oil and molasses. Use 1–2 cups of citrus oil and 1–2 cups of molasses per gallon of vinegar.

Natural apple cider vinegar is used as a mild fertilizer element when watering or spraying foliage.

Yellow Sticky Traps

These are nontoxic bright yellow cards that trap insects with their sticky coating. They are also used to monitor insect populations, and are somewhat effective in greenhouses against whiteflies. Instead use garlic-pepper tea and/or the citrus-based products.

Animal Pests

Deer. These animals are a big problem in Texas. Controls that sometimes work include tall fences, electric fences, human hair in small porous bags, soap in porous bags, cheap perfume, and predatory animal urine. Human urine will also sometimes work.

Raccoons. These are smart little critters, but they can be repelled with strong garlic-pepper tea.

Squirrels. Beats us. If you come up with a good answer, let us know.

Texas Vegetables and Other Food Crops

Aloe Vera

Common Name: Aloe vera
Botanical Name: *Aloe vera*
Family: *Lillaceae*
Type and Use: Tender perennial with edible flowers
Location: Full sun
Planting Dates: Spring
Planting Method: Division, vegetative off-shoots from the mother plant
Harvest Time: When the flowers are young and fresh
Height: Up to 35 inches
Spread: 24 inches
Final Spacing: Use individually or in small clusters
Growth Habits: Upright, succulent rosette of pointed leaves with soft spines. Golden-orange tubular flowers on spikes. Blooms in the fall.
Culture: Needs loose, well-drained soil and moderate to light water.
Troubles and Solutions: Will sunburn easily when moved from a shady nursery or indoors to a full-sun location. The root system is subject to bacterial diseases and rot when overwatered. The shortness of growing season in the northern part of the state can be a problem.
Harvest and Storage: The flowers are edible and delicious. They should be harvested and eaten before they mature for tenderness and the best taste.

Notes: Aloe vera needs greenhouse or very bright conditions indoors and should be moved out to full sun early for a growing season to encourage flower stalks. The gel in the leaves can be used year-round to treat burns and rashes, but only the flowers are edible.

Althea. *See Hibiscus.*

Apricot

Common Name: Apricot
Botanical Name: *Prunus armeniaca*
Family: *Rosaceae*
Type and Use: Deciduous shrub or small tree with edible flower petals
Location: Sun
Planting Dates: Fall to spring
Planting Method: Container transplant, bare root
Harvest Time: Summer, if you are lucky. Ripe when fully colored and slightly soft. Pick the flower petals while in bloom for use in salads and garnishes. Use petals only, not entire flowers.
Height: 15–20 feet
Spread: 15–20 feet
Final Spacing: 20–25 feet
Growth Habits: Small tree, white to light-pink spring flowers, and delicious summer fruit. It's an easy-to-grow tree, but the fruit production is another matter. The early blooming habit often causes a loss of fruit because of late freezes.
Culture: Normal maintenance program using the basic organic program and spraying Garrett Juice with additives of baking soda and garlic.
Troubles and Solutions: Brown rot, cotton root rot, plum curculio, birds, and squirrels. Treat soil with cornmeal at 20 lbs/1,000 sq. ft. Spray foliage with Garrett Juice plus garlic, citrus oil, and potassium bicarbonate. Neem sprays can also be used.
Harvest and Storage: Harvest as soon as fruit is ripe and before the squirrels and birds beat you to it. Eat soon or store in a cool, dry place at 32–40°. Will keep about 2 weeks.
Varieties: Decent varieties for Texas are Bryan, Blenheim, Hungarian, and Moore-park. Manchurian may be the best choice; Mongolian is the worst.

Notes: Beautiful little tree for the landscape, but not a good high-production fruit tree for the orchard.

◀ Aloe vera

Apple

Common Name: Apple

Botanical Name: *Malus pumila*

Family: *Rosaceae*

Type: Deciduous tree with edible flowers and fruit

Location: Full sun

Planting Dates: Year-round

Planting Method: Cuttings or graphs

Harvest Time: Summer through fall. Fruit ripens summer through fall depending on the variety

Height: 8–20 feet. Depends on the species. Some will grow even taller.

Spread: 15–20 feet

Final Spacing: 15–30 feet

Growth Habits: Upright to spreading small- to medium-sized tree. Pink and white spring flowers after the new foliage has emerged. Long-lived, productive, and relatively easy fruit tree to grow in Texas.

Culture: Apple trees need well-drained healthy soil. Fertilize following a basic organic program and spray every two weeks during the growing season with Garrett Juice. Some commercial orchards grow the trees on trellises at very close spacing (30–48 inches on center). Fertilize three times a year with an organic fertilizer at 20 pounds per 1,000 square feet in early spring, early June, and harvest in the fall.

Troubles and Solutions: Cotton root rot, brown rot, aphids, and various other insect and disease pests. Fireblight is a problem on some varieties. Building beneficial life in the soil is the answer to most of these troubles. Garrett Juice plus additives helps, and cornmeal in the soil at 20 pounds per 1,000 square feet is important.

Harvest and Storage: Pick and store apples in dry, cool locations. Eat as soon as possible.

Varieties: Anna in early summer, but it may suffer frost damage in northern part of the state. Dorsett Golden in late spring, but it may suffer frost damage in northern part of the state. Fuji in early fall, ugly but delicious. Golden Delicious in late summer. Mollie's Delicious in mid-summer. Braeburn in fall. Gala in summer through fall. Granny Smith in early fall. Holland is easy to grow, but the taste isn't much.

Notes: Eat them as soon as possible. "An apple a day keeps the doctor away" is an important bit of advice to remember. Apple trees make excellent ornamental and small shade trees to use in the landscape. Eat the flower petals—not the entire flower.

Artichoke, Globe

Common Name: Artichoke
Botanical Name: *Cynara Scolymus*
Family: *Compositae*
Type: Perennial thistle with edible fleshy bracts. Grown as an annual in the northern two-thirds of the state.
Location: Full sun, but can take some afternoon shade in the hotter parts of the state
Planting Dates: Spring, after all danger of freeze is gone
Planting Method: Divisions or seed. Start plants indoors in the winter and set out when all danger of frost is gone.
Harvest Time: Cut the buds when they are small, fist-sized, and still tight. Stems should be soft several inches below the bud.
Height: 3–4 feet
Spread: 2–3 feet
Final Spacing: 2½–3 feet
Growth Habits: Grows easily in warm to hot weather. It can stand only a few degrees below freezing. Shoots die to the ground and rot after one year's growth. It grows back from offshoots.

Culture: In cold temperatures (most of Texas), the root can be dug, stored inside, and kept cool and dry. Brush away the soil and store in burlap bags. Suckers and roots can be potted and held over winter indoors. Protect from cold weather after they are planted in the garden. Prepare the soil with rock minerals and lots of manure compost. Spray regularly with fish emulsion or Garrett Juice. Excellent drainage is needed, but artichoke need plenty of moisture. After the last harvest, cut the stems off at or below the soil surface.

Troubles and Solutions: Possible pests include snails, slugs, caterpillars, and several diseases. Control insects with trichogramma wasps, beneficial nematodes, and citrus-based sprays if necessary.

Harvest and Storage: Cut buds when the size of a small fist by cutting 2 inches below the bottom of the bud. Eat while fresh.

Notes: Artichokes can be a helpful source of nectar for beneficial insects and can be used as an ornamental background plant.

Artichoke, Jerusalem. *See Sunflower.*

Arugula

Common Name: Arugula, Roquette
Botanical Name: *Eruca vesicaria*
Family: *Cruciferae*
Type and Use: Cool-season annual with edible flowers and leaves
Location: Full sun to part shade
Planting Dates: For spring, plant in late winter. For fall, plant in late summer. Successive planting of seeds from early September through April.
Planting Method: Broadcast seed outdoors or start indoors and transplant in late winter. Can be grown in cool greenhouses throughout the winter.
Seed Emergence: 7–10 days
Harvest Time: Early in the season when the leaves are young, tender and flavorful. Old leaves are bitter especially after the weather gets hot. Approximately 40–60 days after planting. Harvest when leaves are 2–4 inches long.
Height: Foliage to 18–24 inches
Spread: 18 inches
Final Spacing: 12 inches

Growth Habits: Flowering stalks go to 3 feet high. Foliage develops in a rosette growth pattern. It bolts in hot weather. Grows very fast and self sows.
Culture: Plant in healthy, well-drained soil. Needs cool weather to prevent bolting. Will grow in partial shade.
Troubles and Solutions: Bolting in hot weather. Bitter taste due to hot weather and bolting. Harlequin bugs, loopers, imported green worms, and flea beetles. Plant in well-prepared, well-drained soil in the correct season. Spray Bt products for caterpillar pests. Use citrus oil-based products for the other insect pests.
Harvest and Storage: Harvest the leaves often when young and tender and before hot weather sets in. Harvest the flowers after bolting and flowering has ruined the flavor of the leaves. Harvest seeds after the flowers have matured.
Varieties: Roquette Salad, Peanut Leaf

Notes: Grown for early spring greens. Good green salad ingredient for a peppery and nutty taste. Arugula reseeds easily. Leaves can be frozen like spinach.

Asparagus

Common Name: Asparagus
Botanical Name: *Asparagus officinalis*
Family: *Liliaceae*
Type and Use: Perennial with edible shoots
Location: Full sun
Planting Dates: Late winter, usually February
Planting Method: Division or crowns. Asparagus can also be grown from seed as some experts recommend in order to avoid diseases that can be in the crowns. This method requires an extra year before harvest. Plant seeds 1 inch deep and 3 inches apart after soaking for 24 hours in liquid seaweed. Move to permanent beds when seedlings are about 12 inches tall.
Seed Emergence: Early spring, but most asparagus is grown from roots. Seed germinates in a range of 60–85°.

Harvest Time: Edible shoots are harvested as they emerge in the early summer.
Height: 4–5 feet
Spread: 6 feet and greater
Final Spacing: 18–24 inches in the rows, rows 5 feet apart
Growth Habits: Fern-like growth, red berries on female plants. Shoots come up from rhizomes.
Culture: Healthy soil and a basic organic program. Highly organic beds and excellent drainage are critical. Overwatering can cause crown rot and loss of new or established plants. Plant crowns (roots) in 3–4 foot beds in late winter. Best planting method is to prepare beds as usual with heavy amounts of compost, lava sand, sugar, organic fertilizer, or manure. Then add earthworm castings, soak roots in seaweed water, spread out, cover the roots

with 3 inches of compost, and then add 6–9 inches of shredded mulch. Partially completed compost can be used. Plantings should last at least 10–15 years, probably longer under an organic program.

Troubles and Solutions: Crown rot, spider mites, slugs, snails, cutworms, and other fungal diseases. None of these troubles are serious if the soil is healthy and drains well. Fusarium root and harmful fungi can be controlled with cornmeal at 20–25 pounds per 1,000 square feet.

Harvest and Storage: Don't harvest many, if any, of the shoots the first year. The plants need to produce foliage to make food to build a strong root system. Go easy on the harvesting of shoots the second year, and even in the third and subsequent years let some of the shoots grow to produce foliage while harvesting other shoots. That's the traditional recommendation. However, according to researchers, you can harvest the first year without hurting future years' yields by planting year-old crowns. Never harvest tall shoots. You can cut the shoots off underground as most books recommend if you want to. Store shoots at 32–40° for 2–4 weeks.

Varieties: Mary and Martha Washington, Ben Franklin, Jumbo Jim, Jersey Gem, UC 157, Jersey Knight and Jersey Giant are all male hybrids developed at Rutgers University.

Notes: Cold weather helps produce larger shoots. Asparagus production is directly related to beneficial fungi in the root systems. Male plants produce more spears; females (with red berries) produce larger spears but have a higher mortality rate.

ASPARAGUS TROUBLE SOLVER

SYMPTOMS	CAUSES	SOLUTIONS
Weak foliage growth	Old, weak crowns used at planting	Replant with fresh crowns
	Wrong soil	For acid soil apply high-calcium lime, fireplace ashes, granite sand, or soft rock phosphate. For alkaline soil, add wood chip compost, leaf mold compost, Texas Greensand, or sulfur
	Poorly drained soil	Improve the bed preparation with compost, lava sand, and sugar
Woody spears	Low fertility	Add compost, earthworm castings, and organic, fertilizer
Misshapen spears	Insect damage or wind damage	Spray Garrett Juice plus citrus oil. Plant a wind break, especially in West Texas.
Spindly spears	Crowns too close	Widen the spacing
	Low soil moisture	Maintain even soil moisture, including for several months following harvest
	Harvesting too long	Stop harvesting
Spots on stems and leaves	Leaf spot or other fungal disease	Spray Garrett Juice plus garlic and/or neem
Declining spear production	Poor cultural care	Add compost, lava sand, sugar, and organic fertilizer
	Harvesting too long	
	Hot weather	Thicken the mulch and foliar feed every two weeks with Garrett Juice

Avocado

Persea Americana is cold tender and will only survive the winter in the southern tip of Texas. It can be grown easily from seed, but then a lot of people ask what to do with it after it is grown. You have three choices: 1) build a tall greenhouse, 2) move to Brownsville, or 3) toss it in the compost pile and plant an adapted plant.

Banana

Common Name: Banana
Botanical Name: *Musa* spp.
Family: *Musaceae*
Type and Use: Tender perennial with edible fruit
Location: Full sun
Planting Dates: Spring through fall
Planting Method: Divisions or transplants
Harvest Time: When bananas are ripe
Height: 5–20 feet (some even taller)
Spread: 5–10 feet
Final Spacing: 5–10 feet
Growth Habits: Very large leaves, thick stems, spreads by suckers to form large clumps. Banana clusters will set and produce in the southern one-third of the state.
Culture: Nothing special, if planted in healthy, well-drained soils. Use a basic organic program. Don't let the roots stay too wet in the winter or they will rot. Bananas need approximately 15 months above 28° to bear fruit.
Troubles and Solutions: Freeze damage and no fruit production in the northern half of the state.
Harvest and Storage: Harvest the fruit whenever and if ever ready. To store the plant for the winter in the northern part of the state, cut the top off and throw into the compost pile after the first light freeze. Cover the stumps with a thick layer of mulch to protect the roots from winter temperatures.

Notes: Bananas can be brought into production in greenhouses. If you have chickens, feed them the discarded banana leaves.

Basil

Common Name: Basil

Botanical Name: *Ocinum basilicum*

Family: *Labiatae*

Type and Use: Annual herb with edible flowers and leaves

Location: Full sun to partial shade

Planting Dates: Spring after last frost

Planting Method: Seed or cuttings

Seed Emergence: 7–14 days

Harvest Time: Harvest the flowers and foliage anytime. Both can be eaten fresh in salads and as garnish or used in teas.

Height: 12–24 inches

Spread: 12–18 inches

Final Spacing: 12–18 inches

Growth Habits: Whorls of flowers ranging in color from white to dark purple. Tender, leafy annual herb. Easy to grow from seed or transplants. Basil reseeds readily. The leaves are soft and fragrant. Square stems.

Culture: Keep the flowers and terminal growth cut back to keep plants compact and healthy. Use a basic organic program and spray at least monthly with Garrett Juice.

Troubles and Solutions: Caterpillars, leaf hoppers, plant bugs, and grasshoppers. Spray for serious infestations with molasses, compost tea, and citrus oil.

Harvest and Storage: Harvest and use fresh anytime or freeze leaves for winter use. Basil leaves picked at the end of the day will last about twice as long as leaves picked early in the morning. Reason: sugars build during the day. Leaves store well at 60° in plastic bags.

Varieties: Many, and they are all good.

Notes: The leaves and flowers can be used in herb teas.

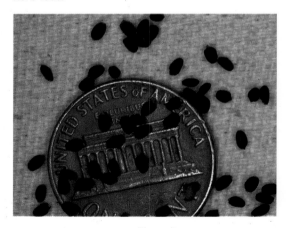

Basil Seed

Beans

Common Name: Bean (Snap, Bush, and Lima)

Botanical Names: Green beans, pintos, snaps, *Phaseolus vulgaris;* Lima beans, *Phaseolus lunatus*

Family: *Leguminosae*

Type and Use: Warm-season annuals with edible flowers and seed

Location: Full sun

Planting Dates: For spring, plant seed after all danger of frost. For fall crop, 12 to 14 weeks before the first average frost. In general, plant lima beans from April 1 to June 15 and July 1 to August 15.

Planting Method: Plant seed ½–1 inch deep about 1-2 inches apart

Seed Emergence: 5–14 days. Bush lima beans are the fastest to emerge and mature. Optimum germination is at 65–85°.

Harvest Time: 55–70 days after planting

Height: 18 inches to 8 feet for the vining types

Spread: 18 inches to 8 feet

Final Spacing: 6 inches to 3 feet. Green beans should be thinned to a spacing of 3–4 inches; limas 4–6 inches. Pole beans should be 8 inches or farther apart. The aggressive climbers should be planted as much as 36 inches apart. Eat the thinned sprouts.

Growth Habits: Low-bush to high-climbing types. Beans are warm-season legumes that have deep growing roots.

Culture: Legumes make a lot of their own nitrogen; therefore, they don't usually need heavy fertilization. Add an organic fertilizer at 15–20 pounds at planting and again in early summer. Plant the seed in the spring, when the soil has warmed, in 16–20 inch wide beds. Limas need the warmest soil of all beans—at least 70°. Additional plantings can be made every 10–14 days for a longer harvest season. Plant beans in single rows and give the climbers something to grow on. Spray Garrett Juice weekly for top production.

Troubles and Solutions: "Crusting" of the soil is never a problem when the plants are mulched well. Planting too early when the weather is still cool is a problem. Beans are fairly drought-tolerant, some more than others, but proper mulch helps them all. Avoid grass hay mulches because of the

SYMPTOMS	CAUSES	SOLUTIONS
Poor germination and emergence	Old seed	Replant with fresh seed
	Cold or wet soils	Plant when soil temperature is 65°
	Soil-borne diseases	Treat seed with Actinovate when planting and/or treat soil with cornmeal
Damaged seedlings	Crusted soil	Lightly sprinkle seedbed during emergence. Use a light mulch of compost.
	Insect injury	Treat plants with appropriate pest control
Slow seedling growth	Cold or wet soils	See above
	Low fertility	Fertilize with organic fertilizer and treat soil
	Nematode damage	with citrus oil or pulp
	Boron toxicity	Treat soil with activated carbon
Seedlings die soon after emergence	Damping-off fungi	Plant at appropriate time and treat soil with compost and cornmeal
	Cutworms or grubs	Treat soil with DE, crushed hot pepper, beneficial nematodes, and sugar
Foliar edges brown	Fertilizer burn	Stop using artificial fertilizer.
	High salts in soil	Stop using synthetic fertilizers. Apply humate and organic fertilizers.
	Root damage	Don't cultivate close to plants and don't walk in beds
	Sunburn	Build strength of foliage by spraying Garrett Juice
	Pesticide burn	Don't overuse organic sprays and don't use any toxic synthetic products
Spots or lesions on leaves, stems, or pods	Fungal or bacterial diseases	Work on improving soil health, treat soil with cornmeal, and spray foliage with Garrett Juice plus garlic and/or potassium bicarbonate
Reddish spots on leaves or pods	Rust	Treat foliage with Garrett Juice with garlic and potassium bicarbonate
Talcum-like powder on plants	Powdery mildew fungus	Work on improving soil health, treat soil with cornmeal, and spray foliage with Garrett Juice plus garlic and/or potassium bicarbonate
Bloom drop and failure to set fruit	High temperatures and/or high humidity	Plant in the proper season and hope for cooler temperatures
	Insects damage on the buds or flowers	Spray with Garrett Juice plus garlic
	Poor soil moisture	Avoid over- or under-watering
Small shriveled pods	Low soil moisture	Maintain even soil moisture during bloom and pod formation and keep soil mulched at all times
Small holes in pods and seeds	Insect damage, flea beetles, etc.	Treat plants during pod formation with natural insecticides and Garrett Juice
Large holes in leaves	Insect damage, caterpillars, or beetles	For caterpillars, release trichogramma wasps or spray Bt products, and for beetles, spray citrus oil product

risk of broadleaf herbicides, especially pichloram. Aphids, fleahoppers, cutworms, stink bugs, and spider mites are common troublesome insect pests. A regular spray with any product that contains seaweed helps greatly. A mix of molasses, compost tea, and citrus oil will control the tough ones. Add baking soda and garlic for diseases such as rust or powdery mildew.

More Problems: There is evidence that all diseases, including viruses, can be controlled by applying cornmeal at 20 pounds/1,000 square feet. Root knot nematodes can be controlled by tilling citrus pulp into the soil prior to planting.

Harvest and Storage: Most bush beans mature in about 8 weeks, climbers take 10–14 days longer. Green beans should be picked when the pods are young and tender and the seeds are still immature and soft. Beans for shells shouldn't be picked until they are full size and starting to change color. Avoid picking the beans when the foliage is wet.

Varieties: The best bush bean choice for our money is "pinto." Other good choices include Contender, Roma, Tendercrop, Topcrop. Pole bean choices are Blue Lake, Kentucky Blue, and Kentucky Wonder.

Notes: Sulfur is a common organic pesticide used on beans. Remember that it will burn the foliage of cucurbits like squash and cucumbers. There is some indication that garlic can be phytotoxic to all legumes. Boron toxicity is definitely a problem.

Other Bean Crops

Broad beans, fava beans, horse beans. These are all names for basically the same large beans (actually vetches) that like cool weather and are best grown as a fall crop. These beans require the same conditions and culture as bush beans. They can be picked and used as green, shelled, or dry beans.

Asparagus or yard-long beans. These produce beans up to 2 feet in length. These are climbing southern pea-type plants that need to be trellised. Oriental intensive gardeners love these beans.

Mung beans. These beans can be planted in succession. Like black-eyed peas, they like the hot weather. Multi crops.

Soybeans. Warm-season bush beans, these beans should be treated like limas but need a longer growing season of about 120 days. They can be used as green beans, shelled, or dry. Very nutritious beans.

Kentucky Wonder Seed

Lima Beans

Lima Bean Seed

Beets

Common Name: Beets

Botanical Name: *Beta vulgaris*

Family: *Chenopodiaceae*

Type and Use: Cool-season biennial, grown as an annual with edible leaves and root

Location: Sun to partial shade

Planting Dates: For spring, 4 to 6 weeks before the last killing frost in the spring, usually February 10–May 15. Initial planting can be followed by successional plantings at 2–3 week intervals. Fall crop should be planted when the summer temperatures have moderated to an average of 80° during the day, usually August 1–September 30.

Planting Method: Seeds ½–¾ inch deep, 1 inch apart

Seed Emergence: Germination in 3–14 days at 68–86°

Harvest Time: About 8 weeks after planting (50–80 days)

Height: 7–12 inches

Spread: 6 inches

Final Spacing: 3–5½ inches for the final spacing

Growth Habits: Rosette of tasty foliage out of a swollen root. Beets are cool-season vegetables that are extremely easy to grow and are often used to teach kids how to grow plants.

Culture: Need well-drained healthy soil. Prepare soil well and add organic fertilizer when plants are about 6 inches tall. Beets do best in raised flat-topped rows. The seed can be planted closely but should be thinned to 3 inches for the final spacing. Beet seed can be planted in single rows,

Beet Seed

multiple rows, or broadcast on top of the beds or hills. Top of beds should be 16–20 inches wide. Plant seed ½–1 inch deep; 1-inch seed depth is too deep in heavy soils. Thin the seedling to 3 inches for best production.

Troubles and Solutions: Nematodes, wireworms, grubworms, cutworms, flea beetles, and leaf diseases. Boron deficiencies are common in non-organic gardens. Use the basic organic program.

Harvest and Storage: Harvest the foliage for salads and to cook as greens or use in salads when it is young and tender. Harvest bulbs when they are 3–4 inches. Store 10–12 weeks at 32–40°.

Varieties: Lutz is the most often recommended variety. Other choices include Pacemaker II, Detroit Dark Red, Chiogga, and Red Ace.

Notes: Beets don't like low pH soils. When thinning the young plants, the tops can be used as greens, cooked or raw, in salads.

BEET TROUBLE SOLVER

SYMPTOMS	CAUSES	SOLUTIONS
Poor establishment	Old seed Cold soil	Use fresh seed and plant only when soil temperatures are above 45°
	Poor soil condition	Smooth and firm the seedbed and add compost and rock minerals to improve soil
	Crusted soil	Cover seed with compost, rather than soil
	Planting too deep	Plant seed ½″ deep in heavy soils and 1 inch deep in sandy soils
Sprouts die	Damping-off fungi	Drop wet seed in cornmeal before planting
	Cutworms	Treat around plants with crushed red pepper and diatomaceous earth
Plants lack vigor and grow slowly	Cold soils	Avoid planting too early in the spring
	Wrong soil	Add high-calcium lime to balance the chemistry of acid soil
	Nematodes	Treat soil with citrus
	Low fertility	Apply light application of organic fertilizer
Spots on leaves	Fungal leaf spot	Work on improving soil health, treat soil with cornmeal, and spray foliage with Garrett Juice plus garlic and/or potassium bicarbonate
Small holes in leaves	Flea beetle damage	Treat foliage of plants with citrus insecticide
Bolting to seed	Warm or hot weather	Plant in the cool seasons
Roots misshapen and cracked	Low soil moisture	Maintain even soil moisture
Undersized roots	Crowded plants	Thin plants to 3 to 4 inches
Rings in interior of roots	Overmature	Harvest when roots are less than 2 inches in diameter
	High temperatures during maturity	Plant for cool temperature maturity
Dark spots in roots	Boron deficiency	Treat soil with **very small** amounts of borax (2–3 lbs. per acre)

Begonia

Common Name: Begonia, Wax Begonia

Botanical Name: *Begonia semperflorens*

Family: *Begoniaceae*

Type and Use: Annual bedding plant with edible flowers

Location: Partial shade to full sun

Planting Dates: Spring, after last frost

Planting Method: Seed or cuttings. Best to plant 4 inch transplants.

Seed Emergence: 1–2 weeks

Harvest Time: Anytime the flowers are present and the toxic chemical pesticides aren't

Height: 6–15 inches

Spread: 12–18 inches

Final Spacing: 9–12 inches

Growth Habits: Waxy leaves and red, pink, or white summer flowers. Begonias bloom throughout the summer. Under an organic program, begonias will sometimes perennialize.

Culture: Begonias need healthy, loose, organic soil. Plant the red-leaf varieties in sun to partial shade, the green-leaf varieties in partial shade to shade. Leggy plants can be cut back in summer for additional blooming. Use a basic organic program and spray often with Garrett Juice.

Troubles and Solutions: Slugs and cutworms. Foliage and flower burn when the tender varieties are used in sunny areas. Treat slugs and cutworms with DE, hot pepper and cedar flakes.

Harvest and Storage: Edible flowers can be picked and eaten or used in teas at anytime with one exception: most bedding plants are commercially grown using toxic pesticides and synthetic fertilizers. The plants need to be grown and maintained in an organic program to be safe to eat.

Notes: The flowers are delicious on sherbet and other desserts, especially cold ones.

Blackberry

Common Name: Blackberry

Botanical Name: *Rubus* spp.

Family: *Rosaceae*

Type and Use: Perennial with edible flowers and fruit

Location: Full sun

Planting Dates: Late winter

Planting Method: Root cuttings planted 2 inches below the surface in clay soils and 4 inches in sandy soil. Use little finger-sized cuttings about 6–8 inches long. Store in plastic bags at 45° if necessary.

Seed Emergence: Early spring

Harvest Time: Summer as the berries mature and are full colored, sweet and release easily. Most varieties will bear fruit for about two weeks or so in late May through early June.

Height: 3–5 feet

Spread: Far and wide if you don't control the plants

Final Spacing: 24–36 inches in rows or 8–15 feet apart in hills. Use three plants per hill.

Growth Habits: Easy to grow in almost any soil

Culture: Plant in full sun in healthy soil. Two-year-old canes bloom and produce fruit and then die after the fruit has matured. Prune the old canes out after harvesting because they will never produce again. Keep the plants cut to form a 3-foot-high hedge. Do not do any winter pruning because the buds are formed in September.

Troubles and Solutions: Double blossom (rosette), anthracnose, redneck cane borer, and a few other minor problems. The worst problem with blackberries is the aggressive spreading characteristic.

Harvest Storage: Harvest the berries as they ripen and turn dark purple. Eat right away or store in the refrigerator at 32–40° for about 2 weeks max.

Varieties: Brazos is probably the best choice. Comanche, Humble, Brison, Choctaw, Navaho, Womack, and Rosborough are also good. It's best to avoid Gem, Lawton, Young, Barpen, Fluit, and the old thornless varieties. The best raspberries for Texas are Doman Red. They should only be grown in sandy, acidic soils.

Notes: Don't allow suckers at the base of plants to spread.

Black Walnut. *See Walnut.*

Blueberry

Common Name: Blueberries, Rabbiteye Blueberries

Botanical Name: *Vaccinium ashei*

Family: *Ericaceae*

Type and Use: Deciduous shrub with edible berries

Location: Full sun to partial shade

Planting Dates: Fall to late winter

Planting Method: Best from small stem cuttings. Plant bare-rooted or container-grown plants from fall to late winter.

Harvest Time: Blueberries start to turn blue weeks before they are ripe. They ripen over a 2–5 week period. The best method is to taste some to see if they are ready. Ripe fruit is plump, has a slight softness, and will fall off the plant easily.

Height: 3–10 feet

Spread: 3–10 feet

Final Spacing: 6–12 feet

Growth Habits: Bushy deciduous shrubs with white spring flowers and purple berries. . They have shallow, fibrous roots similar to azaleas. Plants mature in 7–8 years.

Culture: Blueberries need acidic soils with a pH of no higher than 5.5. They benefit from cross pollination, so use at least three varieties in every planting. Use large amounts of compost, peat moss (one of the few times we recommend peat moss), organic fertilizer, lava sand, Texas Greensand, and sugar. Cottonseed meal is one of the best fertilizers for blueberries. Mulch on the surface of the soil is critical. Roots drying out will ruin plants quickly.

Troubles and Solutions: No major pests have been identified. Poor soil conditions are the only major problem.

Harvest and Storage: Pick and eat fresh or store in the refrigerator 32–40°. Will keep for about 2 weeks.

Varieties: Tifblue, Woodard, Climax and Briteblue

Notes: Even organiphobes recommend using organic fertilizers instead of synthetic ones for blueberries. The artificial products can burn plants, especially young ones. One so-called expert says that nitrate-type fertilizers can kill plants. This is the same guy who says not to use barnyard manures because they contain toxic salts.

Bok Choy. *See Cabbage.*

Borage

Common Name: Borage

Botanical Name: *Borago officinalis*

Family: *Boraginaceae*

Type and Use: Annual herb with edible flowers and leaves

Location: Sun to partial shade

Planting Dates: Spring, after the last frost

Planting Method: Seed and transplants

Seed Emergence: 10–14 days

Harvest Time: Anytime during the growing season

Height: 24–36 inches

Spread: 18–30 inches

Final Spacing: 18 inches

Growth Habits: Fast-growing, fuzzy-leafed herb that can get a little messy looking unless cut back from time to time to maintain compactness

Culture: Needs healthy soil with good drainage. Use a basic organic program and spray occasionally with Garrett Juice.

Troubles and Solutions: Grasshoppers occasionally attack the foliage. Control them with hot pepper products, all-purpose flour, DE, and beneficial fungi products.

Harvest and Storage: Cut and use the flowers and foliage anytime. Leaves are best when young and tender. Flowers can be candied or frozen into ice cubes.

Notes: The foliage can be used for vinegar, drinks, teas, and salads to add a cucumber flavor.

Broccoli

Common Name: Broccoli

Botanical Name: *Brassica oleracea* (*italica*)

Family: *Cruciferae*

Type and Use: A half-hardy biennial, grown as an annual with edible flower clusters and leaves, broccoli is a cool-season vegetable for use in the spring and fall.

Location: Full sun to light shade

Planting Dates: For the spring garden, plant seed weeks before last average frost. Start indoors or in a cold frame around mid-January during the waxing (increasing light) moon cycle. Plant transplants in early spring, broccoli can tolerate and actually likes light frost. For the fall garden, plant 10–12 weeks before first frost. In general, mark your calendar for February 1–March 15 and August 1–31.

Planting Method: Plant ¼–½ inch deep. Press surface lightly but firmly with a board or flat trowel. When the fifth leaf emerges, transplant seedlings to 4-inch pots to hold until planted in the garden.

Seed Emergence: Germination in 3-10 days at 68–86°.

Harvest Time: 50–80 days from transplants. Harvest heads when they are about two-thirds of their potential size. Cut above side buds, which will continue to mature into heads that can be harvested later.

Height: 12–24 inches

Spread: 12–24 inches

Final Spacing: 12–24 inches, although 15 inches is considered to be the ideal spacing

Growth Habits: Leafy vegetable with large flower heads. Leaves and flower heads are edible.

Culture: Cool-weather vegetable that likes healthy well-drained soil and full sun. Continue fertilizing after the first harvest to encourage the secondary heads. Broccoli likes moisture and plenty of fertilizer. Fertilize when the heads begin to form and are about the size of a fifty-cent piece. Sprinkle a half handful of organic fertilizer around each plant.

Troubles and Solutions: Aphids, harlequin bugs, cutworms, green worms, flea beetles, loopers, and boron deficiency. Use Bt products for the loopers, cutworms, and other caterpillars. Spray molasses, manure compost tea, and citrus oil for the other critters if needed. Healthy soil and beneficial insects will prevent most pests.

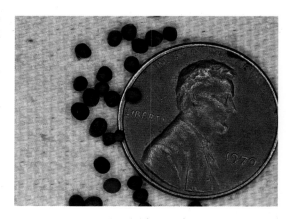

Broccoli Seed

Harvest and Storage: Harvest flower heads when they are large but still firm. When the yellow flowers start to open, they get tough. Eat right away or store in the refrigerator at 32–40° for 1–2 weeks.

Varieties: Packman, Galaxy, Green Comet, Heirloom, Calabrese, Early Green, Purple Sprouting, and Waltham

Notes: Broccoli is nutritious and considered an important health food. Former President George Bush doesn't eat it, but he should. Always use healthy, vigorous plants. Avoid those with tough, woody stems. Set transplants just below the first set of leaves. According to researchers at Johns Hopkins University, broccoli sprouts have up to 50 times more powerful anticancer chemicals than mature broccoli.

BROCCOLI TROUBLE SOLVER

SYMPTOMS	CAUSES	SOLUTIONS
Poor germination	Cold soil	Keep trays in warm location or plant when soil temperature is above 50°
	Seed planted too deep	Plant ¼"–½" deep
	Crusted soil	Break the crust
	Old seed	Use fresh seed
Sprouts die	Damping-off fungi	Avoid treated seed, wet soil, plant at the proper time, and apply cornmeal
	Cutworms, snails, or slugs	Treat around base of plants with DE and crushed red pepper
Stunted or slow growing plants	Low fertility	Apply light application of organic fertilizer
	Wrong soil	Apply high-calcium lime
Holes in leaves	Loopers and other caterpillars	Release trichogramma wasps and spray *Bacillus thuringiensis* for heavy infestations
	Flea beetles	Spray Garrett Juice with garlic
Damage to older leaves	Harlequin bugs	Spray Garrett Juice plus citrus. Time planting so vegetable matures in cool weather. Best to plant in the fall. Maturity is during cool and shorter days.
V-shaped yellow lesions on leaf margins	Black rot bacteria	Apply cornmeal to soil and spray foliage with Garrett Juice plus garlic and/or potassium bicarbonate
Premature flowering	High temperatures	Plant so that maturity will occur during cool weather
	Plant stress	Maintain even moisture and fertility and maintain thick mulch layer
	Incorrect planting time	Check the dates in this book
Hollow stems	Excessive fertility	Fertilize less
	Boron deficiency	Apply Texas greensand @ 40–80 lbs/1,000 sq. ft.
Heads fail to form	Poor variety choice	Plant varieties adapted to Texas conditions
	Climate problems	Plant at the proper time.

Brussels Sprouts

Common Name: Brussels Sprouts

Botanical Name: *Brassica oleracea (gemmifera)*

Family: *Cruciferae*

Type and Use: Biennial, grown as an annual with edible sprouts

Location: Sun to partial shade

Planting Dates: For the fall garden, plant seed 8–10 weeks before first average frost. Cool-season vegetable. Plant late winter for spring crop and late summer, 8 to 10 weeks before the first frost, for a fall crop. Best as a fall crop. Mark your calendar for February 10–March 15 and August 1–31.

Planting Method: Set transplants after the first set of true leaves appears. Plant seeds ¼ inch in the soil.

Seed Emergence: 6–14 days

Harvest Time: Harvest in 90–110 days from seed, 65–75 days from transplant

Height: 12–18 inches

Spread: 12–18 inches

Final Spacing: 14–18 inches, single rows, 18 inches on center

Growth Habits: Supports are sometimes needed when the plants get 10–14 inches tall.

Brussels Sprouts Seed

82

Culture: Plant brussels sprouts so they can mature during cool temperatures, usually 55–65° or cooler. Cover the plants with shade cloth when first planted in the summer. Keep the soil moist as the sprouts begin to form or they will be small and deformed. Remove the lower leaves only if they yellow or wither. Sidedress brussels sprouts after harvesting the first small marble-sized sprouts. Use about a half a handful around each plant.

Troubles and Solutions: Aphids, black rot, cabbage loopers, and imported cabbage worms. Spray molasses and seaweed and release ladybugs for the aphids. Treat the soil with cornmeal at 20 pounds/1,000 square feet for disease problems. Sprouts may not form if the weather is too hot.

Harvest and Storage: Harvest approximately 90–100 days after transplanting. Plant sprouts form near ground level and produce in about two months. Sprouts are mature and ready for harvest when 1–2 inches in diameter. Pull down with a twisting motion to harvest. Store mature sprouts in cool, dry place and eat soon after harvest.

Varieties: Prince, Marvel, Jade, and Cross

Notes: Grows best during long periods of cool weather.

BRUSSELS SPROUTS TROUBLE SOLVER

SYMPTOMS	CAUSES	SOLUTIONS
Sprouts or transplants die	Damping-off fungus	Work on improving soil health, treat soil with cornmeal, and spray foliage with Garrett Juice plus garlic and/or potassium bicarbonate
	Hot weather	Use larger transplants and water more carefully
	Cutworms, slugs, or snails	Treat soil with DE and crushed red pepper
Spindly plants	Excess fertility	Fertilize less at planting time
Stunted plants	Low fertility	Apply additional organic fertilizer and water
	Wrong soil	Apply high-calcium lime to soil
	Dry soil	Maintain soil moisture and mulch layer
Holes in foliage	Cabbage loopers or cabbage worms	Release trichogramma wasps, and treat plants with *Bacillus thuringiensis* as last resort
Yellow or brown spots or lesions	Downy mildew fungus	Work on improving the soil health, treat soil with cornmeal, and spray foliage with Garrett Juice plus garlic and/or potassium bicarbonate
V-shaped lesions on margins of leaves or discolored veins	Black rot bacteria	Work on improving the soil health, treat soil with cornmeal and spray foliage with Garrett Juice plus garlic and/or potassium bicarbonate
Sprouts don't grow	Aphids	Spray molasses water and release ladybugs.
	Heat	Plant at proper time during cooler weather
	Poor variety choice	Use recommended varieties

Cabbage

Common Name: Cabbage

Botanical Name: *Brassica oleracea (capitata)*

Family: *Cruciferae*

Type and Use: Biennial grown as an annual with edible leaves

Location: Sun to partial shade

Planting Dates: For spring, 2 to 4 weeks before last frost. For fall, 10 to 12 weeks before first frost. Use transplants and set just below the first set of leaves. In general, plant February 1–28 and September 1–15.

Planting Method: Plant seed indoors or in cold frame in mid-January. Plant ¼ inch deep.

Seed Emergence: 3–14 days, optimum temperature range 45–85°

Harvest Time: 60–120 days to harvest. Cabbage matures best at 60–65°

Height: 12–24 inches

Spread: 12–18 inches

Final Spacing: 8–18 inches apart. Double rows, 12 inches on center is good for the home gardener; 14–18 inches is considered ideal.

CABBAGE TROUBLE SOLVER

SYMPTOMS	CAUSES	SOLUTIONS
Poor germination and emergence	Old seed	Use fresh seed
	Cold soil	Plant when soil temperatures are 50° or higher
	Crusted soil	Break the crust
	Seed planted too deep	Plant seed ¼–½" deep
	Low moisture	Plant in moist soil and water carefully
Seedlings die	Damping-off fungus	Work on improving soil health, treat soil with cornmeal, spray foliage with Garrett Juice plus garlic and/or potassium bicarbonate, and plant at the correct time
	Cutworms, slugs, or snails	Treat soil around plants with DE and crushed red pepper
Transplants die	Stress	Protect from winds, high or low temperatures, and low soil moisture, and mulch the bare soil
	Damping-off fungi	Work on improving soil health, treat soil with cornmeal, and spray foliage with Garrett Juice plus garlic and/or potassium bicarbonate
Slow growth, poor foliage color	Wet soil or poor drainage	Use raised beds and prepare soil properly
	Acid soil	Add high-calcium lime
	Cold soil	Plant/transplant at right time of year
	Low fertility	Apply light application of nitrogen containing fertilizer
Holes in leaves	Loopers and other caterpillars	Release trichogramma wasps and treat with *Bacillus thuringiensis*
	Flea beetles	Spray with Garrett Juice plus citrus oil
Leaves cupped or wrinkled	Aphids	Spray with Garrett Juice plus garlic
V-shaped lesions on leaf margins or veins discolored	Black rot	Improve drainage, remove infected plants, work on improving soil health, treat soil with cornmeal, and spray foliage with Garrett Juice plus garlic and/or potassium bicarbonate
Lesions or sunken areas on leaves or head	Leaf spot fungus	Work on improving soil health, treat soil with cornmeal, and spray foliage with Garrett Juice plus garlic and/or potassium bicarbonate
Heads don't form	Heat stress	Plant at the proper time Avoid high or low soil moisture, low fertility, etc., when plants are young

(table continued on page 86)

CABBAGE TROUBLE SOLVER (CONTINUED)

SYMPTOMS	CAUSES	SOLUTIONS
Heads split or crack near maturity	Fast growth	Avoid excess fertility
	Wet soil	Don't overwater
Plants bolt	Weather	Bad timing—spring planting was too late
	Transplants too big	Use only transplants with a stem diameter less than pencil size

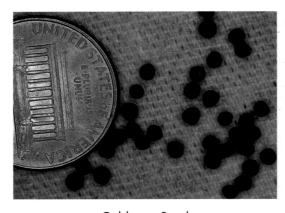

Cabbage Seed

Growth Habits: A cool-weather leafy vegetable grown as an annual has edible foliage and flowers. Cabbage is smooth head-forming or savory (crinkled). Head shape ranges from flat to pointed. Cabbage has a relatively shallow root system.

Culture: Likes cool weather and moist, healthy soil. Keep the soil around plants mulched well. Add compost tea and organic fertilizer to the soil when the inner leaves begin to cup and start to form heads. At this point, keep the soil slightly moist. Can stand temperatures down into the 20s, especially when in an organic program. High fertility encourages firm, healthy heads. Use 25–30 pounds of organic fertilizer per 1,000 square feet. Foliar feed every two weeks with Garrett Juice.

The best time to fertilize cabbage is when heads start to form. In wide rows of cabbage, that's when the leaves of the plants are about to completely shade the row. Use a half handful of organic fertilizer.

Troubles and Solutions: Cabbage looper, imported cabbage worm, aphids, harlequin bugs, splitting heads caused by uneven moisture, and flea beetles. Treat worms with trichogramma wasps and Bt products for severe infestations. Citrus-based sprays are also effective. Splitting can be reduced by root pruning to slow down growth.

Harvest and Storage: Expect about 10–20 heads per 10 feet of double row. Store in the refrigerator or eat right after harvest. Harvest the young leaves of Chinese cabbage anytime. When mature, the leaves and stems can be used for miso soups and stir-frying. Can be stored 4–8 weeks at 32–40°.

Varieties: Early Jersey Wakefield, Sanibel, Gourmet, Ruby Ball, Savory King, Bravo, Green Cup, Stonehead. Chinese cabbage varieties are Michihili, Jade, Pagota, China Pride.

Notes: The chemical experts say there is no control for the common disease black rot. Yes, there is. It's called a basic organic program.

Chinese cabbage is best planted in flats and then planted into the garden soil in early spring or late summer.

Calendula

Common Name: Calendula

Botanical Name: *Calendula officinalis*

Family: *Compositae*

Type and Use: Annual bedding plant with edible flowers

Location: Sun to light shade

Planting Dates: Transplant in the fall or early spring in the northern part of the state

Planting Method: Seed. Sow seed in mid to late summer in pots or flats.

Seed Emergence: 1–2 weeks

Harvest Time: Whenever flowers are present in the spring and fall

Height: 12–15 inches

Spread: 12–15 inches

Final Spacing: 12–15 inches

Growth Habits: Sprawling annual with yellow or orange mum-like flowers

Culture: Start seeds in healthy, well-drained soil. Likes cool to cold weather and hates hot weather.

Troubles and Solutions: Hot weather, slugs, and snails. Plant during the cool seasons and use DE, hot pepper, and cedar flakes for the critters. Also, spray with citrus oil products if needed.

Harvest Storage: Harvest the orange or yellow flowers anytime to use in stews, salads, and as garnish.

Notes: Most common use is as a pot herb.

Cantaloupe

Common Name: Cantaloupe, Muskmelon

Botanical Name: *Cucumis melo*

Family: *Cucurbitaceae*

Type and Use: Annual with edible fruit

Location: Full sun in summer

Planting Dates: For spring, after all danger of frost. For fall, 12–14 weeks before first frost. In general, April 1–30 and July 10–31.

Planting Method: Plant 4–5 seeds ½–1 inch in hills every 18–24 inches on center in rows. Thin down to the two strongest seedlings per hill.

Seed Emergence: 5–14 days after planting at 75–95°

Harvest Time: 60–90 days after planting

Height: 6–8 feet on trellis or cage, 6–8 inches on the ground

Spread: 6–10 feet

Final Spacing: 3–6 feet, row spacing 48–72 inches

Growth Habits: Climbing or crawling vine with yellow flowers and delicious fruit. Fruit primarily sets on secondary or fruiting branches that can be encouraged earlier by pinching out the tips of the primary tip growth.

Culture: Plant on hills or raised rows. Needs healthy well-drained soil and full sun. Use 3–5 plants per hill. To conserve space, grow cantaloupe on trellises or cages. Cut back on irrigation as the melons mature and add lots of trace mineral products like Texas

CANTALOUPE TROUBLE SOLVER

SYMPTOMS	CAUSES	SOLUTIONS
Poor germination and emergence	Old seed	Use fresh seed
	Cold soil	Wait to plant until the soil is 60° or above
	Crusted soil	Break the crust with a rake or other tool
	Seed planted too deeply	Plant ½″ on heavier soils or less
Seedling or transplants die shortly	Damping-off fungus	Work on improving soil health, treat soil with cornmeal, spray foliage with Garrett Juice plus garlic and potassium bicarbonate, and do not plant when soils are cold
	Cutworms, snails, or slugs	Treat soil around plants with DE and crushed red pepper
Stunted growth and yellow foliage	Cold soil	Plant only when soil temperature is 60° or above
	Acid soil	Add high-calcium lime
	Nematodes	Treat soil with citrus pulp prior to planting
	Low fertility	Add organic fertilizer
	Poor drainage	Add compost to loosen soils, plant on raised beds, and add other soil amendments
Flowers don't set fruit	No female flowers	Male blooms appear first; be patient
	Lack of pollinating insects: bees, wasps, flies, etc.	Never use killing sprays for insect and disease control during morning, and set up a beehive or mason bee house
	Excessively lush foliage growth	Cut back on the fertilizer
Seedlings or mature plants wither	Cucumber beetles or squash bugs	Spray with Garrett Juice plus garlic and citrus oil
Leaves curled and distorted	Aphids	Spray with Garrett Juice plus garlic-pepper tea and release lady beetles
Yellow spots on older leaves	Downy mildew fungus	Work on improving soil health, treat soil with cornmeal, and spray foliage with Garrett Juice plus garlic and potassium bicarbonate
Talcum-like powder on leaves	Powdery mildew fungus	Work on improving soil health, treat soil with cornmeal, and spray foliage with Garrett Juice plus garlic and potassium bicarbonate
Small, poor quality fruit	Wrong soil	Treat soil with high-calcium lime
	Low fertility	Add organic fertilizer
	Low moisture	Water carefully and maintain mulch layer
Fruit rots on the vine	Soil fungi	Keep soil mulched, work on improving soil health, treat soil with cornmeal, and spray foliage with Garrett Juice plus garlic and potassium bicarbonate
	Excess soil moisture	Improve drainage and water carefully
Fruit cracks at maturity	Excess fertility	Avoid over-fertilizing
	Soil moisture	Avoid swings in wet and dry soils
Poor flavor	Excess soil moisture	Don't water much as melons mature; use raised beds if soils are poorly drained or you live in high rainfall areas.

Cantaloupe Male (left) and Female (right) Flowers

Cantaloupe Seed

root knot nematodes, aphids, cucumber beetles, squash bugs, flea beetles, garden flea hoppers, and plant bugs. Lack of pollination and soil-borne diseases can also cause trouble. Most of these pests can be controlled with healthy soil and organic fertility.

Harvest and Storage: The melons will slip easily from the vines when mature. Fruit on trellises may need to be supported to prevent damage when they fall away. Store the fruit after it is ripe above 45°. Will keep 1–4 weeks.

Varieties: Ambrosia, Magnum 45, Mission, TAM Uvalde

greensand and soft rock phosphate. Apply organic fertilizer as the plants begin to vine and again when the fruit begins to set. If grown on trellises, fruit will need to be supported when melons reach grapefruit size.

Troubles and Solutions: Poor flavor due to excess soil moisture. Powdery mildew,

Notes: Real cantaloupes have rough, wary skins and do not have the net-let texture. They are more oblong than round and not often grown in Texas. Some people like to pollinate by transferring the male flower pollen to the female flowers with a cotton swab, but that's way too much trouble for me. The female flowers have swollen, immature fruit just behind them.

Carrot

Common Name: Carrot

Botanical Name: *Daucus carota*

Family: *Umbelliferae*

Type and Use: Biennial, grown as an annual with edible roots

Location: Sun to light shade

Planting Dates: For spring, 3–4 weeks before last average frost. For fall, 8–10 weeks before first average frost. Plant seed in late winter for an early summer crop and in mid-summer for a fall-winter crop. In general, February 1–March 20 and August 1–31.

Planting Method: Seed should be broadcast on top of the soil and then gently watered in. Seed can be planted in single rows, double rows, or broadcast. Water often with a light mist until seedlings emerge, but don't water too heavy or too often.

Seed Emergence: Seed germinates in 6–20 days at 68–86°, but will germinate as low as 40°.

Harvest Time: Anytime the roots are large enough to eat. Maturity 70–100 days.

Height: 8–12 inches

Spread: The tops will spread 8–12 inches

Final Spacing: 3–4 seeds per inch, then ½ inch apart, final spacing of 2–4 inches on center. Wide rows are best. Thin the carrot seedlings to 12 plants per square foot. Eat the small ones that are removed.

Growth Habits: Ferny top growth and large, showy white flowers.

Culture: Carrots must have soft, healthy soil and moderate fertility. If the roots hit rock or hard spots in the soil, the carrots will be deformed. Too much fertilizer will encourage top growth instead of roots. Keep plants mulched as they grow. They like cool weather and will grow all winter in these conditions. Mulch the top of roots to prevent "greening." Maintain even soil moisture level as carrots mature. Root length is made the first week, then enlargement happens.

CARROT TROUBLE SOLVER

SYMPTOMS	CAUSES	SOLUTIONS
Seedlings don't emerge	Old seed	Use fresh seed
	Seed planted too deep	Plant ¼" deep in heavy soil; ½" deep in sandy soils
	Crusted soil	Break the crust
	Cold soil	Don't plant if soil is below 45°
	Low soil moisture	Water carefully
	Crusted soil	Cover seed with fine-textured compost
Seedlings die	Damping-off fungus	Avoid treated seed; plant when soil temperature is above 45°
	Cutworms, slugs, and snails	Treat soil with citrus pulp, apply DE and crushed red pepper to the soil surface
Weak growing seedlings	Wet soil	Improve drainage and water carefully
	Cold soil	Don't plant until soil temperature is above 45°; plant in raised beds for earlier warming
	Wrong soil	Apply high-calcium lime
	Low fertility	Apply a light application of organic fertilizer and water lightly
Good top growth, but no carrot	Excess fertility	Cut back on the fertilizer
Misshapen carrots	Crowded plants	Thin plants to 1–1½" apart
	Poor bed preparation	Work soil to depth of 8–10", add compost, lava sand, sugar, and remove all trash, rocks, etc.
	Poor variety choice	Short-rooted varieties are best in much of Texas
	Nematodes	Till citrus pulp into beds prior to planting
Cracked, split carrots	Swings in soil moisture	Maintain soil moisture and mulch layer
Knotty carrots	Root knot nematodes	Till citrus pulp into the soil prior to planting
Plants bolt and flower	Poor planting time	Plant so that small carrots will not suffer temperatures below 45°
Tough, flavorless carrots	Low soil moisture	Maintain soil moisture as carrots mature
	Low fertility	Add organic fertilizer
	Heat	Plant so carrots mature during cool weather
	Lack of trace minerals	Build the soil with compost, volcanic rock, soft rock phosphate, and Texas greensand
Holes or tunnels in carrots	Wireworms or grubworms	Treat soil with sugar and beneficial nematodes
Yellow spots on leaves	Leaf spot fungus or bacteria	Work on improving soil health, treat soil with cornmeal, and spray foliage with Garrett Juice plus garlic and potassium bicarbonate

Carrots Growing in Wide Beds

Troubles and Solutions: Insect pests include grubworms, wire worms, cutworms, snails, slugs, and pillbugs. Other pests include nematodes, bacterial diseases, and rabbits. Armadillos can also be a problem. Build soil health and spray with Garrett Juice as a foliar feed and citrus-based mixes for serious pest infestations. Use hot pepper repellents for animal pests. Cracking can be avoided by not overpowering and over-fertilizing.

Harvest and Storage: Dig the roots anytime they are of edible size. Eat fresh or store in the refrigerator. They can also be stored in the winter by leaving them in the ground. Carrots increase in sweetness and food value in cold weather. They can also be stored in the refrigerator at 32–40° for about 10 weeks or more.

Varieties: Red Cored Chantenay, Nantes, Orland Gold, Imperator, Danvers 126

Carrot Seed

Notes: Carrots are a great source of many vitamins and minerals. Their roots develop in the 4–6-week period after their emergence. Lack of flavor can be caused by moisture stress, high temperature during maturity, or lack of trace minerals in the soil.

Cauliflower

Common Name: Cauliflower
Botanical Name: *Brassica olracea* (*botrytis*)
Family: Cruciferae
Type and Use: Biennial, grown as an annual with edible flower head and leaves
Location: Full sun
Planting Dates: Spring, 2–3 weeks before the last average frost. Fall, 10–12 weeks before the first average frost. Best to use transplants instead of sowing direct. In general, February 10–March 20 and August 1–31.
Planting Method: Seed planted ¼" in the soil. Transplants are best for the home gardener.
Seed Emergence: 5–20 days at 45–85°
Harvest Time: 65–80 days
Height: 12–24 inches
Spread: 15–24 inches
Final Spacing: 14–16 inches in a single row; 5–7 heads per 10 feet of row.
Growth Habits: This is the most difficult crucifer to grow. Of all the cabbage family, it is the least tolerant of freezing weather and hot summer weather. It has a relatively shallow root system.
Culture: Cool temperatures are needed for large, high-quality heads. Even soil moisture is needed to avoid "buttoning" or small heads. Add additional organic fertilizer when the small inner leaves begin to cup and start to form heads. Some gardeners recommend tying the larger outer leaves together over the head as it forms. This will prevent sunlight-caused discoloration of the head. Does fairly well in heavy clay soils.

Because cauliflower heads form so fast, fertilizing when you first see the head usually won't help. Add half a handful of fertilizer when the plant's leaves seem to be as big as they're going to get, usually 5 or 6 weeks after transplanting.

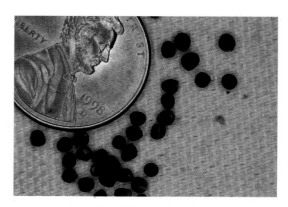

Cauliflower Seed

94

Troubles and Solutions: Hard-to-grow vegetable. Temperature extremes are damaging. Pests include cabbage loopers, aphids, imported cabbage worms, cutworms, and harlequin bugs. Build the soil well with lots of compost and rock powders. Keep the soil mulched well and foliar feed at least every two weeks.

Harvest and Storage: Harvest tender greens anytime. Harvest heads when they are full and firm and about 6–8 inches in diameter. They can be kept 2–4 weeks at 32–40°.

Varieties: Snow Crown, Snow King

Notes: Cauliflower is the least winter hardy of all the crucifers. Avoid odd-looking or woody transplants.

CAULIFLOWER TROUBLE SOLVER

SYMPTOMS	CAUSES	SOLUTIONS
Transplants die	Damping-off fungus	Work on improving soil health, treat soil with cornmeal, and spray foliage with Garrett Juice plus garlic and potassium bicarbonate
	Soil moisture problems	Solve drainage problems and water carefully
	Temperature extremes	Plant at right time; protect plants from cold, heat, winds, drying conditions with mulch, and windbreaks
	Cutworms, slugs, or snails	Treat soil around plants with DE and crushed red pepper
Slow, yellowish plant growth	Poor drainage	Use raised beds and avoid overwatering
	Low fertility	Add organic fertilizer
	Wrong soil	Add high-calcium lime
	Cold soil	Plant in the correct season
Holes in leaves	Cabbage loopers and other caterpillars	Release trichogramma wasps and treat foliage with *Bacillus thuringiensis* as a last resort
Leaves cupped and distorted	Aphids	Spray Garrett Juice and release lady beetles
V-shaped lesions on leaf margins	Black rot bacteria	Work on improving soil health, treat soil with cornmeal, and spray foliage with Garrett Juice plus garlic and potassium bicarbonate
Premature head formation	Cold weather	Avoid exposure of temperatures 45° or below
	Transplants too large	Use small transplants in the spring
	Low fertility	Add organic fertilizer
	Moisture stress	Maintain mulch layer
Poorly formed heads	Heat	Plan for maturity to be before daytime temperatures average above 75°
	Excessive fertility	Avoid overfertilizing
Heads discolored	Exposure to sun light	Tie wrapper leaves above head
Heads loose and rough	Overmature plants	Harvest earlier when heads are tight, about 6–8" in diameter

Celery

Common Name: Celery

Botanical Name: *Apium graveolens*

Family: *Umbelleferae*

Type and Use: Biennial, grown as an annual with edible stalk and leaves

Location: Sun to partial shade. Morning sun and afternoon shade.

Planting Dates: For fall, 14–16 weeks before the first average frost. Use transplants for the home garden. Use 8–12-week-old transplants.

Planting Method: Seed. Sow seed in late winter in flats in organic potting soil no more than ¼ inch deep. Move seedlings to 4-inch pots when 1 inch tall.

Seed Emergence: 12–20 days. Up to 3 weeks at 60–70°.

Harvest Time: 90–120 days

Height: 12–15 inches

Spread: 8–10 inches

Final Spacing: 8–12 inches for double rows, rows 10–14 inches apart, 6–12 inches between plants. A 6–11-inch spacing is considered the most efficient.

Growth Habits: Upright, leafy vegetable with edible stalks. Hard to grow.

Culture: Needs cool temperatures for success. Celery is cold-hardy but will freeze during harsh winters. Avoid moisture stress to young plants. When the plants are about 8 inches, loosely tie the stalks together for compact and upright growth. Use lots of Texas greensand, lava sand, soft rock phosphate, and compost.

Troubles and Solutions: Not easy to grow. Blackheart is a calcium deficiency that is treated with soft rock phosphate at 20–30 pounds. Boron deficiency is common in a

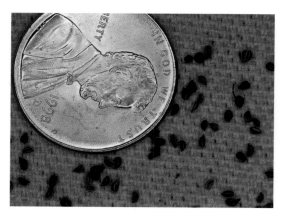

Celery Seed

CELERY TROUBLE SOLVER

SYMPTOMS	CAUSES	SOLUTIONS
Transplants die	Low soil moisture	Maintain soil moisture and mulch around plants
	Heat	Shade plants from intense afternoon sunlight and mist occasionally
	Cutworms, slugs, snails	Treat soil around plants with DE and crushed red pepper
	Damping-off disease	Garlic/pepper helps, work on improving soil health, treat soil with cornmeal, and spray foliage with Garrett Juice plus garlic and potassium bicarbonate
Stunted yellowish growth	Heat	Shade plants from afternoon sun and maintain mulch layer
	Wrong soil	Add high-calcium lime
	Low fertility	Add organic fertilizer
	Wet soil	Plant in raised beds; do not overwater; increase drainage
	Nematodes	Till citrus pulp into beds prior to planting
Poor stalk formation	Plants too far apart	Space plants 6–8"; tie stems together
Yellow spots or lesions on foliage	Blight or mildew fungus	Work on improving soil health, treat soil with cornmeal, and spray foliage with Garrett Juice plus garlic and potassium bicarbonate
Discolored and poorly formed leaves	Calcium deficiency	Add soft rock phosphate
Stems cracked or discolored	Boron deficiency	Treat soil with Texas greensand and natural DE.
Bitter flavor	Heat	Plants should mature before temperatures exceed 75°
Stems tough and pithy	Low soil moisture	Water carefully and keep soil well mulched
	Low fertility	Add organic fertilizer
	Overmature	Harvest while stalks are still tender and succulent
Trails in leaves	Leaf miners	Spray Garrett Juice plus garlic and neem
Leaves cupped or distorted	Aphids	Spray Garrett Juice and release lady beetles
Premature flowers	Exposure to cold	Don't expose plants to 45° or below

chemical program but not in an organic program where the soil is healthy. Bitter taste results from high temperature and lack of trace minerals in the soil.

Harvest and Storage: Harvest 30–40 stalks per 10 feet of row and store in the refrigerator.

Varieties: Utah 5270, Florida 683 Heirloom, Red Stalk

Notes: Celeriac is one-half celery and one-half lettuce. It is also called knob celery.

Chard. *See Swiss chard.*

Chicory. *See Endive.*

Garlic Chives Seed

Chives

Common Name: Chives

Botanical Name: *Allium schoenoprassum*

Family: *Liliaceae*

Type and Use: Hardy perennial with edible leaves and flowers

Location: Full sun to partial shade

Planting Dates: Transplants in the spring. Seed can be started indoors anytime. Outdoors, the seed should be planted in the fall.

Planting Method: Division in the fall and early spring. Seed in the winter indoors. Transplant in the spring.

Seed Emergence: 1–2 weeks

Harvest Time: Harvest anytime when flowers are in full bloom

Height: 12 inches

Spread: 6 inches

Final Spacing: 6–12 inches

Growth Habits: Onion chives have pink or purple flowers in the early summer. They have dark green, flat leaves. Garlic chives have white flowers in the late summer. They have medium green, round leaves.

Culture: Both onion and garlic chives are easy to grow, especially garlic chives. Once planted, garlic chives will be around forever. In fact, if the white flowers are allowed to go to seed, there will be a sea of chives the next year. Both will grow in any soil, but do best in healthy, loose, well-drained soil. Both need modest fertility.

Troubles and Solutions: Overwatering, snails, slugs, pillbugs. Spray biweekly with Garrett Juice when the young pests first begin to make their appearance in the spring. Aggressive spreading can be controlled by cutting flowers to eat or to use for cut flowers. This prevents the scattering of seed.

Harvest and Storage: Cut the flowers when in full bloom and the foliage anytime. Serve and eat fresh.

Notes: Chives can be used to season all food including eggs, soups, and sauces. They can also be eaten fresh in salads.

Cilantro. *See Coriander.*

Citrus

Common Name: Citrus

Botanical Name: *Citrus* spp.

Family: *Rutaceae*

Type and Use: Tropical evergreen trees: orange, grapefruit, lemon, lime, tangerine, kumquat. Fruit and fruit juice.

Location: Full sun

Planting Dates: Anytime as long as protected from freezing weather. Best to plant in warm soil and warm weather in the spring.

Planting Method: Seed or stem cuttings. In Texas, citrus matures at 4–5 years.

Seed Emergence: 2–4 weeks

Harvest Time: When fruit is ripe in late summer

Height: Varies greatly

Spread: Varies greatly

Final Spacing: Varies greatly

Growth Habits: Grow on the south side of the house so plastic can be pulled down from the eve to make a greenhouse-type effect in winter, or move potted plants into a greenhouse or grow citrus in a greenhouse year-round. Generally in Texas, citrus will only bear fruit on the spring bloom.

Culture: Healthy, well-drained, slightly acidic soil. Plant all citrus high with the graft union well above the soil line. Citrus needs little or no pruning; in fact, pruning is detrimental to fruit production. If citrus is left outdoors in the northern part of the state, a greenhouse-like structure with heat must be provided. It is best to grow citrus in containers in most of the state. Protect in the winter, move plants outside into the sun when temperature is over 30°.

Troubles and Solutions: For soil and root diseases, treat soil with cornmeal and use a basic organic program.

Harvest and Storage: Stem should be cut, not pulled. Harvest the fruit when mature and store in a cool place. Eating the fruit fresh from the tree is, of course, best. The flowers that form in the summer can be harvested and eaten any time. Fruit will store on the tree. After ripe and removed from tree, store at above 50°. Will keep 2–6 weeks.

Varieties: Satsuma is the one most often recommended for use in pots, but it still needs protection in the winter. Chang Sha, a tangerine, is hardier and has a much better flavor. It will also come true from seed and grows well on its own root system.

Notes: The peelings of citrus are used to flavor food and drinks. Citrus flowers, especially orange and lemon, are edible and good in teas. Grated peelings are also good in teas. Make sure the fruit is organically grown because the pesticides collect in the rind. Trifoliate orange is a thorny rootstock plant.

Hardy Orange "Trifoliate"

Collards and Kale

Common Name: Collards, Kale

Botanical Name: *Brassica oleracea* (*acephala*)

Family: *Cruciferae*

Type and Use: Biennial, grown as an annual with edible leaves and flowers

Location: Sun to partial shade

Planting Dates: For spring, 4–6 weeks before the last average frost. For fall, 6-8 weeks before the first average frost. In general, February 10–April 30 and August 10–September 30.

Planting Method: Seeds or transplants. Plant seed ¼–½ inch deep. Set transplant deep to the first true leaves.

Seed Emergence: 3–10 days at 68–86°

Harvest Time: 50–85 days

Height: 12–24 inches

Spread: 12–18 inches

Final Spacing: 10–14 inches. Rows should be about 36 inches on center.

Growth Habits: Cool weather leafy vegetables.

Culture: Collard greens need cool weather, loose, well-drained, healthy soil. Normal water and fertility requirements. Collard greens that mature in cool weather will have the best flavor. If color is desired from the kale, don't over fertilize.

Troubles and Solutions: Cutworms, aphids, harlequin bugs, downy mildew, flea hoppers, loopers, and boron deficiency. Release beneficial insects and spray heavy insect infestations with citrus oil-based products. Replace trace minerals with Texas Greensand.

Kale Seed

100

COLLARDS AND KALE TROUBLE SOLVER

SYMPTOMS	CAUSES	SOLUTIONS
Seeds don't grow	Old seed	Use fresh seed
	Cold soil	Plant after soil temperature is above 40°
	Seed planted too deep	Cover seed ¼–½" deep or less
	Soil moisture problem	Improve drainage and water carefully
	Crusted soils	Cover seed with peat or finely screened compost
		Maintain even moisture
Seedlings die	Damping-off fungus	Do not use treated seed and plant in the proper season
	Cutworms, slugs, and snails	Treat with DE, crushed red pepper, and spray with garlic-pepper tea
Slow growth and poor color	Acid soil	Apply high-calcium lime
	Low fertility	Apply light application of organic fertilizer
	Cold soil	Plant when soil temperature is above 40°
Holes in leaves	Loopers and other caterpillars	Release trichogramma wasps and treat with *Bacillus thuringiensis* for heavy infestations
Leaves cupped and wrinkled	Aphids	Spray Garrett Juice
V-shaped lesions on leaf edges and discolored veins	Black rot	Improve seed beds. Work on improving soil health, treat soil with cornmeal, and spray foliage with Garrett Juice plus garlic and potassium bicarbonate
Yellow and darkening spots on leaves	Downy mildew fungus	Work on improving soil health, treat soil with cornmeal, and spray foliage with Garrett Juice plus garlic and potassium bicarbonate
Leaves tough and bitter	Heat	Plant in the right season so plants can mature in cool weather
	Overmaturity	Harvest at a young, tender stage
Bolting plants	Exposure to cold temperatures followed by hot weather	Plant in the proper season and keep plants well mulched

Harvest and Storage: Harvest young leaves as needed for cooking. Flavor is better after a frost. Can be stored up to 3 weeks at 32–40°.

Varieties: Collards—Blue Max; Georgia Champion Kale—Blue Knight, Dwarf Blue, Dwarf Scotch, Dwarf Siberian, Giant Southern. Plant from transplants: Vates, Dwarf Blue Curled, Dwarf Scotch.

Notes: Kale is one of the best winter color plants. Both, especially the collards, do well from seed because they develop a deeper root system. Kale and other greens can be used as cover crops.

Coriander

Common Name: Coriander, Cilantro
Botanical Name: *Coriandrum sativum*
Family: *Apiaceae* (*Umbelliferae*)
Type and Use: Annual with edible foliage, flowers, and seed; very pungent.
Location: Full sun to light shade
Planting Dates: Sow seed after the weather starts to cool in the late summer or early fall and sow a little more seed every few weeks. Can also be planted in late winter.
Planting Method: Sow seed in the fall; thin seedlings to 1 foot. Because of their taproot, they are hard to transplant once established.
Seed Emergence: 7–21 days
Harvest Time: Cut the foliage anytime, the flowers when they are in bloom.
Height: 24 inches
Spread: 18–24 inches
Final Spacing: 12–15 inches
Growth Habits: Lacy herb with white flowers in late spring or early summer. Young foliage is large and flat; the growth is feathery as it matures and starts to form white or mauve flowers. Its pungent fragrance and flowers attract beneficial insects.

Coriander Seed

Culture: Easy to grow from seed. Needs healthy, well-drained soil. Hard to transplant. Needs moderate water and fertility.
Troubles and Solutions: Weevils may attack seed in storage. Store with bay leaves. Spray with garlic-pepper tea to repel garden flea hoppers.
Harvest and Storage: Cut and use the foliage anytime. Collect the seed when mature and brown. Store the seed in glass containers with natural diatomaceous earth added as a drying agent.

Notes: Also called Chinese parsley and cilantro. Seeds are delicious to eat raw. Foliage is used fresh in salads and with various meat dishes. Roots can be used to flavor curries.

Corn

Common Name: Sweet Corn
Botanical Name: *Zea mays* (*saccharata*)
Family: *Gramineae*
Type and Use: Annual with edible seeds
Location: Full sun
Planting Dates: In the spring, after danger of frost. Some gardeners recommend planting when the full moon is near. That would be the second quarter. Others recommend the first quarter. For a fall crop, plant 80–90 days before the first average frost date. In general, March 15–April 30 and June 1–August 15.
Planting Method: Plant seed in the garden soil after it has warmed in the spring. Seed can be started in a greenhouse and transplanted outside later for the earliest possible corn. Use 3–4 seed per foot of row 1–1½ inch deep.

Seed Emergence: 7–12 days at 60–95°
Harvest Time: When corn silks wither (about 18–24 days after first silks appear) and the ears are full. Best technique to tell if the corn is ready is to pull the husks back and look at or taste the corn. When gone past its prime, corn can be used in soups and stews. Sweet corn is best when eaten fresh out of the garden. Harvest is usually in 60–95 days.
Height: 3–12 feet
Spread: 12–18 inches
Final Spacing: Two methods: hills of 4–6 plants 3–4 feet apart, or in rows, 3 feet apart. Thin seedling to 10–12 inches apart.
Growth Habits: Tall growing grass with seed pods that contain deliciously sweet seed we eat as corn.
Culture: Corn needs loose, healthy, well-drained soils. Use lots of compost, organic

Corn Seed

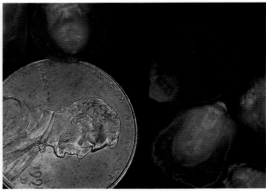

Rainbow Corn Seed

Popcorn

fertilizer, and lava sand for best results. Sugar at 5 pounds per 1,000 square feet and humate at 10 pounds per 1,000 square feet. Plant corn when the soil is 60° or warmer. Make sure young seedlings don't suffer from lack of water. Some gardeners recommend "dirting" the plants when they are about 12 inches high by covering the base of the plants with soil. Mulch is probably better. Corn takes more fertility than most other crops. Sidedress twice: the first time when the plants are about knee-high, the second time when the tassels and silks form. Fertilizer helps to make good ears. Use about half a handful of organic fertilizer per plant or about 3 cups per 25 feet of row.

Troubles and Solutions: Poorly filled ears result from poor pollination. To avoid this, don't plant long, single or double rows. Plant in blocks, hills, or three or more rows. Downy mildew, mosaic virus, and other diseases can be controlled with Garrett Juice plus garlic and potassium bicarbonate, and by applying cornmeal and other biological products to the soil. Corn earworm can be controlled with beneficial nematodes and Bt products. Rolling of leaves can be caused by high temperatures, low soil moisture, excessive fertilizer, soil-borne insect, and disease pests, or too much soil moisture. If you don't want the weeds, pull them and mulch.

Harvest and Storage: Harvest the ears as soon as the silks have turned brown and dry. Open some husks and check. Pull the ears downward and twist off the stalks. This limits damage to plants and ears. For the best flavor, eat the ears as soon as possible. Put in bags and store in the refrigerator if necessary for up to 3 weeks at 32–40°.

Varieties: True Gold, Triple Play, Golden Midget, Calumet, Golden Queen, Sweet G90, Honey and Pears, Kandy Korn, Silver Queen, Golden Queen, Guadalupe Gold, and Stowell's Evergreen

Notes: Don't overcook corn. Cook the ears just long enough to heat the kernels. Or, put ears on the grill—shucks and all. Turn once after shucks are slightly brown. Chop off both ends, shucks will roll off. Then roll ear through pan with butter and "pig out."

Many gardeners worry about weeds in the cornfield. Weeds are more of a cosmetic problem than a production-limiting problem. Often the weeds serve as a green manure crop and can increase soil fertility. Just don't let them get too tall.

SYMPTOMS	CAUSES	SOLUTIONS
Poor germination	Old seed	Always use fresh seed
	Seed planted too deep	Plant seed 1–1½", use greater depth on sandy soils
	Low moisture	Water thoroughly if soil moisture isn't adequate
	Cold soil	Plant after soil is above 50°; for extra sweet varieties, 60°
Plants are yellow and stunted	Cold soil	As above
	Wrong soil	Apply high-calcium lime, granite, and ashes
	Low fertility	Apply organic fertilizer
Leaves have ragged holes	Armyworms	Treat with *Bacillus thuringiensis* as a last resort after releasing trichogramma wasps
Small, stunted, unproductive plants	Seed planted too early	Don't plant until soil temperature is above 50–60° for extra sweet varieties
	Low soil moisture	Maintain soil moisture especially during early stages of plant development
Rolled leaves	Low moisture	Add water as necessary
	Excess fertility	Use only low-salt organic fertilizers
	Heat and bright sunlight	Normal reaction
Small ears	Crowded plants	Thin plants to 10–12", use at least a 30" row spacing
	Low soil moisture	Maintain soil moisture especially from tasseling to maturity
	Low fertility	Add organic fertilizer
Poorly filled-out ears	Single-row planting	Do not plant corn in long, single rows; use several shorter rows
	Low fertility	Add organic fertilizer
	Low soil moisture	Maintain soil moisture especially from tasseling to maturity
	Heat	Plant so that corn will mature before average temperature exceeds 90°
Bicolored kernels	Variety	Some varieties have yellow and white kernels
	Cross-pollination	Yellow corn will produce bicolored ears when it pollinates with white corn
Worms in ears	Corn earworms	Spray Garrett Juice plus garlic and add citrus oil for heavy infestations and Bt sprays
Poor flavor	Overmaturity	Corn matures about 18–24 days after silking; harvest when kernels have white, milky juice
	Heat	Plant so that corn matures when temperatures average 68–75°
	Storage conditions	Eat sweet corn as soon as possible after harvesting; store for short periods in crisper in refrigerator
	Overcooking	Never overcook! Just cook long enough to heat up

Cucumber

Common Name: Cucumber
Botanical Name: *Cucumis sativus*
Family: *Cucurbitaceae*
Type and Use: Annual with edible fruit
Location: Full sun
Planting Dates: For spring, plant seed after all danger of frost. For fall, plant seed 12–14 weeks before the average first frost. In general, April 1–30 and May 31–August 15.
Planting Method: Plant seed ½–1 inch deep after treating with seaweed, vinegar, or other biostimulant. Optimum temperature range is 65–95°. Transplants can also be used.
Seed Emergence: 3–13 days at 65–95°
Harvest Time: 52–70 days
Height: Vining plant, 6–8 feet
Spread: 3–6 feet
Final Spacing: 15–18 inches in rows, 2–3 plants per hill
Growth Habits: Vining plant that climbs by tendrils. Makes a good-looking decorative vine. Male and female yellow flowers. Females have swollen immature fruit behind the flower. Even moisture is important for cucumbers to prevent misshapen fruit.
Culture: Cucumbers need healthy soil and excellent drainage. It is best to grow cucumbers in cages or on trellises to save space. Start more plants than needed and then remove the excess seedings by pinching or cutting so as not to damage the others. Some gardeners hand-pollinate by dabbing the pollen of male flowers onto the females. It is better to encourage bees and other beneficial insects. These vine crops should be fertilized before they start to spread. At this point, they stand up straight. It's easy to get the fertilizer close to the plants where the main roots are. Use half a handful of organic fertilizer per plant.

Troubles and Solutions: Poor flavor is caused by too much soil moisture and/or not available trace minerals in the soil. Powdery mildew is controlled with Garrett Juice and additives. Moisture stress causes misshapen cucumbers. Control leaf miners, aphids, squash bugs, and cucumber beetles with healthy plants and regular foliar feeding with Garrett Juice. Spray heavy infestations with garlic-pepper or citrus oil-based products.

Harvest and Storage: Plan to get 8–12 cucumbers per plant. Harvest when the fruit is the desired size, and if not eaten right away, store in a cool place. Small fruit are more tender than larger ones. Will keep 2–4 weeks.

Varieties: Pickling—Carolina Hybrid, Lucky Strife, Pioneer, Liberty, Saladin, County Fair 81, Miss Pickler; slicing—Carolina Hybrid, Dasher II, Salad Bush, Salad Master, Picklebush, Lemon, Sweet Slice, Slice Master, Sweet Success, Burpless, and Straight Eight

Notes: Yield will definitely be reduced if mature fruit is left on the vine too long. Pickling cucumbers are generally a' little lighter green and rougher in texture.

Cucumber Seed

CUCUMBER TROUBLE SOLVER

SYMPTOMS	CAUSES	SOLUTIONS
Seeds don't grow	Old seed	Use fresh seed
	Cold soil	Plant when soil temperature is above 60°
	Crusted soil	Break the crust
	Seed planted too deeply	Do not plant deeper than 1″–1½″
	Low soil moisture	Add compost and volcanic rock powders, water carefully
Slow growth and lack of vigor	Cold soil	Same as above
	Wrong soil	Apply high-calcium lime in acid soils
	Low fertility	Apply organic fertilizer and lava sand
Young plants die	Damping-off fungus	Do not use treated seed. Avoid planting in cold, wet soil
	Cutworms, slugs, or snails	Treat with DE, crushed red pepper, and spray with garlic-pepper tea
Poor bloom set	Poor insect and wind pollination	Lack of honeybees and other pollinators; avoid spraying garden in morning hours; use varieties (seedless) that do not require pollination
Misshapen fruit	Low soil moisture	Provide adequate soil moisture during blooming and fruiting
	Stress	Plant in the correct season; maintain adequate soil moisture and fertility
Yellow spots on older leaves	Downy mildew fungus	Work on improving soil health, treat soil with cornmeal, and spray foliage with Garrett Juice plus garlic and potassium bicarbonate
Talcum-like material on leaves that later turn brown, wither and die	Powdery mildew fungus	Work on improving soil health, treat soil with cornmeal, and spray foliage with Garrett Juice plus garlic and potassium bicarbonate
Worms found inside fruit	Pickle worms, small off-white worms	Spray Garrett Juice plus garlic and add citrus oil for heavy infestations
Tunnels in the leaves	Leaf miner	Spray Garrett Juice plus garlic and add citrus oil for heavy infestations
Plants stunted, growing slowly, knots on roots	Nematodes	Till citrus pulp into soil before planting
Bitter fruit	Stress	Plant in the right season and maintain adequate soil moisture and fertility
	Lack of trace minerals	Apply humate, lava sand, Texas greensand, and sugar
Poor quality, soft pickles	Improper variety	Use recommended varieties; see appendix

Dandelion

Common Name: Dandelion

Botanical Name: *Taraxacum officinale*

Family: *Compositae*

Type and Use: Perennial with edible leaves, flowers, and roots

Location: Sun

Planting Dates: Year-round

Planting Method: Seed

Seed Emergence: 10–21 days. Mostly germinates in the cool weather of early fall

Harvest Time: Anytime the feathery foliage is present. The seeds are harvested after they mature and turn brown.

Height: 6–12 inches

Spread: 6–8 inches

Final Spacing: 6–8 inches

Growth Habits: Rosette of foliage, yellow flowers followed by a puffball seedhead. Considered a weed and is wild-like in growth.

Culture: Very easy to grow and actually does better in infertile soil. Grows as a weed on most sunny sites.

Troubles and Solutions: Considered a weed. Seed heads grow quickly and can look unsightly in lawns and in planting beds.

Harvest Storage: Harvest the young leaves for use in salads. Cut the yellow flowers when in full bloom to use to make cookies and dandelion wine. Harvest the roots anytime for use in cooking. Buds can be pickled or roasted as a coffee substitute.

Notes: Leaves are rich in vitamins A and C. For those wanting to control this plant, apply corn gluten meal September 15–March 1 at 20 pounds per 1,000 square feet and/or spray with vinegar/citrus herbicides.

Dill

Common Name: Dill, Indian Dill

Botanical Name: *Anethum graveolens*

Family: *Apiaceae*

Type and Use: Annual used for seasoning and a salad ingredient with edible seeds

Location: Full sun

Planting Dates: Plant seed in the spring and every 2 weeks thereafter to have a continuous succession of plants

Planting Method: Seed

Seed Emergence: 10–21 days

Harvest Time: Anytime the feathery foliage is present. The seeds are harvested after they mature and turn brown.

Height: 3 feet

Spread: 6–12 inches

Final Spacing: 12 inches

Growth Habits: Upright growth, blue-green feathery foliage, umbrella-shaped yellow flower heads that produce small oval seed. Stems have hollow stalks.

Culture: Easy to grow in healthy soil. Needs moderate water and fertilizer.

Troubles and Solutions: Strong wind can damage plants unless they are somehow

Dill Seed

supported. Caterpillars of the swallowtail butterfly can attack. The solution is to share instead of kill the caterpillars.

Harvest and Storage: Cut and harvest the leaves during the summer, dry in the shade, and store in a dry place or use fresh.

Varieties: Bouquet, Dukat, Fernleaf, Long Island Mammoth

Notes: Best flavor is in the green, immature seedheads.

Eggplant

Common Name: Eggplant

Botanical Name: *Solanum melongena*

Family: *Solanceae*

Type: Perennial, grown as an annual, with edible fruit

Location: Full sun

Planting Dates: Spring after all danger of frost. For fall, 100–120 days before the first average frost. In general, plant seed April 1–30 and May 31–July 15.

Planting Method: Use 7–8-week-old transplants that are about 5–6 inches tall for best results. 65–80 days from planting. If starting from seed, plant ½ inch deep.

Seed Emergence: 6–21 days at 75–90°

Harvest Time: Harvest the fruit as it matures

Height: 18–24 inches

Spread: 18–24 inches

Spacing: 2–½ feet rows, 3 feet on center, plants 15–18 inches apart

Growth Habits: Large, fuzzy leaves; thick stems; open growth; and fruit in several sizes; basically two colors: purple and white.

Culture: Don't plant too early in the spring. Eggplant does not like cold weather. Do not plant deeply; eggplant does not have the ability to root from stems. It is best to grow in cages because the plants get floppy.

When blossoms or first small eggplants are visible, apply sidedressing. Use half a handful of organic fertilizer per plant.

Troubles and Solutions: Very sensitive to frost. Leaf miners, potato beetles, flea beetles, and spider mites can be controlled with garlic, seaweed, and citrus-based

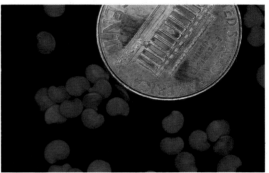

Eggplant Seed

sprays. Nematodes can be eliminated by tilling citrus pulp into the soil prior to planting. Yellows, a virus, is a common leaf disease that can be controlled with a basic organic program and healthy soil. Use cornmeal for a short-term solution. Fire ants have become a major enemy of eggplant. Control them with Garrett Juice plus citrus oil.

Harvest and Storage: Use a knife or pruning shears to avoid damage to plants. Store the fruit in a cool place or eat as soon as possible. Harvest when two-thirds full size to avoid toughness. Expect 7–20 fruit per plant.

Varieties: Florida market, Midnight, Black Night, Black Beauty. Small fruited varieties—Ichiban, Imperial, Kurame; white variety—Casper.

Notes: Member of the nightshade family, which are considered toxic by macrobiotic practitioners. All nightshade plants are reported to create negative response in joints. The small, thin Japanese varieties are most tender and have the best flavor.

EGGPLANT TROUBLE SOLVER

SYMPTOMS	CAUSES	SOLUTIONS
Young plants die and fall over	Damping-off fungus	Plant only when soil is warm and do not overwater; work on improving soil health, treat soil with cornmeal, and spray foliage with Garrett Juice plus garlic and potassium bicarbonate
	Cutworms	Treat with DE, crushed red pepper, and spray with garlic-pepper tea
Poor growth and color	Cold weather and cold soil	Do not plant until average temperatures are 65°, and maintain mulch layer
	Low fertility	Apply organic fertilizer
	Wrong soil	Add high-calcium lime
	Transplants set too deeply	Don't do that
	Poor drainage	Use raised beds, improve drainage, and water carefully
Poor fruit set	Cool, cloudy weather	Wait
	Temperature extremes	Set out transplant in the proper season so blooming will occur during mild weather
	Thrips damage	Spray Garrett Juice plus garlic and add citrus oil for heavy infestations
	Low soil moisture	Water carefully and maintain mulch layer
Small stunted plants	Transplanting too early, when it's too cold	Wait 10–14 days after setting out tomatoes to set out eggplants
	Buying woody transplants	Use only healthy, vigorous plants
Small, misshapen fruit	Low fertility	Sidedress during development of plants and fruits with organic fertilizer
	Low soil moisture	Maintain mulch layer and water carefully
Poor, even brown, fruit color	Overmature fruit	Harvest earlier
	Excessive heat	Water carefully and maintain mulch layer
Bitter fruit	Heat	Plant in the correct season and keep mulched
	Overmature fruit	Harvest fruits earlier
	Mineral deficiency	Add rock minerals and sugar
Yellow individual leaves	Yellows (a virus)	Work on improving soil health, treat soil with cornmeal, and spray foliage with Garrett Juice plus garlic and potassium bicarbonate
Holes along the margins of leaves and reddish larvae	Potato beetles	Spray Garrett Juice plus garlic and add citrus oil for heavy infestations
Small holes in leaves	Flea beetles	Spray Garrett Juice plus garlic and add citrus oil for heavy infestations
Trails or tunnels in leaves	Leaf miners	Spray Garrett Juice plus garlic and add citrus oil for heavy infestations plus neem
Leaves mottled with webbing on lower surfaces	Spider mites	Spray Garrett Juice plus garlic and add citrus oil for heavy infestations; extra seaweed is helpful

Elderberry

Common Name: Elderberry
Botanical Name: *Sambucus canadensis*
Family: *Caprifoliacaeae*
Type and Use: Perennial shrub with edible flowers and berries
Location: Full sun to light shade
Planting Dates: Spring through fall
Planting Method: Cuttings or seed
Seed Emergence: 1 to 2 weeks
Harvest Time: Flowers in the spring and berries in the summer
Height: 10–12 feet
Spread: 8–10 feet
Final Spacing: 6–8 feet

Growth Habits: A deciduous, shrubby, multi-trunk tree or big bush with musk-scented wood and flowers, creamy-white flowers in early summer, and wine-colored berries. Spreads aggressively to become a pest if you aren't careful. Likes moist, semi-shady locations.

Culture: Very easy to grow in almost any soil. Likes moist soil, but needs light fertility.

Troubles and Solutions: Invasive. Be careful where it's planted.

Harvest and Storage: Harvest the berries in the summer and the flowers in the spring. Use both fresh.

Notes: Berries are good for jellies, jams, and pies, if you can get them before the birds do. Use the flowers in teas.

Endive

Common Name: Endive

Botanical Name: *Chicorium endiva*

Family: *Compositae*

Type and Use: Biennial grown as an annual with edible leaves and flowers

Location: Sun to partial shade

Planting Dates: For spring, plant seeds 2–4 weeks before the last average frost. For fall, 8–10 weeks before the first average frost. For best production, use a succession of plantings. In general, February 7–March 15, August 10–September 30.

Planting Method: Broadcast seed or plant in rows ¼ inch deep. Seeds need light to germinate. When the seedlings have 2–3 leaves, thin to 2 inches on center, later thin to 8–10 inches. The small plants that are removed are excellent for use in salads, or eat them fresh in the garden, if you are a grazer like me.

Seed Emergence: 3–10 days in soil temperatures ranging from 40–85°. Lettuce will germinate as low as 35°.

Harvest Time: 60–80 days

Height: 12–40 inches

Spread: 18–24 inches

Final Spacing: 8–12 inches

Growth Habits: Leafy vegetable plant that grows in a similar manner to lettuce. Chicory forms tall slender heads and endive has looser heads similar to leaf lettuce. Very cold-tolerant.

Culture: Endive is related to wild chicory and likes cool weather and growing conditions similar to lettuce. Bitter taste is lessened by freezing temperatures. Warm weather increases bitterness.

Troubles and Solutions: Imported cabbage worms, cabbage loopers, flea beetles, and other insect pests can be controlled with regular foliar feeding, healthy soil, and planting at the right time.

Harvest and Storage: The inner leaves are usually sweeter than the outer leaves. Can be harvested with their roots in the fall and stored in a cool, dark place. Can be grown larger before harvesting in cool weather.

Notes: Chicory is *Cichorium intybus*. The endive you usually get in restaurants is chicory that is blanched by withholding light for 2–3 weeks, which lessens the bitter taste. Radicchio is the red-leafed chicory.

Fennel

Common Name: Fennel
Botanical Name: *Foeniculum vulgare*
Family: *Apiacaeae*
Type and Use: Biennial used often as an annual with edible foliage, flowers, and seed. Will function as a tender perennial.
Location: Full sun to part shade
Planting Dates: Spring to fall
Planting Method: Seeds or transplants in early spring; seeds need to germinate in darkness.
Seed Emergence: 7–14 days at 70°
Harvest Time: Summer
Height: 18–24 inches
Spread: 2–3 feet
Final Spacing: 18–24 inches
Growth Habits: Bronze fennel has coppery-bronze, feathery foliage, yellow umbels of flowers followed by aromatic seeds. Looks like bright green or bronze dill. Grows taller than dill. Sweet fennel has green foliage, and Roman fennel has bronze foliage.
Culture: Fennel likes healthy soil and morning sun for best results. Use moderate water and fertilizer applications. It is an

Fennel Seed

easy plant to grow and works well in the landscape garden.
Troubles and Solutions: Swallowtail butterfly larvae eat the plants, but that's all right—share with them.
Harvest and Storage: Harvest the foliage anytime, and the sweet seed when they have matured and turned brown. Store dry in glass containers. The fleshy stems and foliage are used in salads and in cooking various dishes.
Varieties: Bronze and Florence.

Notes: Fennel has medicinal value in addition to tasting really good.

Fig

Common Name: Fig

Botanical Name: *Ficus carica*

Family: *Moriaceae*

Type and Use: Deciduous tree with edible fruit

Location: Sun to partial shade

Planting Dates: Spring to fall

Planting Method: Transplants from cuttings or suckers. Best stem cuttings are 6–8 inches of the terminal shoots. Make the cuttings in late winter. Bundle the cuttings and put in the soil with tips down. Cover with 2–4 inches of soil. After callusing, the cuttings should be put in propagation rows right side up with 6 inches in the soil and 1 inch above the soil surface. In about a year, the cuttings will have roots and can be transplanted.

Harvest Time: Summer as the fruit matures

Height: 8–10 feet

Spread: 10–12 feet

Final Spacing: 12–20 feet

Growth Habits: 'Celeste' is a large-growing tree with small, very sweet figs with tightly closed eyes. 'Brown Turkey' or 'Texas Everbearing' is a productive tree with medium-sized fruit and basically two crops: one on last year's wood and a smaller, second crop on the new growth. 'Alma' is an A&M vari-ety that is productive, but frost-sensitive and is best used in the southern half of the state.

Culture: Figs don't need much other than an organic program and continuous mulch on the root system. They will grow in all soils, but like healthy soils the best, of course. They need plenty of water. Heavy mulching is very important.

Troubles and Solutions: Nematodes can be a pest but can be easily controlled with cit-rus pulp worked into the soil. Varieties with open eyes are subject to damage from the dried fruit beetle. Birds, raccoons, pos-sums, and squirrels are also problems. Don't plant figs too close to big trees. Don't till the soil around fig trees. Keep the trees heavily mulched.

Harvest and Storage: Harvest as soon as figs have ripened. Figs will easily fall off into your hand. They will not continue to ripen after being harvested. They are not ripe if the sap is white. Figs are excellent dried. Store at 32-40° for 2-3 weeks.

Varieties: 'Celeste', 'Texas Everbearing' ('Brown Turkey'), and 'Alma'. 'Celeste' bears mostly on last year's growth and is subject to winter damage in the northern part of the state. Figs produce fruit without pollenation. Parthenocarpic.

Notes: Shriveled fruit may result from using the wrong variety or from hot, dry weather.

Garlic

Common Name: Garlic

Botanical Name: *Allium sativum*

Family: *Amaryllidaceae*

Type and Use: Herbaceous perennial with edible flowers, leaves, and cloves

Location: Full sun to partial shade

Planting Dates: Fall is best, but can be planted in the spring. In Dallas, I plant between October 1 and 15.

Planting Methods: Cloves or bulblets

Emergence: 7–14 days

Harvest Time: Varies, but should be done as the leaves start to turn brown. It's bad advice to wait until the tops turn brown and fall over. At that point, the bulbs will be overmature and often split open like a flower. At this point, food value will begin to diminish. Garlic can't be stored in the ground as onions can. Watering too long or too-wet soil will cause bulbs to rot. Days to harvest range from 90 to 180.

Height: 12 inches–4 feet, some even taller

Spread: 6 inches

Final Spacing: 4–6 inches

Growth Habits: Considerable variance in the various subspecies. Some have flower heads and some don't. I think garlic is a beautiful plant and useful in the landscape garden, herb garden, and vegetable garden.

Culture: Easy to grow in healthy soil. Good drainage is essential so raised beds, rows, or hills are best. Fertilize at least twice with an organic fertilizer and spray at least monthly with Garrett Juice.

Using (hopefully, organically grown) large bulbs, separate into individual cloves and plant them in prepared soil, 1 inch deep in clay soil, 2 inches deep in sandy soil. Point up is the best, but I'm usually going too fast and lay the cloves on their sides. Soaking the cloves in seaweed and water before planting is helpful. Putting Actinovate and cornmeal in the soil at planting also helps, especially if your garden soil is not alive and healthy yet. Water the cloves in and then cover with about 1½ inch compost.

The garlic sprouts will emerge within a few weeks and the plants will continue to grow into the winter. Don't worry; they won't freeze unless we have an 1983-type winter again. A little browning of the leaf tips is normal. On nights of hard freeze, you can cover the planting with floating row cover.

Garlic

Increase the thickness of the mulch as the plants grow to maintain perfect soil conditions. Every garden should have plants of garlic. It's easy to grow and is one of the most useful plants in the world.

Troubles and Solutions: Few problems if any, when planted in healthy soil and at the right time of the year.

Harvest and Storage: Garlic should be cured slowly indoors, in low humidity, not in wind rows in the garden. Dig the bulbs when the leaves begin to turn brown in the summer and store in a cool, dry place. In order to avoid diseases, bruising, and other causes of spoilage, the bulb wrappers should cover the cloves. A good rule of thumb is to harvest the bulbs when the top has at least 5 leaves. Each leaf represents a bulb wrapper. Each brown leaf means a dead or decaying bulb wrapper.

When wrappers are damaged or gone, the garlic cloves are not necessarily ruined, but they are possibly injured and in danger of spoilage. Do not wash the bulbs, and do not trim off the roots and tops.

Varieties: Texas White, Elephant

Notes: For larger bulbs, cut the flowering stems as they emerge from the foliage. Giant garlic or elephant garlic is actually a leek and has a milder flavor than true garlic. Chew fresh leaves of parsley or sweet basil to cure "garlic breath." The high chlorophyll content helps to neutralize the garlic odor. Garlic tea is an excellent insect control.

Using garlic as an ornamental plant is often overlooked. Plant garlic in the perennial beds, the herb garden, and even in pots because it looks good. The foliage is dark green and the flowers are dramatic. Just don't let the flower heads mature and the bulblets scatter or you will have garlic everywhere! Some garlic does not produce bulblets.

Ginger

Common Name: Ginger

Botanical Name: *Zingiber officinale*

Family: *Zingiberaceae*

Type and Use: Tender perennial with edible rhizomes (hands). It can be used in tea and in many food dishes. Chewing raw is another use.

Location: Sun to partial shade. Semi-shade is best.

Planting Dates: Indoors or in greenhouses anytime. Outdoors in the spring after the soil has warmed and all danger of frost is gone.

Planting Method: In the fall, buy the rhizomes (hands) and cut them into pieces about the size of half a golf ball. Cover the cut surfaces with fireplace ashes or soft rock phosphate (available from garden centers) on newspaper or butcher paper in a cool, dry place until the cut surfaces form a callous. I've learned the hard way that if you plant without taking this step, the pieces will rot in the soil.

Place the callused ginger pieces in the soil at a planting depth so shallow that the pieces still show above the soil line. I use 6–8 inch clay pots. Put the pots in a sunny spot. They can be left outdoors while the weather is still warm, but must go inside during cool nights. Bottom warmth from commercially available heating devices helps to speed up the sprouting. Remember this is a tropical plant and must be kept warm in a brightly lit spot all winter.

In the spring, after all danger of frost has past, the young ginger plants can be moved to larger pots and placed outdoors or planted in garden beds.

Harvest Time: The following fall before temperatures fall below 50°.

Height: 3–8 feet

Spread: 5–8 feet

Final Spacing: 12–36 inches

Growth Habits: Beautiful, fragrant tropical plant with yellow and purple flowers that bloom in late summer. Upright, jointed stems that are similar to bamboo.

Culture: Gingers are heavy feeders, so add organic fertilizers at least three times a year. Healthy, moist soil is needed and regular foliar feeding with Garrett Juice is important. Some of the large ornamental ginger can be cut back in fall and mulched heavily to encourage them to live through the winter, especially in the lower half of the state.

Troubles and Solutions: Freeze damage in most of the state. *Z. officinale* is particularly freeze-sensitive.

Harvest and Storage: Dig the rhizomes in the fall and store in a cool, dry place for use in teas and foods.

Notes: Ginger often prevents motion sickness. Growing and using ginger is good for kids and adults. It is also an important antioxidant.

Ginkgo

Common Name: Ginkgo, Maidenhair Tree
Botanical Name: *Ginkgo biloba*
Family: *Ginkgoaceae*
Type and Use: Deciduous tree with leaves for making tea that research shows to be good for brain functions
Location: Full sun
Planting Dates: Year-round
Planting Method: Transplants
Harvest Time: Green leaves can be harvested all summer. There is some question about how useful the yellow fall leaves are. They're beautiful for sure.
Height: 60 feet or more
Spread: 40 feet or more
Final Spacing: 30–40 feet
Growth Habits: Open-growing shade tree. Good for the herb or vegetable garden because it lets plenty of light through. Bright yellow fall color that doesn't last long. Medium green leaves are uniquely fan-shaped. Light bark and distinctive character.
Culture: Easy to grow in almost all soils, but responds dramatically to an organic program with lots of compost, organic amendments, and shredded tree mulch. It likes moist soil. This tree alone proves how important living soil, mychorrhizal fungi, and absence of high-nitrogen fertilizer and toxic pesticides are to the production of trees.
Troubles and Solutions: Slow-growing when under a traditional chemical program. Solution: don't do that. Ginkgo does not like synthetic fertilizers and pesticides. I've never seen a single insect or disease pests on healthy trees.
Harvest and Storage: Harvest the green leaves anytime in the summer and either use fresh to make into herb tea or dry and store in glass in a cool place. It is best to add a small amount of natural diatomaceous earth to keep the leaves dry.
Varieties: Everyone always suggests buying male plants only, because the female fruit smells bad. The only problem with that advice is that the trees don't start to set fruit until they are at least 15 years old. By that time, it's too late to change. The fruit contains an edible kernel that is very nutritious.

Notes: Ginkgo is a 200-million-year-old tree. Use a few leaves per teapot whenever making herb tea. Ginkgo mixes well with most other herbs.

Grape

Common Name: Grape
Botanical Name: *Vitis* spp.
Family: *Vitaceae*
Type and Use: Deciduous vine with edible leaves and fruit. Fruit is eaten, made into wine, jellies, jams, and other food products.
Location: Full sun
Planting Dates: Fall
Planting Method: Transplants in one gallon cans are best for the homeowner.
Harvest Time: After grapes mature on the vine
Height: High climbing
Spread: Wide spreading
Spacing: 8–10 feet
Growth Habits: Fast-growing climbing vine for structures and support. Large leaves and clusters of sweet-tasting grapes. Grapes range from white to deep purple.
Culture: Relatively easy to grow in healthy soil. Use lots of compost and volcanic rock powders and either mulch heavily or use green manure cover crops such as oats, vetches, and/or clovers in the fall and black-eyed peas (or other peas) or buckwheat in the spring.
Troubles and Solutions: Grasshoppers, caterpillars, and various diseases. The dis-eases can be controlled using a basic organic program, broadcasting cornmeal at 20 pounds per 1,000 square feet, and spraying often with Garrett Juice plus potassium bicarbonate, garlic, and pepper. Birds can be controlled with hot pepper spray products. Grasshoppers can be controlled with biological products that contain *Nosema*.
Harvest and Storage: Harvest the grapes when they are mature (sweet and the seeds are brown) and before the birds and other animals get them. Cut the clusters from vines—don't pull. Store ripe at 32–40° for 4–6 weeks. Leaves are best harvested when young and tender.
Varieties: 'Reliance' (red), 'Flame' (red), 'Concord' (red), 'Mustang' (red), 'Fiesta' (white), 'Niagra' (white). Mustang and Concord are almost black when ripe. Muscadines (*Vitus rotundifolia*) need sandy soil. Our native wild Mustang (*Vitus landicans*) is best for jams and jellies.

Notes: Grapes function as a good landscape vine as well as a food crop. Researchers have recently discovered that a substance in grapes called reservatrol can help the body's cells from becoming cancerous and inhibit the spread of cells that are malignant. Tests of several foods for anticancer properties showed grapes to be the best.

Hoja Santa

Common Name: Hoja Santa, Root Beer Plant

Botanical Name: *Piper auritum*

Family: *Piperaceae*

Type and Use: Herbaceous perennial with edible foliage

Location: Semi-shade. Morning sun and afternoon shade is best.

Planting Dates: Spring to fall

Planting Method: Divisions or transplants

Seed Emergence: We've never grown it from seed.

Harvest Time: The leaves can be harvested anytime during the summer growing season through the first freeze

Height: 4–8 feet

Spread: 6–8 feet

Spacing: 3–8 feet

Growth Habits: Aggressively spreading, large-leafed herb that has interesting small cylindrical white flowers and large stems. The leaves are velvety and the edible part of the plant. They are sometimes 10–11 inches long and as wide.

Culture: Easy to grow but likes moist soil and protection from direct sun in the afternoon, although it will adapt to a full-sun location.

Troubles and Solutions: Freezes in the far northern part of the state. Hail and high winds can damage the large leaves.

Harvest and Storage: Harvest the leaves anytime in the summer. They can be stored dry or frozen.

Notes: Some research shows that eating large quantities of hoja santa is not healthy. So don't eat large quantities. Here's a good recipe: Put into a leaf, pieces of chicken, beef, or fish, some onions, garlic, and peppers, a dash of amino acids, and/or wine. Roll the leaf enchilada-style and bake for an hour at 350° in a casserole dish. This makes a delicious appetizer or main course.

Horseradish

Common Name: Horseradish
Botanical Name: *Armoracia rusticana*
Family: *Cruciferae*
Type and Use: Hardy perennial with edible foliage and roots
Location: Full sun to partial shade
Planting Dates: Spring and fall
Planting Method: Root cuttings. Put the root pieces in the soil with the small ends down and the large end 2–4 inches below the soil level.
Harvest Time: Fall is the best time
Height: 24–40 inches
Spread: 12–18 inches
Spacing: Divisions 1 foot apart in rows 3–4 feet apart.
Growth Habits: Leafy perennial that spreads quickly with long, variously cut leaves. Looks like a big lettuce.
Culture: Deep, healthy soil is best for the production of large thick roots. Fertilize lightly once a year with a 100 percent organic fertilizer. Too much fertilizer and/or water reduces the flavor of the roots. Remove the spikes of tiny white flowers to concentrate the energy in leaves and roots.
Troubles and Solutions: Various leaf-eating insect pests and slugs and snails. Spray at least once a month with Garrett Juice. Add garlic-pepper tea if the pests persist.
Harvest and Storage: Use a spading fork to carefully dig the roots in the fall. Pick and use leaves for salad anytime, but the young spring growth is the most tender and tasty. Roots can be left stored in the ground for several months.

Notes: Some gardeners like to plant horseradish in bottomless buckets to prevent spreading. Plant horseradish near potatoes to help prevent potato diseases.

Jerusalem Artichoke. *See Sunflower.*

Jujube

Common Name: Jujube
Botanical Name: *Ziziphus jujube*
Family: *Rhamnaceae*
Type: Deciduous tree with edible fruit
Location: Full sun
Planting Dates: Spring or fall
Propagation: Transplants and seed
Seed Emergence: 2–3 weeks
Harvest Time: The fruit matures late summer to fall
Height: 25–30 feet
Spread: 15–30 feet
Spacing: 20–30 feet
Growth Habits: Upright-growing tree with clusters of small yellow flowers in early summer and shiny, date-like, red-brown fruit in the fall. Slow to moderate growth, but will spread aggressively to become a real pest.
Culture: Easy to grow in any soil.
Troubles and Solutions: Can spread badly by seed and root sprouts.
Harvest and Storage Instructions: Harvest the fruit after it changes from red to dark brown and eat right away—unless you don't like the taste.

Notes: Fruit tastes a little like dried apples. Leaves can be used in herb tea.

Kale. *See Collards/Kale.*

124

Kohlrabi

Common Name: Kohlrabi

Botanical Name: *Brassica oleracea gongylodes*

Family: *Cruciferae*

Type and Use: Cool-season biennial, grown as an annual with edible leaves and bulb. Bulbs are good for slicing raw in salads or stir frying.

Location: Full sun

Planting Dates: In general, February 20–March 10 and August 15–September 15.

Planting Method: Direct seeding in the garden is best even though kohlrabi does transplant easily. The disturbance of the roots does hurt the bulb development. If you do choose to use transplants, use small plants. Plant in rows, double rows, or hills. Plant seed ¼–½ inch deep. Cover the area with a thin layer of compost to prevent crusting.

Seed Emergence: 6–9 days

Harvest Time: Approximately 50–60 days from planting. Expect about 20–40 bulbs per 10 feet of row.

Height: 10–12 inches

Spread: 10–12 inches

Final Spacing: 6–10 inches

Growth Habits: Kohlrabi is a turnip-like bulb that forms above the ground and has leaves growing from it. It's actually an enlarged stem. It is quite drought-tolerant because of its extensive root system. Very fast growing.

Culture: Kohlrabi's cultural requirements are similar to broccoli. Easy to grow and productive in healthy soil. Likes large amounts of organic matter. Use plenty of compost, lava, soft rock phosphate, and mulch. Fertilize two times per season with an organic fertilizer. It is best to plant in raised beds, rows, or hills. Considered a cool-season vegetable but can stand fairly high temperatures like its close kin, the turnip.

Troubles and Solutions: Bulbs get woody in hot weather or the small seedlings dry out during establishment. Treat aphids with molasses spray and release beneficial insects such as ladybugs and green lacewings. Control cabbage loopers and

Kohlrabi Seed

green worms with the release of trichogramma wasps. Spray serious infestations with citrus-based mixes. Control downy mildew and other diseases with Garrett Juice plus additives and cornmeal in the soil at 20 pounds per 1,000 square feet.

Harvest and Storage: Harvest the leaves anytime and eat fresh in salads or cook as greens. Harvest the bulbs when they are 2–3 inches or slightly larger. Fall crops can be harvested at a larger size. Will keep more than 6 weeks at 32–40°.

Varieties: Grand Duke, White Vienna, Purple Danube, Super Schmeltz, Grand Duke hybrid, and White Vienna

Notes: Tough bulbs can result from stress. The stress can be caused by too much or too little water, too much or too little fertilizer, or soil compaction or salt buildup.

125

KOHLRABI TROUBLE SOLVER

SYMPTOMS	CAUSES	SOLUTIONS
Seed fails to emerge	Old seed	Use only fresh seed
	Seed planted too deep	Don't plant deeper than ½″
	Low soil moisture	Maintain soil moisture
	Cold soil	Don't plant seed until soil temperature is at least 45°
	Crusted soil	Cover seed with compost and water by sprinkling lightly
Slow growth and poor color	Cold, wet soil	Plant in raised beds, improve drainage, and water carefully
	Low fertility	Add organic fertilizer
	Wrong soil	Add high-calcium lime
Seedlings die	Damping-off fungus	Don't plant too early or in wet soil; do not use treated seed; work on improving soil health, treat soil with cornmeal, and spray foliage with Garrett Juice plus garlic and potassium bicarbonate
	Cutworms	Treat with DE, crushed red pepper, and spray with garlic-pepper tea.
Stunted plants and failure to bulb	Transplants are a problem	Plant from seed and if transplanting, use small plants
	Cold and wet soil	Don't plant too early and use raised beds for best drainage
	Poor soil moisture	Add organic amendments and mulch; mulch to conserve moisture; too much water can cause the same effect
	Crowded conditions	Thin seedlings to a spacing of 6″
	Low fertility	Apply an organic fertilizer
Bulbs are tough and woody	Stress	Avoid low soil moisture, high temperatures, low fertility, and competition from other plants
	Overmature plants	Harvest when bulbs are about 2" in diameter
Bolting to flower	Exposure to prolonged cold then heat	Plant so the bulb can be harvested during cool weather
Holes in leaves	Loopers or other caterpillars	Release trichogramma wasps and treat foliage with *Bacillus thuringiensis* as a last resort
Stunted plants and deformed leaves	Aphids	Spray plants with Garrett Juice and release lady beetles
Yellow spots that darken on leaves	Downy mildew fungus	Work on improving soil health, treat soil with cornmeal, and spray foliage with Garrett Juice plus garlic and potassium bicarbonate
Rough, misshapen bulbs	Fresh manure	Best to compost barnyard manure before using

Leek

Common Name: Leeks, Giant Garlic, Sand Leek

Botanical Name: *Allium scorodoprasum*

Family: *Amarllidaceae*

Type and Use: Perennial bulb with edible bulb and leaves used for salads, soups, and many other dishes

Location: Full sun to light shade

Planting Dates: Plant the large bulbs in the fall for harvest in the early summer. They can also be planted late summer for harvest in the winter and early spring.

Planting Method: Plant the bulbs as deep as twice their diameter. Plant seed about ½-inch deep. Cover the seed with a thin layer of compost. Transplants work well if you can find them.

Seed Emergence: Seeds emerge 1–2 weeks after planting

Harvest Time: In the early summer when the plant has matured but before the leaves start to brown and before the weather turns hot

Height: 18 inches–3 feet

Spread: 8–10 inches

Final Spacing: 4–6 inches

Growth Habits: Leeks are related to and look like giant green onions with very tall, dark-green flat leaves.

Culture: Same as for onions and garlic. Healthy soil and a basic organic program. Let the soil stay on the dry side as the plants mature. Some gardeners like to blanch the stems by piling soil up on the plant. They like the white color that results and think that it improves the quality. It doesn't, and we think it's a silly thing to do. Add organic fertilizer to leeks when they're 8–12 inches tall. Use several big handfuls of compost high around each stem. This provides a slow release of nutrients and blanches the stalks white and tender. Use 2 to 3 handfuls compost mounded around each plant.

Troubles and Solutions: Few problems, if any, other than slugs and snails occasionally. Spray and dust with hot pepper products. Thrips are sometimes a pest but can be controlled with seaweed and neem.

Harvest and Storage: Harvest the entire plant and either eat as soon as possible or store in the refrigerator at 32–40°. Will last 8–10 weeks.

Varieties: American Flag, Electra, Titan

Notes: Like onions and garlic, leeks are among some of the most healthy foods.

Buttercrunch Lettuce

Lettuce

Common Name: Lettuce

Botanical Name: *Lactuca sativa*

Family: *Compositae*

Type Use: Cool-season annual with edible leaves

Location: Sun to partial shade

Planting Dates: For spring, plant seeds 2–4 weeks before the last average frost. For fall, 8–10 weeks before the first average frost. For best production, use a succession of plantings. In general, February 7–March 15, August 10–September 30.

Planting Method: Broadcast seed or plant in rows on top of the soil. Seeds need light to germinate. When the seedlings have 2–3 leaves, thin to 2 inches on center; later thin to 8–10 inches. The small plants that are removed are excellent for use in salads, or eat them fresh in the garden, if you are a grazer like me. Lettuce seed can't emerge through the slightest crust.

Seed Emergence: 3–10 days in soil temperatures ranging from 40–85°. Lettuce will germinate as low as 35°.

Head Lettuce

Harvest Time: 25–70 days

Height: 12–18 inches

Spread: 12–18 inches

Final Spacing: 6–12 inches

Growth Habits: Leafy, cool-season vegetable. For the best quality, lettuce needs to mature during cool temperatures.

Culture: Thrives in healthy soil. Use lots of compost, rock powders, soft rock phosphate, and organic fertilizers. Soil moisture

Leaf Lettuce

is also important. Avoid having lettuce mature in hot weather to avoid bitterness and bolting. Lettuce and carrot seeds are the most difficult seeds to sprout. The slightest crust will stop them.

Troubles and Solutions: Cutworms, loopers, and imported cabbage worms can be controlled with Bt products or the release of trichogramma wasps. For aphid, spray Garrett Juice or molasses water and release lady beetles. Slugs, snails, flea beetles, and garden fleahoppers can be controlled with garlic-pepper tea, citrus products, or neem products.

Harvest and Storage: Harvest small thinning plants anytime. Harvest leaves before they mature. Lettuce can be cut and allowed to grow again. Cut leaves can be stored at 32–40° for 1–3 weeks.

Varieties: Green Ice, Salad Bowl, Black Seeded, Simpson, Ruby, Red Sails, Oak Leaf, Little Gem, Winter Density, Butter

Leaf Lettuce Seed

Crunch, Four Seasons, Tom Thumb (for pots), Red Salad Bowl, Prizehead, Red Sails; Romaine—Paris Island, Valmaine

Notes: A high source of silica. The leaf-type lettuces are the easiest to grow. Different types include leaf lettuce, butterhead, romaine, and iceburg.

SYMPTOMS	CAUSES	SOLUTIONS
Seeds don't emerge	Old seed	Always use fresh seed
	Cold soil	Don't plant too early
	Heat	Won't germinate in hot soil so keep soil moist and apply light mulch of compost over seed row
	Seed planted too deeply	Plant no deeper than ¼–½"
	Low soil moisture	Mulch seed with thin layer of compost and firm soil over seed row
Weak seedlings with poor color	Cold soil	Do not plant too early in the spring
	Low fertility	Apply organic fertilizer
	Acid soil	Apply high-calcium lime
Seedlings die	Damping-off fungus	Don't plant too early and use raised beds for best drainage. Never use treated seed. Work on improving soil health, treat soil with cornmeal, and spray foliage with Garrett Juice plus garlic and potassium bicarbonate.
	Cutworms	Treat with DE, crushed red pepper, and spray with garlic-pepper tea
Spindly and weak plants	Crowded plants	Thin the seedlings to the recommended final spacing
Failure to head	Poor variety choice	Some varieties will not form heads
	High temperatures near maturity	Mulch
	Crowded plants	Thin plants to the proper final spacing
Bolting	Cold weather	Avoid prolonged, low temperatures and avoid planting too early in the spring
	Heat	Don't plant too late in spring and too early in summer and fall, keep soil moist, and mulch during high temperatures
Bitter taste	Stress	Low fertility, low soil moisture, high temperatures can cause bitter flavor
	Lack of trace minerals	Apply sugar, rock powders, and humate and spray with Garrett Juice
Leaves ragged, torn, holes present	Loopers or other caterpillars	Treat foliage with *Bacillus thuringiensis* as a last resort after trying the release of trichogramma wasps
Plant lice beneath	Aphids	Spray plants with Garrett Juice and release lady beetles
Yellow spots on leaves	Downy mildew fungus	Work on improving soil health, treat soil with cornmeal, and spray foliage with Garrett Juice plus garlic and potassium bicarbonate
Fuzzy, gray mold on leaf surface	Botrytis	Work on improving soil health, treat soil with cornmeal, and spray foliage with Garrett Juice plus garlic and potassium bicarbonate

Lovage

Common Name: Lovage

Botanical Name: *Levisticum officinale*

Family: *Umbelliferae*

Type and Use: Perennial with seeds that can be used in breads and cookies. Good salt substitute. Use like celery.

Location: Partial sun, but morning sun is best

Planting Dates: Plant anytime, but spring is best

Planting Methods: Seeds, divisions

Harvest Time: Harvest leaves anytime. Will freeze well, and can be dried. Pick leaves just before bloom. Dig roots in the fall.

Height: 3–5 feet

Spread: 2 feet

Spacing: 12–18 inches

Growth Habits: Umbels of small yellow-green flowers followed by many aromatic seeds. Large dark-green leaves, celery-scented leaves, and yellow stems.

Culture: Easy to grow in any well-drained soil. Use like celery. Use seeds in breads. Stems, seeds, and large, parsley-like leaves have a pungent celery flavor. Plant is totally winter-hardy. It has glossy, deep-green leaves that are cut and divided, and somewhat flat clusters of greenish-yellow flowers. It likes a rich soil with plenty of humus.

Troubles and Solutions: Cutworms, caterpillars, hot weather, and afternoon sun will burn plants.

Harvest and Storage: Good to nibble on fresh out of the garden. Chew on the seeds when they turn brown.

Notes: Use the leaves fresh, but cook the stalks.

Melons. *See Cantaloupe.*

Mint

Common Name: Mint

Botanical Name: *Mentha* spp.

Family: *Labiatae*

Type and Use: Perennial herb for use in salads and teas

Location: Sun to partial shade

Planting Dates: Anytime

Planting Methods: Plant transplants spring to fall. Mint propagates easily from stem cuttings.

Seed Emergence: 7–14 days

Harvest Time: Anytime leaves are needed

Height: 1–3 feet

Spread: Unlimited

Spacing: 12–18 inches

Growth Habits: Aggressively spreading ground cover herb with highly aromatic leaves. It roots at every mode. Stems are square.

Culture: Low fertilizer requirements, moist soil. Some afternoon shade is helpful. Cut back regularly to remove the flowers. Likes loose, well-draining soils. Plant mint in bottomless pots to prevent spreading.

Troubles and Solutions: A few chewing insects can be controlled with regular sprayings of Garrett Juice and the release of beneficial insects. Add potassium bicarbonate for minor disease problems.

Harvest and Storage: Cut the foliage throughout the growing season and use fresh in salads and teas. Dry and store in glass for the winter. Freeze and store in the freezer.

Notes: It is best to grow mint in pots or hanging baskets to prevent the plant from spreading and becoming an invasive pest.

Peppermint

Mulberry

Common Name: Mulberry
Botanical Name: *Morus rubra*
Family: *Moraceae*
Type and Use: Deciduous tree with edible fruit
Location: Full sun to fairly heavy shade
Planting Dates: Spring and fall
Planting Method: Can be grown from seed or transplants. Seed can be planted outdoors immediately after harvest or in the spring after being stored in the refrigerator in winter. Can also be propagated from semi-hardwood cuttings.
Seed Emergence: 2 to 6 weeks
Harvest Time: Summer, when the fruit is ripe
Height: 30–50 feet
Spread: 40–60 feet
Final Spacing: 20–30 feet

Growth Habits: Handsome tree with large glossy leaves and heavy production of delicious blackberry-like fruit. Red is the most common, but a dwarf white variety exists that tastes even better.
Culture: Very easy to grow in almost any soil. Requires moderate water and fertility.
Troubles and Solutions: Birds eat the fruit and make a mess on pavement and cars. Plant trees away from the house. Webworms are controlled by the trichogramma wasps released in the early spring.
Harvest and Storage: Collect the blackberry-like fruit when it is ripe and eat fresh or freeze for later use. Mulberries are almost black when ripe—unless they are the white variety.

Notes: The fruitless mulberry is a worthless big weed and should not be planted.

Mustard Greens

Common Name: Mustard Greens
Botanical Name: *Brassica juncea*
Family: *Cruciferae*
Type and Use: Annual with edible leaves and seed
Location: Full sun to partial shade
Planting Dates: For spring, plant seeds 3–6 weeks before the average last frost. For fall, plant 6–8 weeks before the first average frost. In general, February 20–March 31 and August 10–October 31.
Planting Method: Plant seeds in rows or by broadcasting on top of the soil and 1 inch apart. Tamp the seed into the soil after sowing.
Seed Emergence: 3–8 days
Harvest Time: 30–70 days
Height: 12–24 inches
Spread: 6–12 inches
Final Spacing: 6–8 inches
Growth Habits: Leafy vegetable that can be cooked or eaten raw. Mustard likes cool weather. It is cold-hardy down to about

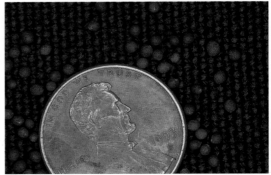

Mustard Seed

20°. Can usually be grown all winter in most of Texas. Small yellow flowers are edible.
Culture: Easy to grow in any healthy soil. Mustard likes lots of organic matter. Mix plenty of compost into the soil before planting as well as lava sand and soft rock phosphate. Fertilize at least once during the season with an organic fertilizer. Spray foliage at least biweekly with Garrett Juice.

MUSTARD GREENS TROUBLE SOLVER

SYMPTOMS	CAUSES	SOLUTIONS
Seedlings fail to emerge	Old seed	Always plant fresh seed
	Seed planted too deep	Never plant seeds more than ¼" deep
Poor seedling growth and color	Low fertility	Apply organic fertilizer
Spindly or stemmy plants	Crowded growing conditions	Thin plants to 3–4"
Small holes in leaves	Flea beetles	Spray Garrett Juice plus garlic and add citrus oil for heavy infestations
Skeletonized leaves	Harlequin bugs	Don't let grow into the hot weather
Ragged leaves	Cabbage loopers or other Caterpillars	Release beneficial insects and treat foliage with *Bacillus thuringiensis* as a last resort
Yellow spots on leaves and moldy growth on lower leaf surface	Downy mildew fungus	Work on improving soil health, treat soil with cornmeal and spray foliage with Garrett Juice plus garlic and potassium bicarbonate
Plants bolt to flower	Heat and long days	Plant at right time so plants can mature in cool weather
Hot or bitter taste	Heat; plants are in stress and ready to bolt	Same as above
Yellow leaves with green veins	Iron or magnesium deficiency	Add Texas greensand, volcanic rock, humate, and sul-po-mag

Mustard greens like raised rows to increase the drainage. Mulch between rows.

Troubles and Solutions: Aphids are controlled by planting at the right time in healthy soil. Spray molasses and water, and then release lady beetles for occasional infestations. Flea beetles can be controlled with Garden-Ville Fire Ant Control formula. Downy mildew and white rust can be controlled with Garrett Juice plus potassium bicarbonate and/or garlic. Garlic-pepper tea helps control all the above pests. Use Bt sprays for cabbage loopers. Harlequin bugs attack when the plants go into stress because of hot weather.

Harvest and Storage: Harvest by the cut-and-come again technique or by removing the entire plant and planting additional seed. Greens are usable at any size. Young leaves are best for salads and fresh eating. Older leaves should be cooked. Harvest the seed when the pods turn brown. Young seed pods are also edible. Flavor is better after the first frost. Can be stored at 32–40° for 1-3 weeks.

Varieties: Green Wave, Osaka Purple, Red Giant, Tendergreen II, Florida Broad Leaf, Southern Giant Curled, Mizuma, and Tendergreen

Notes: *B. hirta* is white mustard, *B. nigra* is black mustard. Their seeds are used to make table mustard. *B. juncea* is brown mustard. Black mustard seed is the hottest.

Nasturtium

Common Name: Nasturtium

Botanical Name: *Tropaeolum* spp.

Family: *Tropaeolaceae*

Type and Use: Annual with edible leaves, buds, flowers, and flower stems

Location: Full sun to partial shade

Planting Dates: Early spring and late summer. Nasturtium does best in cool weather, but cannot stand hard freezes.

Planting Method: Plant seed in late winter or early spring. Protect seedlings against late freezes. Plant seed ½ inch deep in organic potting soil.

Seed Emergence: 1 to 2 weeks

Harvest Time: Harvest the leaves, buds, and flowers anytime they are present, but don't overdo it and kill the plant.

Height: 1–3 feet or more

Spread: 2–4 feet or more

Final Spacing: 12–24 inches

Growth Habits: Round leaves and yellow-to-orange flowers in the cool parts of the growing season. Fast-growing annual with either single or double flowers.

Culture: Easy to grow in pots or garden in healthy soil. Harvest leaves and flowers regularly to encourage more compact growth.

Troubles and Solutions: Aphids are controlled with healthy soil, molasses spray, and release of lady beetles. Freezing weather can kill plants.

Harvest and Storage: The buds, flowers, and leaves can be frozen and stored for later use, but they are better eaten fresh in salads or while you are just grazing in the garden.

Notes: Excellent source of vitamin C. Plant for annual cutflower beds, pots, and hanging baskets.

Okra Seed

Okra

Common Name: Okra

Botanical Name: *Hibiscus esculentus*

Family: *Maluaceae*

Type and Use: Annual with edible flowers and seed pods

Location: Full sun

Planting Dates: Plant seeds in the spring after all danger of frost. The best time is when the soil is between 75–90°. In general, April 1–June 15.

Planting Method: Soaking the seed in water for 24 hours before planting speeds germination. Adding a couple tablespoons of seaweed and/or vinegar works even better. Sow seeds at 4–5 per foot of row and ½–¾ inch deep.

Seed Emergence: 4–14 days in warm soil, 70–95°. Mine usually germinates from 12–14 days.

Harvest Time: Harvest the young pods daily. Pods should be about 3–5 inches long. Once they get large and tough, they are no longer edible. They can usually be harvested 50–70 days after planting, 4–6 days after the first flower blooms.

Height: 8–15 feet

Spread: 5–6 feet

Final Spacing: Thin seedlings to 6–9 inches, rows 3–4 feet apart. Some gardeners like to thin out farther to 12–18 inches.

Growth Habits: Upright growth that's aggressive after the soil has warmed in the spring. Large leaves, edible yellow flowers, and spiny stems.

Culture: Okra enjoys hot weather and is easy to grow (if you control the root knot nematodes with citrus) in healthy, well-drained soil. Okra does like to be fertilized a couple of times with organic fertilizer, but does not require large amounts of water. Lava sand and soft rock phosphate will help to increase yields. Also, Texas Greensand should be used in alkaline or high-calcium soils. Maintain a thick mulch layer around plants after they start to grow. Fertilize when the plant blossoms in the spring. If you have a long harvest of okra, fertilize again about a month later. Use a handful of compost and organic fertilizer per plant or 3 cups per 25 feet of row.

Troubles and Solutions: Curled or crooked pods are usually caused by insects like stink bugs. Control with citrus sprays. Will not germinate in cool soil. Don't get in a hurry. "Wet feet" can be avoided by planting in healthy well-drained soil. Aphids are controlled with a molasses-water spray followed by the release of lady beetles. Fire ants are controlled with citrus sprays. Nematodes are controlled by tilling orange, grapefruit, and other citrus pulp into the soil before planting the seed. Control cutworms with DE around seedlings. Fungal diseases can be controlled with Garrett Juice, garlic tea, and potassium bicarbonate. Cotton root rot can be controlled with biological products such as Actinovate and Plant Health Care. Okra needs full sun all day. Even cloudy days cut production.

Harvest and Storage: Okra provides a long harvest season. Pick the young pods when they are young and tender. Store if necessary in the refrigerator but be sure to eat the pods fresh. Expect about 20–30 pods per plant. Harvest daily or at least every other day. Leaving pods on the plant to mature shuts down new pod formation. Watch out for the spines.

Okra seed is about the easiest to save. Just let the pod completely dry on the stalk, then cut it off with pruning shears. Store it someplace out of the weather. Mice, weevils, and other critters ignore it, and it keeps almost forever. Mixing okra seeds with other seeds while in storage seems to repel weevils and other pests.

Varieties: Emerald, Burgundy, Clemson Spineless, Louisiana Green Velvet, Annie Oakley, Red Velvet, and Beck's Big

Notes: Okra can be cut back in midsummer to create more bushy plants. Fertilize with organic fertilizer immediately after cutting back. Okra can be grown in dry land or without irrigation in some years.

OKRA TROUBLE SOLVER

SYMPTOMS	CAUSES	SOLUTIONS
Poor germination and emergence	Old seed	Only use fresh seed
	Seed planted too deep	Plant okra seed ½–¾″ deep
	Lack of soil moisture	Plant seed in moist soil
	Cold soil	Wait to plant okra until the soil temperature is above 68°
Seedlings die quickly	Damping-off	Plant in the correct season; do not treat seed and avoid overwatering
	Cutworms	Treat with DE, crushed red pepper, and spray with garlic-pepper tea
Slow growth and poor color	Cold soils	Will grow slowly if night-time temperatures are 50° or lower
	Low fertility	Fertilize with nitrogen fertilizer
	Wrong soil	Apply high-calcium lime
	Wet soil	Improve drainage and water carefully
Poorly shaped pods	Acid soil	Add high-calcium lime
Bent or twisted pods	Insect stings on pods and often stink bugs	Spray Garrett Juice plus garlic and add citrus oil for heavy infestations
Slow growth and few blooms	Low fertility	Add organic fertilizer
	Cool temperature	Wait for warmer weather; don't plant so early or late
Stunted slow growth and poor color	Nematodes	Work citrus peels into the soil or drench with diluted citrus oil
Plants die overnight, foliage remains on plant	Cotton root-rot fungus	Treat soil with biological products such as cornmeal, Actinovate, and other microbe products
Plants too tall to harvest	Variety size	Plant dwarf varieties and cut back plants in mid to late summer for bushier plants.

Onion

Common Name: Onion
Botanical Name: *Allium cepa*
Family: *Amaryllidaceae (Liliaceae)*
Type and Use: Biennial, grown as an annual in the cool seasons for edible greens and bulbs
Location: Sun to light shade
Planting Dates: For spring, plant seeds 3–4 weeks before the last average frost. For fall, plant seeds 8–10 weeks before the average first frost. Plant transplants in late winter or very early spring. In general, plant seeds February 7–March 10 and October 1–November 30. Sets and plants can be transplanted February 1–March 17. For big onions, plant seed October 1 and transplants with 8–10 inch spacing in December.
Planting Method: Broadcast seed or plant in rows ¼–½ inch deep. The small bulbs or sets should be planted in rows 1 inch deep. Set transplants in shallow garden

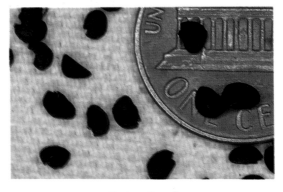

Onion Seed

soil. When using transplants, choose plants only ½ inch in diameter or less.
Seed Emergence: Shoots appear in 7–21 days. Seed germinate at 50–95°.
Harvest Time: Harvest the green onions (scallions) at anytime. Harvest the bulbs when the bulbs have swollen and the tops have died back. Sets usually take 35–45 days; seeds take 85–200 days.

Height: 8–30 inches

Spread: 8–12 inches

Final Spacing: 1 inch apart for seeds and 2–4 inches apart for sets. Some gardeners go as far as 4–8 inches.

Growth Habits: Cool-season bulb that has dark green strap-like foliage and bulb. Onions are related to lilies. They have round clusters of small flowers on hard stems.

Culture: Plant onions in raised rows for best results. Soil should be healthy and well-drained. Add lots of compost, lava sand, sugar, and organic fertilizer. Dairy manure can be used but should be tilled into the soil about two months before planting. Thin out plants to avoid crowding and use the removed plants to plant elsewhere or eat. Onions have small root systems so put the fertilizer close to plants and be sure to keep the soil moist—not too wet, just moist.

Onion seed can be planted in the fall in well-prepared garden soil that's full of compost, rock powder, and organic fertilizer. Onions will definitely start to grow before freezing weather. If it's a relatively mild winter, freezes won't severely damage young onions and they will take off in the spring and produce big, beautiful onion bulbs. During hard freezes, small onions can be covered with loose hay or floating row cover. Another method of starting onion seeds in the fall is to plant them in pots, but keep the small plants in a cool place, greenhouse, or well-lit garage until late winter when they can be set out in the garden without fear of freezing. That's about the same procedure you use when you buy transplants from the nursery in the winter. Seed doesn't cost much; give both techniques a try.

Onions, leeks, and tomatoes need plenty of time to develop a strong root system. That's why I start them so early.

Ignore the rule about fertilizing at bloom time with onions because they don't bloom until their second season. Fertilize them when they are 6–8 inches tall and every couple of weeks after that

until the bulbs start to expand. Onions can take quite a bit of fertilizer. Give them plenty because the size of the onion bulb is determined by how much green top the plant has. Bulbs are made with energy stored in the green leaves. The more green top, the bigger the bulbs. Use 2 to 3 cups of organic fertilizer per 10 feet of row 16 inches wide. Don't fertilize onions if their tops have started to fall.

Troubles and Solutions: Damping-off can be controlled by planting in well-drained soils and avoiding overwatering. Crowded conditions results in spindly, weak plants. Slugs, snails, and cutworms are controlled with natural diatomaceous earth, cedar flakes, hot pepper, and/or fireplace ashes. Fungal and bacterial diseases can be controlled with a basic organic program. Thrips are controlled with the release of beneficial insect and garlic-pepper-seaweed sprays.

Harvest and Storage: Some varieties of onions can be stored by leaving them in the garden soil. When removed from the soil, store bulbs in a cool, dry place. They will keep for months.

Varieties: White Grano is a reliable early type. 502 Yellow and Grano are sweet, mild, earlier, and a better keeper than 1015-Y. Other varieties include Texas Super Sweet, Granex (yellow and white), Burgundy, later than Grano but a good keeper and Red Granex (red). For green onions try Southport White, Bettsville Bunching, White Knight, Crystal Wax, Southport Red Globe, and Torpedo Red Bottle.

Notes: Leeks are big onions that are often mistakenly called elephant garlic. All alliums are good eating and good for you.

Onions should always be on your menu. Not only are onions delicious in soups, salads, vegetables, and on hamburgers, they are good for your health. Onion has the same, but lower, doses of garlic's antibacterial and antifungal properties. Onions in the diet is said to reduce cholesterol in people with high-fat diets. They also can lower blood pressure and help keep arteries clean.

ONION TROUBLE SOLVER

SYMPTOMS	CAUSES	SOLUTIONS
Seedlings fail to germinate and emerge	Old seed	Use fresh seed only
	Seed planted too deep	Plant seed ½–¾" deep using greater depth on sandy soils
	Cold soil	Best if soil temperature is above 50°
	Poor soil moisture	Plant seed in moist soil
	Crusted soil	Onion seeds are weak germinators; sprinkle lightly as emergence time nears and mulch with a very thin layer of screened compost
Weak seedlings with poor color	Cold soil	Plant seeds earlier
	Wet soil	Improve drainage and water carefully
	Wrong soil	Acid calcium, granite sand, or fireplace ashes
	Low fertility	Apply organic fertilizer
Seedlings die quickly	Damping-off fungus	Work on improving soil health, treat soil with cornmeal, and spray foliage with Garrett Juice plus garlic and potassium bicarbonate
	Cutworms	Treat with DE, crushed red pepper, and spray with garlic-pepper tea
Sluggish and slow growing	Low fertility	Apply organic fertilizer
	Lack of soil moisture	Water carefully and maintain mulch around plants at all times
Small or no bulbs form	Wrong variety	Plant short-day varieties; intermediate-day-length varieties can be used in North Texas
	Planted at wrong time	Plant at the recommended time
	Low soil moisture	Water carefully and maintain a thin layer of mulch
	Heavy or droughty soils	Add lots of compost and other organic amendments
	Planted sets	Sets are usually not the right varieties for bulbs but good for green onions
	Low fertility	Add organic fertilizer
Spotty foliage or brown foliage tips	Thrips	Spray Garrett Juice plus garlic and add citrus oil for heavy infestations with neem
Brown spots on leaves, older leaves fall over	Downy mildew fungus	Work on improving soil health, treat soil with cornmeal, and spray foliage with Garrett Juice plus garlic and potassium bicarbonate
Purple lesions on leaves	Purple blotch fungus	As above
Bulbs rot	Soil-borne fungi or bacteria	Work on improving soil health, treat soil with cornmeal, and spray foliage with Garrett Juice plus garlic and potassium bicarbonate
Tops fall over	Sign of maturity	Harvest bulbs and place in dry protected area to cure; onions can be left in the soil
Bulbs rot in storage	Immature bulbs	Harvest when bulbs mature as indicated by fall of tops
	Fungi or bacteria	Let tops die completely before removing, then leave at least 1" of neck on bulb

Oregano

Common Name: Oregano, Wild Marjoram
Botanical Name: *Origanum* spp.
Family: *Labiatae*
Type and Use: Perennial to evergreen ground cover with edible foliage and flowers
Location: Full sun to partial shade
Planting Dates: Transplants anytime. Seed can be started indoors in the winter and set out a few weeks before the last average frost.
Planting Method: Transplants or seed
Seed Emergence: 8–14 days
Harvest Time: Cut and use the foliage anytime, the flowers while in bloom.
Height: 8–30 inches
Spread: 15–24 inches
Final Spacing: 12–18 inches
Growth Habits: Dense, low-growing to upright herb that produces round leaves on slightly fuzzy stems, white to purple flowers, and tiny seed. The low-growing forms are sprawling and can be planted under taller-growing plants.
Culture: Easy to grow in well-prepared, healthy soil. Many of the species and varieties are cool-tolerant and make good semi-permanent plantings.
Troubles and Solutions: Very few when grown under an organic program.
Harvest and Storage: Cut and use the foliage and/or the flower fresh or place in plastic bags to use later. Because oregano grows year-round in most of Texas, it usually doesn't make sense to use anything but fresh cuttings right from the garden.

Notes: Oregano can be used in salads, to flavor foods, and as a tea ingredient.

Papaya

Common Name: Papaya

Botanical Name: *Carica papaya*

Family: *Caricaceae*

Type and Use: Tropical fruit tree with fruit production in the southern half of the state

Location: Sun

Planting Dates: Plant seed indoors in the fall and set plants out in the spring after danger of frost.

Planting Method: Seed or transplants

Seed Emergence: 7–15 days

Harvest Time: If you are lucky, harvest the ripe fruit in the fall.

Height: 8–10 feet

Spread: 5–6 feet

Final Spacing: 4–6 feet

Growth Habits: Papaya has a straight trunk and a crown of very large, deeply cut leaves on long stems. Fruit on female plants. Both male and female plants are needed for fruit production. Papaya plants have the ability to change sex. Fruit production is best when plants are started from seed in the winter and set outside in beds after the last frost.

Culture: Feed with organic fertilizer every 30 days and spray foliage weekly with Garrett Juice.

Troubles and Solutions: These plants can't take any frost, but that's about it.

Harvest and Storage: If you plant the seed early enough to set out large plants in the spring, you will have ripe fruit by fall. Eat it as soon as harvested.

Notes: It is best to start new plants every year rather than trying to over-winter established plants in a greenhouse. Papaya can also be grown at home from seed. Go to the grocery store and buy a ripe papaya and enjoy the fruit. Hopefully you can find one that is organically grown. Scoop out the black BB-sized seeds and put them on paper to dry. Once they have shriveled and fully dried, treat with a spray made by adding 1 teaspoon of liquid seaweed and 1 teaspoon of natural apple cider vinegar to a quart of water. Use a quart spray bottle and spritz the seed. Then plant at a depth about twice the length of a seed—about ¼ inch. Put the pot or flat in a bright, sunny spot and the seed will germinate easily. Bottom heat is beneficial. Outside is okay during warm days but remember again that this plant is tropical and will easily freeze. The little papaya plants can be moved to larger pots in the spring and moved outdoors or they can be planted in the garden in full sun. By starting the plants early indoors, you may get some fruit, but they will rarely mature in north Texas, unless of course they are in a greenhouse. On the other hand, papaya is a beautiful ornamental plant that adds a different texture of garden foliage. Start the seed for the next year before the current plants freeze in the fall.

Parsley

Common Name: Parsley

Botanical Name: *Petroselium crispum*

Family: *Umbelliferae*

Type and Use: Biennial, often grown as an annual for the edible foliage

Location: Full sun with afternoon shade

Planting Dates: Late winter for spring and early summer plants. Plant seed or transplants in late summer for fall plants.

Planting Method: Seed or transplants. Soak seed in seaweed water overnight before planting.

Seed Emergence: Up to 3 weeks. Normal time is 11–28 days at 50–85°.

Harvest Time: 75–80 days after planting

Height: 8–18 inches

Spread: 8–12 inches

Final Spacing: 12 inches

Growth Habits: Leafy vegetable or herb. Foliage ranges from flat-leafed to curly. Curly parsley grows to 10 inches, Italian flat-leaf grows to 18 inches.

Culture: Easy to grow if planted at the right time. Parsley likes cool weather. It also likes healthy, moist, well-drained soil. Keep seed heads cut off to maintain compact plants. Occasional light feedings with organic fertilizer is better than heavy shots. Keep the soil mulched with compost. When parsley blooms, it dies. Pinch off shoots as they emerge.

Parsley Seed

Troubles and Solutions: The lime-green, black, and cream-colored swallowtail butterfly larvae (Parsleyworm) should be hand-removed if they get piggy and start eating too much. These beautiful butterflies are as important as the parsley. Plant enough so they can have their share.

Harvest and Storage: Anytime there's foliage to use. It is best to use fresh, but parsley can be stored in the refrigerator.

Varieties: Gigante D'Italia, Single-Leaf Italian, Frisca Curly Parsley, Moss curled, Evergreen, plain Italian

Notes: Parsley is said to aid the growth of tomatoes and roses. It can be eaten fresh to serve as a breath freshener.

Passion Flower

Common Name: Passion Flower, Passion Vine, Maypop

Botanical Name: *Passiflora incarnata*

Family: *Passifloraceae*

Type and Use: Perennial vine with edible fruit and leaves and flowers for use as sleepy-time tea

Location: Sun to partial shade

Planting Dates: Spring and fall, but container-grown plants can be planted any time

Planting Method: Transplants are available in 1- and 5-gallon containers

Seed Emergence: Don't know. We've never grown it from seed.

Harvest Time: Year-round from containers. Spring and fall are the best times.

Height: High climbing

Spread: Wide spreading

Final Spacing: 5–8 feet

Growth Habits: Beautiful, although aggressively spreading vine with deeply cut foliage and colorful and intricately detailed flowers. Several different flower colors are available. Climbs by tendrils. Blooms all summer.

Culture: Easy to grow in any well-drained healthy soil. Passionvine dies to the ground and returns in the spring, although there are many tropical choices as well.

Troubles and Solutions: Most common pest is the Gulf fritilary butterfly larva. These butterflies are beautiful, so let them have some of the foliage. Hand-pick if they become too plentiful. They're slow and easy to catch.

Harvest and Storage: Harvest the foliage and flowers anytime to use in teas. The fruit should be harvested after it matures. The color of ripe fruit ranges from yellow to red. Be careful; the fruit of some varieties tastes pretty bad.

Varieties: Over 100 available

Notes: As with all the plants, don't eat unless you grow them with organic techniques. For more information, read *Passion Flowers* by John Vanderplank.

Pawpaw

Common Name: Pawpaw, Custard Apple, Wild Banana

Botanical Name: *Asimina triloba*

Family: *Annonaceae*

Type and Use: Deciduous tree with edible fruit and distinctive tropical-looking foliage texture

Location: Shade to partial shade

Planting Dates: Plant seed in fall

Planting Method: Cuttings, layering, seed

Seed Emergence: Slow; germinate the next spring

Harvest Time: Late summer

Height: 15–30 feet

Spread: 15–20 feet

Final Spacing: 10–15 feet

Growth Habits: Purplish-green flowers in April. Fruit is 3–5 inches, banana-shaped, and green when young, brown or black when mature; edible in the fall.

Culture: Small tropical-looking tree. Native to the deep acid soils of east Texas. Very large fan-shaped leaves turn yellow in the fall. Young shoots and leaves are covered with rusty down.

Problems and Solutions: Leaf-eating ants. Hard to transplant large specimens; however, small plants are fairly easy.

Harvest and Storage: Pick when fruit is ripe. The outside will be coppery-brown and the inside creamy-yellow. Keep fruit in cold storage until fully ripe for sweet taste.

Notes: *Asimina parviflora* is the dwarf pawpaw.

Peach

Common Name: Peach
Botanical Name: *Prunus persica*
Family: *Rosaceae*
Type and Use: Deciduous tree with edible flowers and fruit
Location: Full sun
Planting Dates: Spring or fall
Planting Method: Transplants, balled and burlapped, bare-rooted, or container-grown. Can be grown from seed, but the fruit probably won't be very good.
Seed Emergence: Do not plant from seed
Harvest Time: Summer when fruit is ripe
Height: 15 feet
Spread: 15 feet
Final Spacing: 25–30 feet
Growth Habits: Small tree with early spring flowers and summer fruit
Culture: The peach tree is one of the hardest-to-grow fruit trees in Texas. Peaches require lots of tender, loving care. The problems can be controlled with organic techniques. Super healthy soil is imperative, mulch on the soil is critical, and foliar feeding is a must. Prune out the two-year-old gray shoots in late winter.

Troubles and Solutions: Most of the disease problems can be minimized with the basic organic program. Flare-ups can be knocked back with Garrett Juice plus garlic and potassium bicarbonate. Insect pests can be controlled with Garden-Ville Fire Ant Control or other citrus-based products.

Harvest and Storage: Harvest the fruit when slightly soft to the touch and ripe. Eat immediately or store in a cool, dry place.

Varieties: Denman, Harvester, Redskin, Ranger, Loring, Sentinel, Spring Gold, Magestic, and Bicentennial. Avoid Alberta, June Gold, and Sam Houston. See charts in Appendix.

Peanut

Common Name: Peanut, Goober
Botanical Name: *Arachis hypogae*
Family: *Leguminosae*
Type and Use: Annual legume with edible peas that develop underground. Yes, they are peas, not nuts.
Location: Full sun
Planting Dates: Spring, after all danger of frost is passed
Planting Method: Seed removed from the pods and planted in warm soil, well after the last freeze. Soil temperature should be at least 65° at 3–4 inches for 5 consecutive days. Seeds should be planted 2–½ inches deep, 4 inches apart.
Seed Emergence: 9-50 days, depending on the variety
Harvest Time: Fall
Height: 15–20 inches
Final Spread: 15–20 inches
Final Spacing: 10–15 inches
Growth Habits: Low-growing annual legume with a central upright stem. Peanuts have yellow or white flowers and underground pods that form on the roots. The pods contain the edible peanut.

Culture: Peanuts need sandy soil and moderate moisture and a long growing season. The sandy soil is more important for ease of harvest than for growth. They are very tender to frost. Drainage is also critical. Bacteria inoculum is available specially for peanuts. Peanuts are heavy feeders and need lots of calcium, phosphorus, and potassium.
Troubles and Solutions: Insects generally are not too much of a problem. Try to keep night lights away from peanut plantings. Leaf eating insects can be controlled with any citrus-based sprays. Soil-borne diseases are controlled with cornmeal at 20 pounds per 1,000 square feet. Sulfur spray every 5 days will also help control fungal diseases.
Harvest and Storage: Dig peanuts in late summer and let air-dry before storing in a cool, dry place.
Varieties: Spanish, Valencia, Runner, and Virginia

Notes: Peanut vines should be left to increase the nitrogen and carbon of the soil. A good place to learn more about peanuts in Texas is the Texas A&M research station in Stephenville.

Pear

Common Name: Pear

Botanical Name: *Pyrus pyrifolia*

Family: *Rosaceae*

Type and Use: Deciduous tree with edible flowers and fruit

Location: Full sun

Planting Dates: Spring or fall

Planting Method: Transplants, balled and burlapped, bare-rooted, or container-grown. Containers are the best choice. Can be grown from seed, but the fruit probably won't be very good.

Seed Emergence: Do not plant from seed

Harvest Time: Summer, when the fruit is ripe

Height: 15–25 feet

Spread: 15 feet

Final Spacing: 15–20 feet

Growth Habits: Upright-growing fruit tree with white flowers in the spring and summer fruit

Culture: This is one of the easiest-to-grow fruit trees for Texas. Pears need less pruning than plums and peaches. Removal of the dead and damaged wood is about all that's needed.

Troubles and Solutions: Avoid fireblight by cutting back on the nitrogen fertilizer and spraying with Garrett Juice plus potassium bicarbonate and garlic. The traditional solution is to spray with Streptomycin while the plant is in bloom. Insect pests are minimal and can be controlled with citrus sprays.

Harvest and Storage: Harvest the fruit when slightly soft to the touch and ripe. Eat as soon as possible or store in a cool, dry place.

Varieties: Orient, Ayers, Kieffer, and Moonglow. Monterrey is an excellent choice for the southern half of the state. Asian pears include Twentieth Century and Shinseiki. Avoid planting Bartlet.

Note: There is some evidence that soft rock phosphate in the soil will help control fireblight. Avoid using high nitrogen synthetic fertilizers.

149

Pea

Common Name: Pea
Botanical Name: *Pisum sativum*
Family: *Leguminosae*
Type and Use: Annual with edible seed and seed pods for the cool seasons
Location: Full sun
Planting Dates: For spring, plant seed 4–6 weeks before the last average frost. For fall, plant seed 8–10 weeks prior to the first average frost. In general, February 1–March 15 and September 1–October 31.
Planting Method: Seed (peas), 1–½ inches deep
Seed Emergence: 5–12 days, 68° is ideal. Seed will germinate very slowly if the soil temperature is below 60°.
Harvest Time: Harvest the pods when they are young and tender. Plants will start to bloom and grow pods after about 50 days. Harvest the first pods about 20 days after the blooms. Harvest time will usually be between 50–80 days.
Height: 2–6 feet
Spread: 2–6 feet
Final Spacing: 2–3 feet, rows should be 30–48 inches apart
Growth Habits: Legume with small orchid-like flowers followed by edible pods. All peas need support to climb. Chicken wire or welded wire make good supports for peas. Cages similar to those used for tomatoes can also be used.
Culture: Peas are a cool-season annual and like moist, cool soil. English peas are grown only for their seed. Snap peas can be harvested and eaten as pods or seed. Build soil with lots of compost, lava sand, sugar, Texas greensand, and organic fertilizer. Inoculating the seed with rhizobium bacteria (available at feed stores and garden centers) helps the roots fix nitrogen from the air. This black powder can be applied dry or wet.
Troubles and Solutions: Healthy soil will control chlorosis, and cornmeal will control soil-borne diseases and help with foliage diseases. Aphids are controlled with molasses and water spray and release of

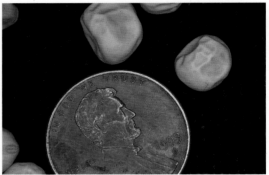

Pea Seed

ladybugs. Control cutworms with DE (diatomaceous earth), hot pepper, and Bt products.
Harvest and Storage: Harvest the pods when they are young and tender. It's best to eat them right away, but if not, store them in the refrigerator at 32–40° for up to two weeks. English peas should be shelled just prior to being cooked.
Varieties: English peas—Oregon Trail Green, Green Arrow, Axton, Thomas Little Marvel, Wando, snow peas—Dwarf Gray Sugar, Melting Sugar, snap peas—Sugar Ann, Sugar Bon, and Sugar Pop.

Notes: These cool-season peas are the true peas. The southern peas include black-eyed, crowder, and purple hull. They are actually beans. Some so-called experts recommend treating seed with fungicides. Those toxic poisons are not needed in an organic program. See Southern Peas for more information.

PEA TROUBLE SOLVER

SYMPTOMS	CAUSES	SOLUTIONS
Seeds fail to germinate, seedlings emerge	Old seed	Always use fresh seed
	Seed planted too deep	Plant 1½" deep using the greater depth on sandy soils
	Cold soil	Soil temperature should be 50°
	Poor soil moisture	Water before planting if soil is dry
Seedlings emerge headless	Crusted soil	Sprinkle soil lightly at first indication of seedling emergence to prevent soil from crusting and mulch with a thin layer of compost
Seedlings die quickly	Damping-off fungus	Avoid wet soils; plant at proper time to encourage rapid germination and emergence of seedlings; work on improving soil health, treat soil with cornmeal, and spray foliage with Garrett Juice plus garlic and potassium bicarbonate
	Cutworms	Treat with natural DE, crushed red pepper, and spray with garlic-pepper tea
Sluggish growth and lack of color	Wrong soil	Add high-calcium lime
	Low fertility	Add organic fertilizer
	Wet soil	Improve drainage and water carefully
Yellow foliage with green veins	Chlorosis	Apply Texas Greensand and Sul-Po-Mag
Plants don't climb	Low temperature	Tendrils can fail to grasp if temperature is below 50°
Flowers abort	Excess fertility	Don't fertilize so much
	Cold temperature	Cold weather will cause blooms to abort
	High temperature	Hot, dry temperatures will cause flowers to set
	Moisture stress	Don't let soil dry out during blooming
Talcum-like substance on leaves	Powdery mildew fungus	Plant resistant varieties and avoid crowded growing conditions
Wrinkled foliage and small insects present on undersurface of leaves	Aphids	Spray plants with Garrett Juice and release lady beetles
Mottled foliage and stunted plants	Virus	Discard affected plants; work on improving soil health, treat soil with cornmeal, and spray foliage with Garrett Juice plus garlic and potassium bicarbonate
Peas starchy and have poor flavor	Heat	Peas need to mature before daytime temperatures exceed 75°
	Overmature pods	Harvest at early maturity
Tough and fibrous pods	Overmature pods	Harvest before peas begin to enlarge and while pods are tender

Pecan

Common Name: Pecan

Botanical Name: *Carya illinoinensis*

Family: *Juglandaceae*

Type and Use: Deciduous shade tree with edible nuts

Location: Full sun

Planting Dates: Year-round from containers, bare-rooted in the winter

Planting Method: Bare-rooted or from containers. Roots must be cut if they have circled in the container. Can be planted from seed also; although, the nuts may be smaller and have thicker shells but better taste and higher quality oil.

Choose a well-drained site with plenty of room. Pecans get big. Whether the tree is bare-rooted, balled and burlapped, or container-grown, measure the depth of the root system and dig a wide, ugly hole that's only as deep as the roots. Backfill with the soil from the hole (no amendments) and settle the soil with water (no tamping). Cover the disturbed area with a mix of lava sand and compost. Top that 1-inch-mixture layer with 3–5 inches of shredded hardwood bark or shredded native tree trimmings. Don't use common pine bark mulch. It's not as good for the tree and usually doesn't stay in place anyway because it is bad about washing and blowing away. Staking, wrapping the trunk, and cutting the top back to match the root loss are all common recommendations and are very bad advice. None of these procedures do any good. In fact, they are all detrimental to proper tree establishment and growth.

Seed Emergence: Pecan roots emerge from seed (nuts) over winter, and the top starts to grow in the spring as the temperatures warm.

Harvest Time: When the nuts start to fall from the trees in the fall

Height: 80–100 feet

Spread: 80–100 feet

Final Spacing: 30–60 feet, 60 feet × 60 feet in orchards is ideal

Growth Habits: Large-growing and long-lived tree. The structure is normally irregularly spreading. The fall color is yellow but not spectacular.

ORGANIC PECAN AND FRUIT TREE PROGRAM

FRUIT AND NUT SPRAY PROGRAM
(Garrett Juice)

Compost tea   Label directions or, if homemade, 1 cup/gallon of water
Blackstrap molasses   1–2 tablespoons/gallon
Seaweed   1–2 tablespoons/gallon (liquid), 1 teaspoon/gallon (dry), or
                               label directions
Natural apple cider vinegar   1 tablespoon/gallon

Optional Ingredients

Garlic tea   ¼ cup/gallon or label directions (for disease and insect pests)
Baking soda or   1 rounded tablespoon/gallon (for disease)
  potassium bicarbonate
Liquid biostimulants   per label (Agrispon, AgriGro, Medina, Bioform, or similar
                               product)
Fish emulsion   2–3 tablespoons per gallon (may not need when using
                               compost tea)
Citrus oil   ¼ cup per gallon (make by soaking orange and grapefruit
                               peelings in water). Use 1–2 ounces per gallon of
                               commercial concentrate.

FRUIT SPRAY SCHEDULE

1st spraying at pink bud
2nd spraying after flowers have fallen
3rd spraying about June 15th
4th spraying last week in August
Additional sprayings are optional; weekly is ideal.

FERTILIZING PROGRAM FOR PECANS AND FRUIT TREES

Round #1   February 1–15. Organic fertilizer at 20 pounds/1,000 square feet
               (i.e., Garden-Ville, GreenSense, Maestro-Gro, Sustane Bradfield, Bioform
               Dry, or natural meals or manure compost.) Lava sand at 80 pounds/1,000
               square feet, and sugar at 2–5 lbs./1,000 square feet

Round #2   June 1–15. Organic fertilizer at 20 pounds/1,000 square feet and Texas
               Greensand at 80 pounds/1,000 square feet

Round #3   September 15–30. Organic fertilizer at 20 pounds/1,000 square feet, and
               Sul-Po-Mag at 20 pounds/1,000 square feet or soft rock phosphate if in
               acid soils.

Note: Once soil health has been achieved, the schedule can probably be cut to
               one application a year.

Large-scale pecan orchards can use manure or compost at 2 tons/acre per year along
with establishing winter green manure cover crops. Lava and other rock powders can be
applied anytime of the year.

(table continued on page 154)

ORGANIC PECAN AND FRUIT TREE PROGRAM (Continued)

INSECT RELEASE

Trichogramma wasps Weekly releases of 10,000–20,000 eggs per acre or residential lot starting at bud break for three weeks.

Green lacewings Release at 4,000 eggs per acre or residential lot weekly for one month.

Ladybugs Release 1,500–2,000 adult beetles per 1,000 square feet at the first sign of shiny honeydew on foliage.

Very little pruning is needed or recommended. Maintain cover crops and/or natural mulch under the trees year-round. Never cultivate the soil under pecan and fruit trees.

Culture: Pecan trees are easy to grow in most soils. They will grow better in deep soil, but can even grow in white rock. To ensure a productive crop with few insect and disease troubles, use a basic organic program that includes organic soil building and foliar feeding with Garrett Juice plus additives of garlic and potassium bicarbonate. Zinc is recommended often but rarely needed in an organic program. Control insect pests with a basic organic program and the release of lady beetles, green lacewings, and trichogramma wasps. The same techniques serve to indirectly control the disease pathogens that attack the foliage and nuts. Severe insect infestations can be stopped with citrus sprays.

Harvest and Storage: Pick up pecans as they drop in the fall. Sometimes shaking or thrashing the trees is necessary to loosen the nuts from the tree. Nuts can be stored in a dry, cool place and for a longer time, shelled or unshelled, in the freezer.

Varieties: Best are natives and other small nut trees like Caddo and Kanza. See Appendix for more information.

Notes: Native trees are the best. They are, in general, more durable, faster growing, longer lived, less trouble and the nuts are higher quality even though they are smaller and harder to shell.

Pecans on an Unadapted Tree. Nuts have Scab Disease.

Death Caused by Circling Roots in Container

Peppers

Common Name: Peppers

Botanical Name: *Capsicum* spp.

Family: *Solanaceae*

Type and Use: Perennial, usually grown as an annual, with edible fruit.

Location: Full sun to fairly heavy shade. Morning sun and afternoon shade is best.

Planting Dates: Spring, after all danger of frost, about 2 weeks after tomatoes are planted. Fall, about 2½ months before first average frost.

Planting Method: Peppers transplant easily and that is the most common method, although they can be grown easily from seed. For spring, plant after last frost.

Seed Emergence: 10–14 days at 65–95°

Harvest Time: 60–100 days

Height: 12 inches–6 feet

Spread: 18–36 inches

Final Spacing: 18–24 inches

Growth Habits: This is a nightshade vegetable that varies greatly in size and heat of peppers. Small white flowers are followed by fruit in many sizes, colors, and flowers.

Culture: Easy to grow in most any healthy soil. Use lots of compost, lava sand, Texas greensand, sugar, and soft rock phosphate. Mulch heavily and spray often with Garrett Juice. Fertilize twice a year with an organic plant food. Peppers are very sensitive to fertilizer. They need it in small doses only at bloom time. Use about half a handful of organic fertilizer per plant.

Troubles and Solutions: Sunburn on the fruit can be avoided by planting in afternoon shade. Leaf miners and spider mites are controlled with healthy soil, Garrett Juice, and garlic tea. Add potassium bicarbonate for disease problems. Nematodes will no longer be a problem if citrus pulp is tilled into the beds before planting. A basic organic program prevents most pest problems.

Harvest and Storage: Don't break peppers from the plant. Cut them off to prevent

155

Habañero Peppers—the Hottest!

damage to the stems and the rest of the plant. Peppers can be stored in a cool, dry place for a good long time, but they are best eaten fresh. All peppers turn red or yellow, but they can also be harvested green.

Varieties: Hot—Cayenne, Chili Piquin, Habañero, Poblano, Bolivian Rainbow, Jalapeño, Serrano, Tobasco, Spanish Spice, Purple Peruvian; Sweet—Big Bertha, Red Pimento, Red Jupiter, Yellow Top Banana, Golden Bell Yellow, Nardello, Lilac—purple. Emerald Giant—red Jingle Bells—heavy producer—good for beginners.

Bell and Hot Peppers.

Notes: Peppers are good for you in that they can help blood circulation and are good for digestion. On the other hand, macrobiotic practitioners say that all nightshade vegetables are bad for the joints, so ease off if you have arthritis. Peppers are loaded with vitamins and minerals, plus they just taste good. The juice from hot peppers like jalapeño, cayenne, and habañero can be used with garlic juice to make an effective organic pesticide. Peppers make lovely ornamental landscape plants. The small fruiting varieties can be used as potted plants, and the chile piquins will perennialize in north Texas under an organic program. All peppers are actually perennial plants, but most will freeze out at the first frost.

When choosing your peppers, remember that color has nothing to do with how hot they are. The amount of capsaicin in a pepper can be scientifically measured by the Scoville Organoleptic Test.

Jalapeño Pepper Seed

This test measures the number of units of water it takes to make a unit of pepper lose all traces of heat. The hottest chile pepper known, the habañero, checks in at an incendiary 150,000 to 300,000 Scoville units, but it looks so tame, like a tiny orange pumpkin. California Wonder is commonly sold but has disease problems.

PEPPER TROUBLE SOLVER

SYMPTOMS	CAUSES	SOLUTIONS
Transplants are sluggish and lack vigor	Cold soil	Plant after the soil is above 55°
	Wet soil	Plant in raised beds and avoid excessive watering
	Low fertility	Add organic fertilizer
	Wrong soil	Add high-calcium lime
Spindly, weak plant	Low fertility	Add organic fertilizer and spray foliage with Garrett Juice
Stunted plants	Setting out too early	Wait until the soil temperature is above 55°
	Dry roots of transplants	Soak roots in seaweed water before planting
	Low fertility	Add organic fertilizer and spray with Garrett Juice
Poor bloom set	Low fertility	Add organic fertilizer
	Heat	Fruit will set best between 60 and 80°; above 90° bloom drop is common
	Poor pollination	Pick off the first flowers to form
Small, misshapen fruits with thin walls	Heat	As above
	Low fertility	Add organic soil and spray foliage with Garrett Juice
Fruit doesn't set until fall	You planted too late	Summer heat caused blossom drop, fruit set occurred when weather cools
Trails in leaves	Leaf miners	Spray with Garrett Juice and garlic and neem
Yellow areas on lower leaves, webs and tiny insects on lower surface of leaves	Spider mites	Spray with Garrett Juice and garlic pepper and add extra seaweed
Brown or yellow spots on leaves	Leaf-spotting fungi or bacteria	Work on improving soil health, treat soil with cornmeal, and spray foliage with Garrett Juice plus garlic and potassium bicarbonate
Plants stunted; leaves twisted and mottled	Pepper mosaic virus	Compost infected plants, control insect pests, and use resistant varieties; spray Garrett Juice plus garlic and add citrus oil for heavy infestations
Plants stunted and knots on roots	Nematodes	Till citrus pulp into the soil prior to planting
Water soaked areas on side of peppers	Sunscald	Exposure to direct sun, provide afternoon shade
Peppers develop chocolate color	Normal ripening	Peppers change color as they ripen, eventually turning red, yellow, or purple

Perilla

Common Name: Perilla, Beefsteak Plant
Botanical Name: *Perilla frutescens*
Family: *Labiatae*
Type and Use: Annual with edible foliage
Location: Full sun to light shade
Planting Dates: Spring after the last frost
Planting Method: Seed
Seed Emergence: 1–2 weeks
Harvest Time: Anytime during the summer
Height: 3 feet
Spread: 3 feet
Final Spacing: 6–12 inches
Growth Habits: Aggressive annual that spreads readily from seed. It has purple flowers and either burgundy, purple, or green leaves. Perilla is often confused with opal or black coleus.

Culture: Very easy to grow in almost any soil. Be careful where you plant it—it might be in your downhill neighbors' yards next year.

Troubles and Solutions: Perilla reseeds so easily, it can become a pest.

Harvest and Storage: Harvest and eat fresh or store in the refrigerator. Leaves can be frozen for use in the winter.

Varieties: Green leaf—Green Shiso, Green Cumin. Purple or red—Red Shiso

Notes: Also called Beefsteak Plant. The leaves are used to flavor meat and vinegars. Many Japanese dishes serve a perilla leaf.

Persimmon

Common Name: Persimmon
Botanical Name: *Diospyrus virginiana*
Family: *Ebenaceae*
Type and Use: Deciduous tree with edible fruit
Location: Full sun
Planting Dates: Anytime of the year if from a container, but fall is the best time
Planting Method: Transplants of container-grown trees grow best. Bare-rooted plants can be planted in the fall and winter.
Seed Emergence: Can be grown from seed after storing about 2 months in the refrigerator. It is better to plant nursery-grown plants.
Harvest Time: The fruit ripens in the fall. It has its best flavor when it easily releases from the tree. The fruit will often be sour until after the first frost.
Height: 60 feet
Spread: 30 feet
Final Spacing: 20–40 feet
Growth Habits: Tall-growing shade tree, insignificant flowers, large, shiny leaves, and small pink to yellow 1-inch fruit in the fall. Dark heavily fissured bark. Really good-looking fruit and shade tree. Oriental persimmons are much smaller trees, but have larger fruit.
Culture: Easy to grow in almost any soil. Fertilize with organic fertilizer. Twice a year is plenty. Foliar feeding will help fruit production and limit insect pests.
Troubles and Solutions: Primary insect pest is the webworm, which can be managed by releasing trichogramma wasps in the spring at leaf emergence. A succession of releases throughout the growing season is best. Heavy infestations can be controlled with Bt sprays.
Harvest and Storage: Harvest the fruit when ripe and after the first freeze for the best taste. Eat immediately because they don't store well.
Varieties: *Diospyrus texana* is the smaller-growing and small-fruited Texas native persimmon. *Diospyrus kaki* is the smaller-growing Japanese species. Some of the best selections for Texas include 'Eureka,' 'Hachiya,' 'Tane-nashi,' and Tamopan. 'Fuyu' or 'Fuyugaki' are the non-astringent recommendations for the southern half of the state. 'Izu' is also non-astringent and more cold-tolerant.

Notes: Other common names are common persimmon and Eastern persimmon.

159

Plum

Common Name: Plum

Botanical Name: *Prunus salicinia*

Family: *Rosaceae*

Type and Use: Deciduous fruit tree with edible flowers and fruit

Location: Full sun

Planting Dates: Fall for bare-rooted plants, but container-grown plants can be planted year-round

Planting Method: Cuttings and graphs

Seed Emergence: 2–4 weeks

Harvest Time: When fruit is ripe in the summer

Height: 20 feet

Spread: 15–20 feet

Final Spacing: 20–25 feet

Growth Habits: Small upright to spreading deciduous tree. Pink to white spring flowers are followed by summer fruit.

Culture: One of the easier-to-grow fruit trees. Use a basic organic program and spray at least monthly (more is better) with Garrett Juice or other organic foliar feeding spray. A small amount of pruning in winter is okay, but not essential. Easy to grow in most soils except white rock.

Troubles and Solutions: Diseases such as bacterial stem canker and brown rot can be controlled with a basic organic program. The first spray of Garrett Juice plus garlic and potassium bicarbonate should be made at pink bud and the second after the flowers have fallen from the tree, then once a month, at least, for the rest of the growing season. Borers and plum curculio are controlled by keeping the trees out of stress. Mulch on the root system is critical. Tree Trunk Goop also helps. Other problem pests are aphids, bacterial stem canker, brown rot, peach tree borer, and plum curculio.

Harvest and Storage: Harvest the flowers when in bloom and the fruit in the summer. Plums are ripe when they take on a deeper red color and are slightly soft to the touch. Pick fruit when it is slightly soft and eat fresh or store in a cool, dry place.

Varieties: Best for Texas are 'Methley,' 'Morris,' and 'Bruce,' and 'Santa Rosa.' *Prunus Mexicana* is our native plum. It is much easier to grow, but the fruit is not that good for eating. It's mostly good for making jams and jellies from the fall-maturing fruit.

Notes: Rabbits love the shoots pruned from this and other fruit trees.

Pomegranate

Common Name: Pomegranate
Botanical Name: *Punica granatum*
Family: *Punicaceae*
Type and Use: Bushy deciduous shrub with red-orange flowers in summer and edible fruit
Location: Sun to partial shade
Planting Dates: Year-round
Planting Method: Transplants from containers
Seed Emergence: Can be grown from seed but the resulting shrub will usually be an inferior quality. The plant can be propagated from softwood cuttings or root suckers.
Harvest Time: In the fall, after skin has become red and leathery in texture
Height: 10–15 feet
Spread: 8–10 feet
Spacing: 6–8 feet
Growth Habits: Bushy deciduous shrub with red-orange flowers in summer. Bare and ugly in the winter so, if you are trying landscape with edible plants, be careful where you plant pomegranate.
Culture: Plant in prepared beds for best results. Water and fertilizer requirements are minimal. Positive drainage is important. Spray often with mixes that contain vinegar and seaweed to help the flowers set fruit.
Troubles and Solutions: Few, if any, other problems than difficulty in setting and producing fruit. Poor pollination is the main cause. Many of the plants sold in nurseries are ornamental only and will never have fruit.
Harvest and Storage: Harvest the fruit when it has turned red and leathery in the fall. It can be stored indoor in a cool, dry place.
Varieties: 'Albescens' is a white flowering selection. 'Wonderful' is supposedly one of the commonly available fruit setting varieties.

Notes: Some people eat all of the crunchy seeds. I like to just suck the juicy stuff off the seed. Pomegranates can be very messy to eat.

Potato

Common Name: Potato
Botanical Name: *Solanum tuberosum*
Family: *Solanaceae*
Type and Use: Perennial, grown as an annual for its edible root tuber. All other parts of the plant are toxic.
Location: Full sun
Planting Dates: Many gardeners plant on Washington's birthday (used to be February 22). Others plant potatoes as early as January. Potato shoots can be frozen back without much damage to the crop. Official planting dates for spring are 2–3 weeks before last frost; for fall, 12–16 weeks before first frost. In general, February 7–March 15 and July 25–August 25.
Planting Method: Ruth Stout, gardening author, and many other gardeners recommend planting the entire seed potato. Others like to cut the potatoes into 2–3 ounce pieces about the size of golf balls. Each piece must have an "eye." Coat the cut surfaces with sulfur or fireplace ashes and allow to callous before planting.
Seed Emergence: Potatoes come up within as quick as a week, but usually 15–20 days when daytime temperatures are between 60–75°.
Harvest Time: 90–120 days
Height: 18–24 inches
Spread: 24–36 inches
Final Spacing: 8–16 inches between pieces in a row and 36 inches between rows
Growth Habits: Leafy vegetables that sometimes flowers in cool weather, potatoes are tubers and are actually modified stems, not roots. The tubers will tend to swell out of the soil. When they do, the sunlight hits them, they turn green and will give you a tummy ache. Keep them covered with soil or mulch.
Culture: Fertilize fairly heavily when planting rather than doing a lot of sidedressing later. For best production, keep the soil slightly moist. Foliar feed with Garrett Juice at least monthly. For best produc-

tion, cover potato plantings with a thick layer of natural mulch. Some gardeners recommend "dirting" or piling soil up on the potatoes as they grow. Adding more mulch is better. Potatoes need ample amounts of nitrogen, phosphorus, potassium, and magnesium. They prefer acid soil, so add lots of compost and sulfur at 5 pounds per 1,000 square feet.

Sidedress potatoes about 6 or 7 weeks after planting. The plants should be blooming by this time. Sidedress before hilling (if you choose to do that) so you can cover the fertilizer with soil as you hill. Use half a handful of organic fertilizer per plant or 3 cups per 25 feet of row.

Troubles and Solutions: Control Colorado potato beetles, flea beetles, garden flea hoppers, and aphids with a basic organic program, citrus product sprays, neem sprays, and the release of beneficial insects. Hand-pick the first potato beetles to appear. Control nematodes and wireworms (the larvae of click beetles) with citrus pulp and sugar. Root fungi and other soil problems can be controlled with compost, biological products, and cornmeal. Leaf fungi troubles can be controlled with potassium bicarbonate.

Harvest and Storage: Harvest when the foliage starts to turn brown or, even better, just before the foliage starts to turn. Dig and eat as new potatoes as soon as they are large enough. If you get lucky and get a fall crop, cut the tops off after they freeze and leave the potatoes in storage in the ground. How long to leave them depends on moisture. If too wet, the tubers will rot. Frozen tubers will rot. Ideal storage temperature is 40°. Potato fruit flowers and sprouts contain toxic substances. Foliage needs to turn completely brown or the potatoes won't store well. Large-scale farmers don't wait. They mow the foliage and dig 7–10 days later, which sets the skin so the potatoes don't rot. Cure potatoes in a dark place above 50° and then store for as long as six months at 40–48°.

Varieties: White—Kennebec, Red Norland; Red—Pontiac, Red Lasota. Yukon Gold tastes like it is already buttered. Other interesting choices include Yellow Finn, Purple Viking, and All Blue. Red potatoes produce better than white ones in Texas.

Notes: The best part of the potato is the skin, but unless you use a totally organic program, don't eat the skin. The skin of the potato is the main storage area for pesticides and other contaminants. The same goes for other fruits and vegetables. Fall potato crops are difficult in Texas.

POTATO TROUBLE SOLVER

SYMPTOMS	CAUSES	SOLUTIONS
Seed potatoes don't sprout	Natural dormancy	Let seed potatoes experience alternating temperatures
	Soil disease	Treat seed pieces prior to planting and treat soil with cornmeal, sulfur, or fireplace ashes
	No eyes on cut seed pieces	Make certain each piece has at least one eye; best to use entire potatoes

(table continued on page 164)

◄ Potatoes Being Harvested

POTATO TROUBLE SOLVER (Continued)

SYMPTOMS	CAUSES	SOLUTIONS
Spindly weak-color plants	Seed planted too close	Plants should have an in-row spacing of 8–12″
	Low fertility	Add organic fertilizer
	Cold wet soil	Make sure drainage is good
Large plants with excessively lush growth	Heat	Plants will grow best at temperatures between 45–75°; avoid planting too late in the spring
	Excessive fertility	Cut back on your fertilizing
Holes in leaves, striped bugs	Potato beetles	Hand-pick the first bugs to appear or spray Garrett Juice plus garlic and add citrus oil for heavy infestations.
Foliage curled and yellow, small green insects under leaves	Aphids	Spray plants with Garrett Juice and release lady beetles
Brown or black spots on leaves and/or stems	Blight fungi	Work on improving soil health, treat soil with cornmeal, and spray foliage with Garrett Juice plus garlic and potassium bicarbonate
Plants wilt suddenly and die	Soil-borne fungi	Work on improving soil health, treat soil with cornmeal, and spray foliage with Garrett Juice plus garlic and potassium bicarbonate
Rough, corky potatoes	Potato scab fungus	Work on improving soil health, treat soil with cornmeal, and spray foliage with Garrett Juice plus garlic and potassium bicarbonate and apply Texas greensand
Rough, pimply, usually small	Root knot nematodes	Drench the soil with orange oil or till citrus pulp in prior to planting
Rough, small pits on surface of tubers	Wireworms	Same as above
Knobby, misshapened potatoes	Heavy soil	Add lots of compost, lava sand, sugar, and Texas Greensand; plant potatoes above ground
	Fluctuating soil moisture	Maintain uniform moisture; don't let soil get dry, especially near time of maturity
Small potatoes and weak overall yield	Wrong variety used	Red LaSoda and Pontiac are preferred red varieties; Kennebec is one of the best white potatoes
	Late planting	Plant early because potatoes don't set well at soil temperatures above 85°
	Planting too deep	Plant just under or on top of the soil and cover with thick layer of mulch

Pumpkin

Common Name: Pumpkin
Botanical Name: *Cucurbita pepo*
Family: *Cucurbitaceae*
Type and Use: Annual with edible flowers and fruit
Location: Full sun
Planting Dates: Pumpkins can be planted anytime after the last frost, but to time your planting for Thanksgiving and Halloween, you have to do a little planning. If the variety needs 100 days to mature, pick the harvest date and count back 100 days or a few more for a cushion. In general, April 1–July 31.
Planting Method: Plant the seeds after all danger of frost is gone and the soil temperature is at least 70°. Use 4–6 seeds every 6 feet in rows about 8 feet apart, about 1½ inches in the soil and a little deeper in sandy soil.
Seed Emergence: 5–14 days when the soil is between 70–95°. Within 10 days of emergence, thin the seedlings down to two per hill. Pinch them off instead of pulling them up to avoid hurting the two winners.
Harvest Time: 85–160 days
Height: High climbing and/or spreading. Can grow 12–15 feet and cover 200 square feet of the garden.
Final Spacing: 24 inches–6 feet
Growth Habits: Large stems and foliage, large yellow flowers. Pumpkins and squash are similar; the main difference is the stem. Pumpkin stems are tough and angular, while squash stems are round and more tender. Pumpkins have large root systems.
Culture: Pumpkins grow best in loose, coarse-textured soils; however, they will grow and be productive in almost any well-prepared soil. Mix in lots of compost, lava sand, Texas Greensand (in alkaline soils), and soft rock phosphate. Mulch the bare soil around the young plants as they start to grow. Fertilize three times with organic fertilizer and spray Garrett Juice at least monthly. Pumpkins have normal water requirements.
Troubles and Solutions: Poor pollination can be solved by encouraging biodiversity,

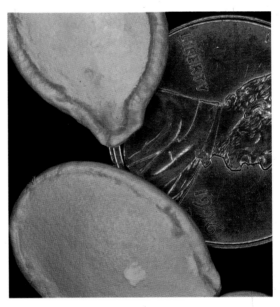

Pumpkin Seed

especially bees and other beneficial insects. Some gardeners like to dab the male flowers on the female flowers (those with the swelling behind the flower). That's okay, but way too much trouble for me. The organiphobes say to only spray in the late afternoon when honeybees are not active. That's nuts! Don't use poisons at all—ever! Treat for mosaic virus, powdery mildew, downy mildew, and other diseases by building soil health and spraying with Garrett Juice plus garlic and potassium bicarbonate. Treat aphids with sugar water and by releasing ladybugs.
Harvest and Storage: Pick pumpkins when they are the size and color you need and always leave a 2–4 inch stem stub. Well, at least an inch. Leaving no stem stub invites disease. Pumpkins can still be harvested after frost. For long-term storage, cure them in the sun for a week and then move to a cool, dry place. For winter storage, the skin should be hard. They will store up to six months at 45–50°.
Varieties: Autumn Gold, Jack O' Lantern, Jackpot, Big Max, Funny Face, Spirit, Small Sugar and Jack-O-Lite

Notes: Don't plant other vegetables close to pumpkins. They will get run over.

SYMPTOMS	CAUSES	SOLUTIONS
Seeds don't germinate	Old seed	Always use fresh seed
	Cold soil	Plant after soil temperatures is above 70°
	Seed planted too deep	Plant 1–1½″ deep, and use greater depth on loose, sandy soils
	Low soil moisture	Moisten soil before planting
Plants die soon after emergence	Damping-off fungus	Do not use treated seed and don't plant when soils are cold
	Cutworms	Treat with DE, crushed red pepper, and spray with garlic-pepper tea
Stunted plants	Wrong soil	Add high-calcium soil and granite sand and fireplace ashes
	Low fertility	Use organic fertilizer
	Cold soil	Pumpkins grow slowly until the soil warms
	Heavy, poorly drained soils	Add organic amendments: compost, lava, sugar, and earthworm castings
Mottled and distorted leaves	Virus	Remove sick plants, work on improving soil health, treat soil with cornmeal, and spray foliage with Garrett Juice plus garlic and potassium bicarbonate
Poor fruit set	Poor pollination	Lack of honeybee and other insect activity
	Low soil moisture	Maintain soil moisture during bloom
Small, misshapen fruit	Low soil moisture	Maintain moist soil as fruits mature
	Virus infection	Remove sick plant, work on improving soil health, treat soil with cornmeal, and spray foliage with Garrett Juice plus garlic and potassium bicarbonate
	Heavy, poorly drained soils	Add liberal amounts of compost, lava sand, sugar, and earthworm castings
White talcum-like matter on leaves	Powdery mildew fungus	Work on improving soil health, treat soil with cornmeal, and spray foliage with Garrett Juice plus garlic and potassium bicarbonate
Yellow spots on older leaves wither and die	Downy mildew fungus	Work on improving soil health, treat soil with cornmeal, and spray foliage with Garrett Juice plus garlic and potassium bicarbonate
Small insects on lower leaf surface	Aphids	Spray plants with Garrett Juice and release lady beetles
Plants wilt suddenly, worms in stems	Squash vine borer	Spray Garrett Juice plus garlic and add citrus oil for heavy infestations
Numerous brown insects	Squash bugs	Spray Garrett Juice plus garlic and add citrus oil for heavy infestations
Spotted or striped beetles on foliage	Cucumber beetles	Spray Garrett Juice plus garlic and add citrus oil for heavy infestations
Fruits rot quickly after harvest	Improper storage	Cure in sun for several days before storing in a cool, dry area
	Pulled from plant	Harvest by cutting stem with sharp knife; leave 3–4″ long stem attached to fruit

Purslane

Common Name: Purslane, Moss Rose
Botanical Name: *Portulaca oleracea*
Family: *Portulacaceae*
Type and Use: Annual with edible foliage and flowers
Location: Sun to partial shade
Planting Dates: Spring
Planting Method: Seed or transplants in the spring after frost danger is gone
Seed Emergence: I bet fast, but not sure. The seeds are tiny. I just buy transplants or let the wild ones sprout and grow.
Harvest Time: Harvest the foliage anytime.
Height: 2–6 inches
Spread: 12–18 inches
Final Spacing: 12 inches

Growth Habits: Low-growing and spreading succulent annual herb
Culture: Drought-tolerant and heat-loving. Not much needed to maintain a healthy crop.
Troubles and Solutions: Few problems, if any.
Harvest and Storage: Foliage and stems can be picked and eaten fresh. Pick the flowers fresh and use as garnish.
Varieties: 'Goldberg,' *P. grandiflora* is the ornamented bedding plant.

Notes: Also called moss rose and portulaca. This tasty herb is loaded with vitamin C and other vitamins and minerals. The organiphobes still recommend spraying this great food with broadleaf weed killers. The so-called weed has more food value than the hybrid flower varieties. However, both are good.

Radish

Common Name: Radish
Botanical Name: *Raphanus sativus*
Family: *Cruciferae*
Type: Annual or biennial grown as an annual with edible greens and roots
Location: Sun to partial shade
Planting Dates: For spring, plant seeds 4–6 weeks before the last average frost. For fall, plant seeds 6–8 weeks before first average frost. They grow so fast, they can almost be planted anytime. In general, January 20–April 30 and September 1–November 15.
Planting Method: Seed only. Broadcast or plant in rows ½ inch deep. Use 3–4 seeds per inch and then thin the stand about 3–4 days after emergence.
Seed Emergence: Radishes germinate quickly. Usually 3–7 days at 45–90°. About 85° is ideal.
Harvest Time: 20–35 days after planting. Some of the winter types take longer.
Height: 3–12 inches
Spread: 4–6 inches
Final Spacing: 1–4 inches
Growth Habits: Very fast growing annual vegetable. The swollen root of the plant is the edible part.
Culture: Radishes like cool soil and need moderate amounts of water and fertilizer. Radishes can be grown in any healthy soil, in garden beds, or in containers. Fertilize with an organic product about two weeks after emergence.
Troubles and Solutions: Control slugs, snails, and cutworms with hot pepper products, diatomaceous earth, cedar flakes, and garlic-pepper-seaweed spray. Wireworms and nematodes can be controlled with citrus pulp tilled into the seedbed prior to planting the seed. Failure to bulb can be solved by thinning the crowded seedlings. Radishes become pithy if left in the soil after maturity. Flea beetles and aphids can be controlled with Garden-Ville Fire Ant Control, other citrus sprays, or sugar followed by the release of lady beetles.
Harvest and Storage: It is best to eat radishes soon after harvesting. Store them if

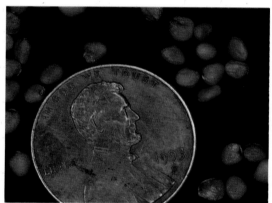

Radish Seed

needed in the refrigerator. An ice bath prior to storing helps.
Varieties: 'Gala,' 'Red Ball,' 'Easy Red,' 'French Breakfast,' 'White Icicle,' 'Red Prince,' 'Champion,' 'Snow Belle,' 'Black Spanish,' 'Cherry Belle,' 'Crimson Giant,' 'White Round,' 'Easter Egg,' 'Plum Purple,' and many others

Notes: Radishes are the fastest of all the edible plants to grow and an excellent choice to get children started in gardening. They are also used as companion plants with summer vegetables to help control troublesome insects.

RADISH TROUBLE SOLVER

SYMPTOMS	CAUSES	SOLUTIONS
Seeds don't germinate	Old seed	Always use fresh seed
	Cold soil	Plant after the soil is above 45°
	Planted too deep	Radish seeds should be planted ½–¾" deep. Use greater depth on lighter soils
Seedlings lack vigor and color	Wrong soil	Apply high-calcium lime
	Wet soil	Avoid overwatering and improve drainage
Small holes in leaves	Flea beetles	Spray Garrett Juice plus garlic and add citrus oil for heavy infestations
Small, football shaped insects on underside of leaves	Aphids	Spray with Garrett Juice and release lady beetles
Roots don't bulb	Crowded plants	Thin stand 2–3 days after emergence
	Low light, fertility, or moisture	Adjust as needed
Roots "pithy" and off-flavored	Heat	Plants should mature before temperatures exceed 80°
	Overmaturity	Harvest at peak of maturity
	Cold	Temperatures should average above 50° for best quality
Radishes cracked and misshapened	Overmaturity	Harvest earlier
	Use of uncomposted manure	Avoid using fresh manure immediately before planting, apply several months earlier or compost it first
Bolting	Heat, long days	Plant during the cool season
	Cold-induced dormancy	Avoid prolonged periods below 45°
Hot taste	Overmaturity	Harvest earlier

Raspberries. *See Blackberries.*

Rhubarb

Common Name: Rhubarb

The experts say that rhubarb can't be grown in Texas. If you want to give it a try, rhubarb is planted from seed or root divisions. Use the same timing as for horseradish and don't harvest any stalks until the second growing season. It is a cold-hardy perennial, but has a tough time with our hot summers.

Rose

Common Name: Rose

Botanical Name: *Rosa* spp.

Family: *Rosaceae*

Type and Use: Perennial with edible flowers and fruit (hips). Old roses are the best choices especially for producing large hips.

Location: Full sun for best production

Planting Dates: Year-round if container grown. Bare-rooted plants should be planted in the winter months.

Planting Method: Plant container-grown or bare-rooted plants in well-prepared beds containing lots of compost, lava sand, Texas Greensand, cornmeal, cedar flakes and soft rock phosphate.

Seed Emergence: Not grown from seed

Harvest Time: Flowers anytime, and hips in the fall after they turn red

Height: 3–10 feet

Spread: 3–10 feet

Final Spacing: 3–5 feet

Growth Habits: Growth varieties include low-spreading to tall bushes. The old roses, or Heirlooms, are much better looking plants than the hybrids, and the flowers and hips are better for eating and using in teas.

Culture: Roses need extra amendments in the bed preparation. Beds should contain more compost, volcanic material, rock phosphate, alfalfa meal, and other organic amendments than most other plants. The beds should be raised or mounded and the bare soil should be mulched year-round. The best mulch for roses is 1 inch of aged pecan shells followed by 3–4 inches of shredded native cedar. Feed three times, and spray Garrett Juice with garlic weekly.

Troubles and Solutions: Aphids are controlled with a basic organic program and the spray of sugar water followed by the release of lady beetles. Thrips are controlled with neem products and garlic-pepper-seaweed tea. Rose diseases such as black spot and powdery mildew are controlled with Garrett Juice plus garlic and potassium bicarbonate.

Harvest and Storage: Harvest the petals to use in salads, as garnish, and in teas when they first start to open. Harvest the hips when they turn red in the fall.

Rose Hip

Varieties: The best choices for useable hips include Old Blush, *Rogosa* spp., 'Duchesse de Brabant,' 'Souvenir de la Malmaison,' 'Mutabilis,' 'Katy Road Pink,' 'Dortmund,' 'LaMarne,' 'Marie Pavie,' and 'Belinda's Dream." *Rosa rugosa* "Hansa" and *Rosa cania* are especially good.

Notes: To use the vitamin C-loaded hips, cut them into pieces and pour hot water over them. Let steep for 2–4 minutes and enjoy a delicious and healthy tea. Hips can also be mixed with herbs.

Milligrams of vitamin C per 100 grams of rose hips:

Rosa rugosa	3,000
Rosa laxa	3,000–4,000
Rosa acicularis	1,800–3,500
Rose cinnamomea	3,000
Rosa conina	711–1,338
Rosa mollis	1,260
Rosa mipponensis	1,180
Rosa multiflora	250

Rusty Blackhaw Viburnum. *See Viburnum.*

Shallots. *See Onions.*

Roses should only be grown organically because they are one of the best medicinal and culinary herbs in the world. When they are loaded with toxic pesticides and other chemicals, that use is gone, or at least it should be. Drinking rose hip tea after spraying the plants with synthetic poisons is a very bad idea. For best results with roses, follow this program.

Selection. Choose adapted roses such as antiques, Austins, and well-proven hybrids. The old roses will have the largest and most vitamin C-filled hips. Rugosa roses have the most vitamin C.

Planting. Prepare beds by mixing the following into existing soil to form a raised bed: 6 inches compost, ½–1 inch lava sand, 20 pounds of alfalfa meal, 20 pounds cottonseed meal, 40 pounds of soft rock phosphate, 20 pounds of Sul-Po-Mag, 4 pounds of sulfur per 1,000 square feet, and 5 pounds of sugar per 1,000 square feet. Soak the bare roots or rootball in water with 1 tablespoon of seaweed per gallon and 1 tablespoon of natural apple cider vinegar or biostimulant. Settle soil around plants with water; do not tamp.

Mulching. After planting, cover all the soil in the beds with ½ inch of earthworm castings followed by 2–3 inches of shredded hardwood bark or other coarse-textured mulch. Do not pile the mulch up on the stems of the roses.

Watering. If possible, save and use rainwater. If not, add 1 tablespoon of natural apple cider vinegar per gallon of water. If all that fails, just use tap water, but don't overwater. Avoid salty well water.

FERTILIZING PROGRAM

Round #1 February 1–15. 100% organic fertilizer at 20 pounds per 1,000 square feet such as Garden-Ville, GreenSense, Maestro-Gro, Sustane or natural meals or manure compost, lava sand at 80 pounds per 1,000 square feet., and sugar at 5 pounds per 1,000 square feet.

Round #2 June 1–15. Organic fertilizer at 20 pounds per 1,000 square feet, Texas Greensand at 80 pounds per 1,000 square feet or soft rock phosphate if in acid soil areas.

Round #3 September 15–30. Organic fertilizer at 20 pounds per 1,000 square feet, Sul-Po-Mag at 20 pounds per 1,000 square feet.

SPRAY PROGRAM
(Garrett Juice)

Compost tea	Label directions or, if homemade, 1 cup/gallon of water
Blackstrap molasses	1 ounce/gallon
Seaweed	1 ounce/gallon (liquid), 1 teaspoon/gallon (dry) or label directions
Apple cider vinegar	1 ounce/gallon

Optional Ingredients

Fish emulsion	2–3 tablespoons/gallon (may not be needed when using compost tea)
Garlic tea	¼ cup/gallon or label directions
Baking soda	1 rounded tablespoon/gallon or per label
Liquid biostimulants	Agrispon, AgriGro, Medina, Bioform, or similar product
Citrus oil	¼ cup per gallon (made by soaking oranges and grapefruit peelings in water). 1–2 ounces per gallon of commercial concentrate.

Sorrel

Common Name: Sorrel

Botanical Name: *Rumex acetosa*

Family: *Polygonaceae*

Type and Use: Perennial with edible foliage.

Location: Full sun to light shade

Planting Dates: Spring through fall

Planting Method: Transplanting in the cool season is the best method

Seed Emergence: 3–14 days at 70°

Harvest Time: Harvest and use the leaves in salads anytime. The younger leaves are more tender and tasty.

Height: 12–24 inches

Spread: 24 inches

Final Spacing: 12–15 inches

Growth Habits: Leafy, upright, top growth, deep roots. Growth is in clumps similar to spinach and lettuce.

Culture: Easy to grow in any soil. Flower stems are fast growing and tall and should be cut away.

Troubles and Solutions: Slugs and snails can be controlled with cedar flakes, DE, hot pepper products, and garlic-pepper tea spray.

Harvest and Storage: Cut and use the leaves anytime. They can be stored in the refrigerator, but are much better eaten fresh in salads or used to flavor other foods. Good to use with or instead of lettuce on sandwiches.

Varieties: *Rumex crispus* is curly dock. *Rumex acetosella* is wood or sheep sorrel.

Notes: Also called French sorrel. Contains lots of vitamin C. Delicious salad addition.

Texas Pinkeye Peas

Southern Pea

Common Names: Southern pea, Field, Crowders, Black-eyed, Purple hulls, and Creams

Botanical Name: *Vigna sinensis*

Family: *Leguminosae*

Type and Use: Annual with edible peas (seed)

Location: Full sun

Planting Dates: After the last frost in the spring and after the soil has warmed to 70°. Fall crops are planted 90–120 days before the first average frost. In general, April 1–August 15.

Planting Method: For best results, plant seed (peas) in raised beds, 16–24 inches wide and 36–48 inches apart. Treat the seed with seaweed and rhizobia bacteria (nitrogen-fixing bacteria). There should be enough moisture in the soil for germination. Put seeds into furrows 1½ inches deep in sand or 1 inch in clay. Sow at 4–5 per foot of row and cover with garden soil. Thin to 4–8 inches when 3–4 inches tall.

Seed Emergence: 5–10 days in warm soil

Harvest Time: About 70–90 days after planting. Southern peas can be harvested at three stages: 1) green snap, 2) green mature, and 3) dry.

Height: Varies greatly

Spread: Varies greatly

Final Spacing: Bush type—4–6 inches, vining type—8 inches

Growth Habits: Peas germinate poorly in cool soil, so don't get in a hurry. Southern peas are either bush-type or climbers.

Culture: Warm weather vegetable that is relatively easy to grow. They are legumes so the natural nitrogen helps to reduce fertilizer inputs. Peas grow well in most soils but best in loose, well-drained healthy soils. In clay soils, use compost, lava sand, Texas greensand, sugar, and organic fertilizer. In sandy soils, use soft rock phosphate or high-calcium lime instead of Texas greensand. Mulch around plants to prevent crusting. Raindrops hitting bare soil is a major cause of crusting and com-

paction. Fertilize the second time after the first harvest. Most southern peas don't like high fertility. Plant in the sorriest soil of your garden.

Troubles and Solutions: For iron chlorosis, apply Texas Greensand. For cutworms and other caterpillars, use citrus based products or Bt products. For aphids, weevils, stink bugs, and thrips, control with a basic organic program, citrus sprays, neem sprays, and Garrett Juice plus garlic-pepper-seaweed. Soil-borne diseases are controlled with cornmeal at 20 pounds per 1,000 square feet and/or other biological products. Control nematodes with citrus pulp. Too much or too little water can drastically reduce production. Keep the soil fairly moist and well-mulched.

Harvest and Storage: Harvest peas when they are young as snap peas, harvest as green mature once the color starts to change on the beans, and wait for full maturity for harvesting dry peas. They will store best and the longest as dry mature peas. Snaps and green matures should be stored in the refrigerator if not eaten right away.

Varieties: 'Big Red Ripper,' 'Texas Pink-Eye,' 'Black-eye #5,' 'Purple hull', 'Crowder,' 'Silver skin,' 'Cream 40,' 'Zipper,' 'Calico'.

Notes: Also called cow peas, field peas, black-eyed peas, purple hulls, creams and crowders. Avoid seed that has been treated with toxic fungicides. They are often pink in color—sometimes blue. There is a difference in beneficial nodules and the domestic root knot nematodes. Beneficial, nitrogen-fixing nodules are loosely attached to the outside of roots. The harmful nematodes cause swelling of the roots from the inside.

Black-eyed Peas

SOUTHERN PEA TROUBLE SOLVER

SYMPTOMS	CAUSES	SOLUTIONS
Poor germination	Old seed	Pea seeds lose viability quickly; always use fresh seed or store in refrigerator
	Cold soil	Wait to plant until soil is above 65°
	Planted too deep	Plant seed 1–1½" deep, using greater depth on lighter textured soils
	Crusted soil	Use a thin layer of compost as mulch and water carefully
Seedlings die	Damping-off fungus	Plant when soils are warm and avoid overwatering; never use treated seed; add compost; decomposing organic matter reduces problems related to damping-off
	Cutworms, snails	Treat with DE, crushed red pepper, and spray with garlic-pepper tea

(table continued on page 176)

◄ Red Ripper Peas

SOUTHERN PEA TROUBLE SOLVER (Continued)

SYMPTOMS	CAUSES	SOLUTIONS
Weak seedlings	Cold soil	Plant when soils are warm
	Wrong soil	Add high-calcium lime and granite sand or fireplace ashes
	Wet soil	Improve the drainage, add compost and other organic amendments, and water carefully
Yellow leaves with green veins	Chlorosis	Add Texas Greensand and Sul-Po-Mag; adding sulfur will help naturally occurring iron and magnesium in soil become available to plants, compost will also help
Bottom leaves yellow; plants lack vigor	Low fertility	Inoculate seed to help nitrogen "fixing" bacteria to develop and apply organic fertilizer
	Cold or wet soils	Raise beds, add lots of compost, avoid overwatering, and hope for good weather
Good foliage but few blooms	Heat and long days	Plant at the correct time
	Excess soil moisture during early stages of growth	Avoid overwatering and improve the soil
	Excess fertility	Avoid excessive fertilizer
Flowers drop, few pods are formed	Moisture stress	Maintain soil moisture while plants are blooming
Twisted seedlings, leaves curled	Thrips and stink bugs	Spray Garrett Juice plus garlic and add citrus oil for heavy infestations
Worms in pods and seed	Pea weevil or pea	Spray Garrett Juice plus garlic and add citrus oil for heavy infestations
Discolored lower leaves webbing on lower surface	Spider mites	Spray Garrett Juice plus garlic-pepper tea plus citrus oil; seaweed by itself also works
Red or orange spots on leaves	Rust fungus	Work on improving soil health, treat soil with cornmeal, and spray foliage with Garrett Juice plus garlic and potassium bicarbonate
Plants wilt suddenly and die	Fusarium wilt fungus	Work on improving soil health, treat soil with cornmeal, and spray foliage with Garrett Juice plus garlic and potassium bicarbonate
Plants are stunted and have knots on roots	Nematodes	Drench soil with citrus oil or till citrus pulp in beds prior to planting
Plants stop producing pods	Mature pods are left on plant	Harvest frequently

Spinach

Common Name: Spinach
Botanical Name: *Spinacia oleracea*
Family: *Chenopodiaceae*
Type and Use: Annual with edible foliage
Location: Sun to partial shade
Planting Dates: For spring garden, 4–6 weeks before the last average frost. For the fall garden, 8–10 weeks before the first average frost. In general, January 10–March 15, or as soon as the soil has reached 50°, and September 10–October 31.
Planting Method: Broadcast the seed or plant in rows 4–6" apart, ⅛–¾ inch deep. Soaking the seeds overnight is helpful. Tamp the soil lightly after installing the seeds.
Seed Emergence: 7–20 days at 60°. The range is 45–75°. Spinach seeds germinate poorly in warm soils. Seeds will actually go dormant if temperatures are more than 77°. Germination can be sped up by putting the seed in water and leaving in the refrigerator for 24–48 hours.
Harvest Time: 40–70 days, before the weather turns hot and as soon as the leaves are an edible size.
Height: 8–12 inches
Spread: 8–12 inches
Final Spacing: 3–8 inches
Growth Habits: Spinach is a relatively shallow-rooted leafy vegetable that bolts easily in warm weather and warm soil.
Culture: Spinach likes temperatures between 50–60°. Prepare beds with compost, lava sand, sugar, and soft rock phosphate. Add Texas greensand to alkaline soils and high-calcium lime (calcium carbonate) to acid sandy soils. Fertilize the soil at planting time with organic fertilizer and again after the first major harvest of leaves. Spray at least monthly with Garrett Juice. Give spinach room. Crowded conditions cause stemming and poor quality plants. Spinach also doesn't like highly acid soils. Mulch is very important.
Troubles and Solutions: Bolting can be avoided by growing in cool weather. Flea beetles, aphids, and spider mites are controlled with a basic organic program. Spray

Spinach Seed

for heavy infestations with citrus-based products. Cutworms, loopers, and green worms can be controlled with trichogramma wasps released during the spring growth or more short-term with Bt sprays. Spring plantings tend to bolt and go to seed easier than fall crops. Warm temperatures and long days encourage bolting. Grub worms are controlled with beneficial nematodes. White rust fungi can be controlled with Garrett Juice plus garlic tea and potassium bicarbonate.

Harvest and Storage: Harvest the foliage anytime the leaves are large enough to use. Small leaves are more tender. Smooth-leaf types are thought to be best for canning; the crinkled-leaf (savory) types are best for fresh use. Eat right away or store in the refrigerator for up to two weeks at 32–40°.

Varieties: There are smooth and crinkled leaf varieties available. 'Melody,' 'Bloomsdale,' 'Hybrid 7,' 'Iron Duke,' 'Long Standing,' and 'America' are good varieties. A good choice for plants from transplants is 'Coho.' Summer spinach (not really spinach) include New England (a bush type), 'Malibar' (a climber), 'Dixie Savoy,' and 'Fall Green II.' These are frost tender.

Notes: Spinach is good tasting and good for you either raw in salads or cooked. Other vegetable gardening books may tell you to add total-nitrogen fertilizers. What a totally silly idea. Nitrogen-only fertilizers contain no trace minerals and no organic matter.

Spinach, Malabar

Common Name: Malabar spinach
Botanical Name: *Basella alba*
Family: *Basellaceae*
Type and Use: Twining herbaceous vine with edible foliage
Location: Sun to partial shade
Planting Dates: Spring after the last frost
Planting Method: Seeds, cuttings, or transplants. Very easy to germinate from seed.
Seed Emergence: 2 to 3 weeks
Harvest Time: When the leaves are young and tender
Height: Will climb or spread to 8–20 feet easily in season

Spread: Same as above
Final Spacing: 6–8', but one or two plants is more than enough
Growth Habits: Succulent dark green vine with brightly distinctive red stems and leaf veins. Fast growing and aggressive.
Culture: Easy to grow in any well-drained soil. Requires normal amounts of water and fertilizer.
Troubles and Solutions: Spreads by seed and can become a pest although the seedlings pull up easily if you get them early.
Harvest and Storage: Pick the young tender leaves and use fresh or store at 32–40° for up to two weeks.

◄ Spinach

Spinach, New Zealand

Common Name: New Zealand Spinach

Botanical Name: *Tetragonia tetragonioides*

Family: *Tetragoniaceae*

Type and Use: Annual vegetable with edible foliage. Not a true spinach.

Location: Full sun to partial shade, but best in full sun

Planting Dates: Plant about the same time you plant okra and black-eyed peas. Weather and soil must be warm for germination.

Planting Method: Transplant or seed. Plant 3–4 seeds every 12 inches, ½–¾ inch deep. Seeds should be soaked before planting.

Seed Emergence: Seeds are slow to germinate. Best to soak them in seaweed water overnight before planting. Then they will germinate in 7–10 days.

Harvest Time: Anytime during the summer growing season. This spinach matures in about 55 days.

Height: 2 feet

Spread: 3 feet

Final Spacing: 12–24 inches

Growth Habits: Grows and produces well in the summer months. Tastes like regular spinach, but milder. Very sensitive to frost, but will produce well until the first hard frost.

Culture: This spinach likes more fertilizer than regular spinach. Pinch out the growing tips of plants to encourage wide branching and leaf production.

Troubles and Solutions: Few, if any, pest problems. Slugs and snails can be controlled with hot pepper products. Control aphids with molasses-water spray and the release of lady beetles.

Harvest and Storage: Cut and store in the refrigerator prior to using.

SPINACH TROUBLE SOLVER

SYMPTOMS	CAUSES	SOLUTIONS
Seeds don't germinate	Soil too warm	Do not plant spinach in the fall until soil temperature is 75° or less
	Soil too cold	In the spring, soil temperature should be about 45°
	Old seed	Always use fresh seed
	Seed planted too deep	Seed should be planted about ½″ deep, slightly deeper on sandy soils
	Low soil moisture	Soil should be moist at planting to ensure germination; water before planting if necessary
Seedlings die after emergence	Damping-off	Work on improving soil health, treat soil with cornmeal and spray foliage with Garrett Juice plus garlic and potassium bicarbonate
	Cutworms	Treat with DE, crushed red pepper, and spray with garlic-pepper tea
Slow growth and lack of good color	Cold soil	Plant at the correct time of year
	Wrong soil	Add high-calcium soil, granite and fireplace ashes
	Low fertility	Add organic fertilizer
	Wet soil	Use raised beds, improve soil drainage, and avoid overwatering
Stemmy plants	Crowded plants	Thin to 4–6″
Off-flavor, bitter taste	Plants about to bolt	Plant at the correct time
Plants stunted with poorly developed leaves	Aphids	Spray plants with Garrett Juice and release lady beetles
White pustules on lower surface of leaves	White rust fungus	Work on improving soil health, treat soil with cornmeal, and spray foliage with Garrett Juice plus garlic and potassium bicarbonate
Grayish mold on underside of leaves, yellow areas on upper leaf surface	Blue mold fungus	Work on improving soil health, treat soil with cornmeal and spray foliage with Garrett Juice plus garlic and potassium bicarbonate
Plants stunted, yellow and often die	Fusarium wilt fungus	Work on improving soil health, treat soil with cornmeal, and spray foliage with Garrett Juice plus garlic and potassium bicarbonate
Holes in foliage, small green worms present	Cabbage loopers	Release trichogramma wasps, treat foliage with *bacillus thuringiensis* as a last resort
Small holes in foliage	Flea beetles	Spray Garrett Juice plus garlic and add citrus oil for heavy infestations
Plants flower prematurely and go to seed	Heat and long days	Plant at the correct time; use bolt-resistant varieties for planting in late winter to early spring

Summer Squash Yellow Straight Neck

Squash

Botanical Name: *Curbita* spp.

Family: *Cucurbitaceae*

Type and Use: Annual vegetable with edible flowers and fruit

Location: Full sun

Planting Dates: For spring, plant after all danger of frost. For fall, plant 12–14 weeks before the first average frost. In general, April 1–May 15 and July 10–August 15. Butternut will split and leak if planted in spring. It's better to plant for the fall garden in central and south Texas.

Planting Method: Seed is the most common method, but squash can also be started from transplants. Plant 3–5 seeds per hill about ½–1 inch deep.

Seed Emergence: 3–10 days at 68-85°

Harvest Time: In summer, usually 42–70 days. In winter, 80–120 days. Harvest summer squash anytime. The young fruit are delicious. Don't harvest winter squash

Tahitian Squash

until they are fully mature. Squash can be a very early crop if started in pots and transplanted.

Height: High climbing or bush form

Spread: Wide spreading

Final Spacing: Hills or rows 4–5 feet apart. Plants 24 inches to 6 feet.

Hand Pollenation of Squash

Growth Habits: Squash is a big, dramatic-leafed annual vegetable that varies greatly in growth characteristics. It is fast-growing and has several problems.

Culture: Plant in well-prepared, healthy soil. Use as many plants as you have room for. Pests seem to hit the smaller plantings for some reason. Use lots of compost, lava sand, and mulch. Add Texas Greensand in alkaline soils and high-calcium lime (calcium carbonate) in sandy acid soils.

Fertilize when flower buds or flowers have formed. Use a handful of organic fertilizer per plant.

Troubles and Solutions: Garden fleahoppers, flea beetles, cucumber beetles, aphids, and squash bugs are controlled with citrus sprays or biological sprays. Control cutworms and other caterpillars with Bt products. End nematode problems with citrus pulp tilled into the soil prior to planting the seed. Powdery mildew, viruses, and

Tatume Squash

other diseases are controlled with a basic organic program and weekly sprays of Garrett Juice plus garlic and potassium bicarbonate.

Harvest and Storage: Harvest and eat summer squash anytime the fruit is large enough to eat. Summer squash can be stored a short time in cool, dry places. Winter squash should only be harvested after it has totally matured. It has a longer storage life. Cut it from the vine only after the skin has hardened.

Varieties: Summer varieties include Tatume, Butterbar, Dixie, Zucchinni, Early Pro Lific Yellow, Straightneck, Miltipik, President Senator, Royal Acorn, Spaghetti, Yellow Crookneck, Pattypan. Multipik is supposed to be the most immune to pests. Winter varieties include Early Butternut, Acorn, Tahitian, Turbin, Buttercup, Hubbard, and Table Ace. Tahitian is a very large heirloom squash. The seeds are in the big end. Cut off as much as needed to

Yellow Crookneck Squash Seed

cook and eat while leaving the rest in the refrigerator for later. This is the best squash for making pumpkin pie.

Notes: Some gardeners help pollination by using a cotton swab to dab the pollen of the male flower onto the female flowers. Females are those with a swelling behind the petals. Yields are greatly reduced if mature fruit is left on the plants.

SQUASH TROUBLE SOLVER

SYMPTOMS	CAUSES	SOLUTIONS
Seed fails to germinate	Old seed	Always use fresh seed and/or store seed in refrigerator
	Cold soil	Don't plant until soil temperature is at least 60°
	Seed planted too deep	Plant seed 1½–2″ deep, using greater depth in sandy soils
	Low soil moisture	Moisten soil before planting
Slow growth, poor vigor, poor color	Cold or wet soil	Use raised beds, improve soil drainage, and avoid overwatering
	Wrong soil	Add high-calcium lime in acid soils, Texas Greensand in alkaline soils
	Low fertility	Add organic fertilizer
	Low soil moisture	Add water and mulch around plants
Plants stunted, knots on roots	Nematodes	Drench soil with citrus oil or till citrus pulp into soil
Plants wilt in the afternoon but recover	Normal reaction to Texas heat	Provide afternoon shade
Plants wilt and are damaged	Low soil moisture	Water and mulch the bare soil
	Nematodes	Drench soil with citrus oil or till citrus pulp into the soil
	Vine borers	Spray Garrett Juice plus garlic and add citrus oil for heavy infestations
	Squash bugs	Spray Garrett Juice plus garlic and add citrus oil for heavy infestations
Plants bloom but fail to set fruit	Male flowers only	Wait for the female flowers
	Lack of pollination	Honeybees not active for several reasons: cloudy, wet weather, pesticides, mites, natural lack of honeybees; transfer pollen with swab or small brush
Fruits shrivel or fail to enlarge	Lack of pollination	As above
Whiskers develop on fruit, rot follows	Fruit rot fungus	Work on improving soil health, treat soil with cornmeal and spray foliage with Garrett Juice plus garlic and potassium bicarbonate
Fruit becomes multi-colored, leaves are distorted and mottled	Squash mosaic virus	Control transmitting insects, spray Garrett Juice plus garlic and add citrus oil for heavy infestations
Talcum-like growth on leaves	Powdery mildew fungus	Work on improving soil health, treat soil with cornmeal, and spray foliage with Garrett Juice plus garlic and potassium bicarbonate
Yellow areas on older leaves that soon turn brown	Downy mildew fungus	Work on improving soil health, treat soil with cornmeal, and spray foliage with Garrett Juice plus garlic and potassium bicarbonate
Fruit tough with hard seed	Summer squash could be overmature	Harvest often when the fruit is young and tender
	Normal for winter squash	Winter squash should be harvested after skin turns hard

Strawberry

Common Name: Strawberry

Botanical Name: *Frageria virginiana*

Family: *Rosaceae*

Type and Use: Short-lived perennial with edible fruit

Location: Full sun

Planting Dates: Perennial—December–February, Annual—February–April

Planting Method: Transplant only

Seed Emergence: Not a seed-grown plant for the average home gardener

Harvest Time: Usually it is not recommended to allow the fruit to develop the first year, but I say, eat any you can get.

Height: 6–8 inches

Spread: 12–18 inches

Final Spacing: 12–18 inches

Growth Habits: Low-spreading fruit crop with white flowers that grows by spreading runners

Culture: Needs well-drained, highly organic soils. Raised beds are best. Strawberries can be grown in containers. Matted row or perennial beds should be planted in the winter (December-February). Strawberries are harvested about 16 months later in April or May. Annuals are planted in the fall (early November) and harvested the next spring (February–April).

Troubles and Solutions: Slugs and snails are the most common pests. Use cedar flakes, hot pepper, and DE (diatomaceous earth) around the plants. Spider mites are controlled by watering properly—not too much or too little. Flare-up infestations can be controlled with garlic-pepper-seaweed tea. Various soil-borne diseases are controlled with cornmeal at 20 pounds per 1,000 square feet. Leaf and fruit fungal diseases are controlled with Garrett Juice plus garlic and potassium bicarbonate.

Harvest and Storage: Harvest whenever the fruit is red all over and ripe. Store in the refrigerator, after ripe at 32–40°, but strawberries don't last long, so eat them quick. Might last 1–5 days.

Varieties: Best perennials (matted row) include 'Sunrise,' 'Pocahantas,' 'Cardinal,' and 'Alstar.' Best annuals include 'Sequoia,' 'Chandler,' 'Fresno,' 'Tiogo,' Tangi,' and 'Douglas.'

Notes: Strawberries are known to have cancer-fighting capabilities. Unfortunately, most of the strawberries are not grown with organic techniques. Pesticides accumulate heavily in strawberries. Easy solution: grow your own organic strawberries.

Sunflower

Common Name: Sunflower

Botanical Name: *Helianthus* spp.

Family: *Compositae*

Type and Use: Annuals and perennials with edible flowers, seed, and roots

Location: Full sun

Planting Dates: Plant seed or root tubers of perennials such as Jerusalem artichoke in the spring after the last frost.

Planting Method: Plant seed or tuber pieces in well-drained soil in full sun in the spring.

Seed Emergence: Both seed and tubers emerge quickly to grow into large plants.

Harvest Time: Harvest the flower petals anytime, the seeds after the flower heads have matured and dried, the edible tubers in the fall.

Height: 3–12 feet

Spread: Annuals grow as single plants; perennials spread by runners

Spacing: Seeds should be planted 18–24 inches, clumps of perennial at 18–36 inches.

Growth Habits: Tall-growing and coarse for the most part. Maximillian is the most refined looking and often the best choice for residential gardens.

Culture: Plant in well-drained soil and fertilize monthly for the largest flower heads. Soil amendments are not that important for sunflowers.

Troubles and Solutions: Too large and coarse for many residential locations. Solution: don't plant them there. The perennials spread and can become invasive.

Harvest and Storage: Harvest the flower petals anytime to use as an interesting garnish. Gather and eat the mature seed after the flower head has dried.

Varieties: The common sunflower is *Hedera annua*. Maximilian sunflower (with edible tubers) is *Hedera* maximilian. Sunchoke or Jerusalem artichoke is *Hedera tuberosa* and has the largest edible tubers.

Notes: The tubers of Maximilian and Jerusalem artichoke taste like water chestnuts. They are delicious and can be used just like potatoes. Maximilian sunflower is an excellent landscape perennial.

Sweet Corn. *See Corn.*

Sweet Potatoes

Common Name: Sweet Potatoes
Botanical Name: *Ipomoea batatas*
Family: *Convulvuloceae*
Type and Use: Perennial, grown as an annual, with edible root tubers
Location: Full sun
Planting Dates: After all danger of frost is gone and the soil temperature is about 70°. In general, April 5–June 31.
Planting Method: About 40 days prior to the targeted planting date, place sweet potato seed roots on their sides in moist sand. Cover with a mix of sand and compost. Maintain a temperature of about 80°. Water to keep the mix moist. After the "slips" appear, add more mix. When the slips reach a height of 8–10 inches, remove them with a twist and plant soon after. A cool, cloudy day is the best timing. Plant them 3–4 inches deep and 10–12 inches apart, and they will grow easily. Plant unrooted slips either end down in raised beds. Roots are planted down if they exist.
Shoot Emergence: 6–10 days
Harvest Time: 100–150 days. Expect 2–3 pounds of potatoes per plant after the second month of growth. Harvest anytime once they have reached a useable size.
Height: 12–15 inches
Spread: Wide spreading
Final Spacing: 10–12 inches
Growth Habits: Fast-growing and vining vegetable that has good-looking foliage
Culture: Sweet potatoes do the best in acid, sandy soils but will grow fairly well in all soils. The sweet potato weevil is not much of a problem in sandy soils. Loose, well-drained soil is needed. Use moderate amounts of compost, lava sand, and soft rock phosphate. Sweet potatoes are fairly drought-tolerant once established. Mulching is important to help maintain an even soil moisture. Mulch will also keep the vines from rooting. Without mulch, the vines should be moved every 7–10 days. Vines will root in good soil and make potatoes if not moved. After the second month of growth, try to keep the soil as evenly moist as possible, but not overly wet.

If the vines outgrow the space, pinch out the growing tips to prevent further spreading. This is not usually necessary with the 'Vardaman' variety.

Troubles and Solutions: Stunted plants from cold weather can be prevented by not planting too early. Avoid overwatering to avoid disease problems. Sweet potato foliage wilts easily during hot days, but this is not necessarily a sign of dryness. Maintain even moisture as the roots mature to avoid cracking and misshapen potatoes. Small, stringy roots are caused by overfertilizing. Rough, misshapen roots result from overwatering. Sweet potato weevils are ¼ inch reddish ant-like weevils with dark heads. Whitish larvae (grubs) do most of the damage. Root knot nematodes can be eliminated with citrus pulp tilled into the soil prior to planting the slips. Various diseases can be controlled with cornmeal added at 20 pounds per 1,000 square feet.

Harvest and Storage: Expect to harvest 60 or more pounds from a 15-foot row. Harvest the roots when the soil is on the dry side to avoid rotting. Do it whenever the potatoes are big enough to eat and before temperatures have fallen below 50°. Sweet potatoes can be left in the ground until needed. For the best results, dig the roots when the soil is dry. Eat the damaged ones first. Do not wash or brush the soil away; this can easily damage the roots. Let the roots dry on news- or butcher paper for 3–4 hours, then store in containers in a warm, humid place for about two weeks.

SWEET POTATO TROUBLE SOLVER

SYMPTOMS	CAUSES	SOLUTIONS
Slips die quickly after setting out	Damping-off fungus	Work on improving soil health, treat soil with cornmeal, and spray foliage with Garrett Juice plus garlic and potassium bicarbonate
	Cutworms	Treat with DE, crushed red pepper, and spray with garlic-pepper tea
	Dry soil	Soil should be moist at planting time; water well at planting time
Plants are sluggish and lack good color	Cold soil	Wait until soil temperature is above 60°
	Wet soil	Use raised beds and don't overwater
	Wrong soil	Sweet potatoes grow poorly if soil is too acidic; adjust by adding high-calcium lime, fireplace ashes and granite
Plants lack vigor and grow slowly	Low fertility	Add organic fertilizer
	Wet soil	Use raised beds and don't overwater
	Tight soil	Add compost, lava sand and sugar
Roots are stringy and small	Excess fertility	Reduce fertilizer
	Secondary rooting	Do not let vines root; move the vines around, mulch with shredded material
Roots are rough and misshapen	Tight, heavy soils	Add compost and plant on top of the soil; cover with a thick blanket of mulch
	Excessive soil	Improve drainage and don't water so much
Tunnels in roots	Sweet potato weevils	Drench soil with citrus oil or till citrus pulp into the soil
Roots cracked and pitted	Nematodes	Drench soil with citrus oil or till citrus pulp into the soil
Rotting in storage	Improperly cured	Cure potatoes in warm humid area for about 2 weeks; eat roots that are damaged during harvest
	Storage rot fungi	Work on improving soil health, treat soil with cornmeal, and spray foliage with Garrett Juice plus garlic and potassium bicarbonate

Wet burlap over the containers works well. After curing, store at about 55°. They will last at least three months.

A week or two before you plan to harvest, allow the soil to dry out. Do not wash them or try to remove any soil that may cling to them. Wash them after curing or when you're ready to use them. Be sure to use any cut or bruised potatoes as soon as possible after harvest. Expect to harvest 60 or more pounds from a 15-foot row.

Varieties: 'Jewel,' 'Centennial,' 'Vardamau' 'Vardaman' is the best variety for small gardens. It's about 3 feet long, and its red-veined leaves are unusually attractive.

Notes: The ideal slips have 5–6 leaves, a stocky stem, and are 8–10 inches long. Sweet potato vines have been used to smother nutgrass.

Swiss Chard

Common Name: Swiss Chard
Botanical Name: *Beta vulgaris*
Family: *Chenopodiaceae*
Type and Use: Annual with edible stems and leaves
Location: Full sun to partial shade
Planting Dates: For spring, plant the seed 3–4 weeks before the last average frost. For fall, plant 6–8 weeks before the first frost average date. In general, February 20–May 10 and June 1–September 15.
Planting Method: Broadcast seed or plant in rows ½–¾ inches deep
Seed Emergence: 7–10 days after planting in soil temperature of 50–85°
Harvest Time: 55–65 days throughout the growing season
Height: 18–24 inches
Spread: 18 inches
Final Spacing: 18-inch rows, 12 inches apart in the row for cut-and-come-again or 12-inch rows at 6 inch for a one-time harvest of the whole plant
Growth Habits: Swiss chard or chard is a relative of the beet and has similar habits and needs. Chard is a beet without a bottom.
Culture: Chard likes cool temperatures but tolerates some hot weather. Culture is about the same as beets. I think chard is much easier to grow than beets. Fertilize the beds at planting time with compost, lava sand, and soft rock phosphate. Fertilizer a second time after the first harvest. For better germination, soak the seed overnight before planting. Planting in rows is considered better than broadcasting.

Fertilize chard after harvesting "crew-cut" style. Cut the plants 1 inch above the ground and use an organic fertilizer. Use one handful for each foot of wide row 16 inches wide.
Troubles and Solutions: Aphids and flea beetles are sometimes a minor nuisance and are easily controlled with citrus sprays or regular foliage feeding with Garrett Juice.
Harvest and Storage: Use cut-and-come-again harvest on the foliage whenever it is large enough. Swiss chard does not store

Swiss Chard Seed

well. Eat fresh. Cool quickly after harvest if storage is necessary. Chard can be harvested after the outer leaves are 4–5 inches long. For the best flavor, wait at least 60 days. Heavy harvesting will limit the production life of the plant.
Varieties: 'White Rib,' 'Lucullus,' 'Rhubarb,' 'Ruby,' 'Fordhook,' 'Broadstem Green'

Notes: Chard can be eaten fresh in salads or cooked like other greens. An excellent alternative to chard is sugar beet greens. Sugar beets can be planted from seed in late winter and their greens are delicious. Finding the seed (especially seed that hasn't been treated with toxic chemical fungicides) is sometimes tough.

Tomato

Common Name: Tomato
Botanical Name: *Lycopersicom esculentum*
Family: *Solanaceae*
Type and Use: Tender perennial, grown as an annual, with edible fruit
Location: Full sun
Planting Dates: For transplants use the following schedule: Plant after all danger of frost in the spring and 12–14 weeks before the first average frost in the fall. In general, April 1–May 20 and July 1–August 5.
Planting Method: Plant transplants by laying the plant down sideways or planting deeply. Tomatoes are able to root from the stems. The sideways method is best in heavier clay soils.
Seed Emergence: If you start your tomatoes from seed, here's the plan. Plant the seeds indoors in organic potting soil, ¼–½ inch deep, in a well-lit or greenhouse condition. They will germinate in 5–14 days at about 68–85°. Keep the seedlings cool and in bright light to keep them from getting spindly.

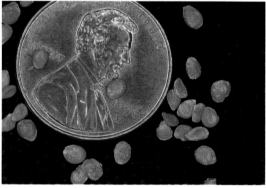

Roma Tomato Seed

Harvest Time: Harvest in summer when the fruit starts to ripen and turn red, usually 55–90 days after planting. Picking the fruit as the color first starts to change will help prevent birds, squirrels, and other critters from eating the fruit before you get it.
Height: 3–15 feet
Spread: 3–15 feet
Final Spacing: 36–48 inches
Growth Habits: Succulent upright-to-spreading perennial that functions as an annual in Texas for two reasons: one, it freezes easily,

191

A Wonderful Medley of Tomatoes on the Table

and two, it plays out with age as it develops insect and disease problems. Bush (determinate) and vining (indeterminate). Tomatoes do not like evening temperatures above 75°. And guess what? We have a lot of that. Tomatoes are wind pollinated—not by bees.

Culture: Plant tomatoes in well-prepared soil with lots of compost, lava sand, rock phosphate, and organic fertilizer. In sandy soil, add high-calcium lime. In alkaline soil, add Texas Greensand. It's also a good idea to add fish meal or cottonseed meal and alfalfa meal. For maintenance ease and increased production, use metal cages. Concrete reinforcing wire mesh makes excellent cages for tomatoes and other vegetables. Fertilize three times per growing season because tomatoes are heavy feeders. Flowers will not set in temperatures below 55° or over 92°. Try adding a handful of Epsom salts or Sul-Po-Mag under new transplants to increase fruit production. Zeolite and soft rock phosphate also can be used this way. Try pinching the flowers off for the first 6–8 weeks of some tomato plants. Some gardeners report good success with this technique.

Sidedress at the first blossoms or when the first small green tomatoes have formed so the fertilizer goes toward nourishing the fruits. Use a handful of organic fertilizer per plant.

A good nitrogen fertilizer is corn gluten meal. It not only adds nutrients, it also keeps some weed seed from getting established.

Troubles and Solutions: Southern blight (which is usually misdiagnosed as early blight) is the most common tomato pest. It can be limited with weekly sprayings of Garrett Juice plus garlic and potassium bicarbonate. Use lots of compost and mulch to prevent tomato pinworm. Eliminate blossom-end rot with even soil moisture and calcium supplements: soft rock phosphate and alfalfa products in alkaline soils, high-calcium lime in acid, sandy soils. Red Christmas tree ornaments hung on plants before the fruit starts to ripen will repel birds. Aphids, spider mites, and flea hoppers are controlled with Garrett Juice and citrus sprays. Use an ultraviolet light such as mineral prospectors use to find hornworms. They fluoresce brilliantly. Hand remove

Tobacco Hornworms

hornworms and treat for all diseases by applying cornmeal to the soil.

Harvest and Storage: Expect 5–20 pounds per plant. For the best taste, pick the tomatoes after they have ripened on the vine and store indoors in a dry, cool place, not in the refrigerator. Tomatoes can also be picked after they have started to blush in color. This helps to prevent animal damage and the fruit will continue to ripen indoors.

Varieties: 'Celebrity,' 'Carnival,' 'Salsa,' 'SuperFantastic,' 'Better Boy,' 'Porter,' 'Viva Italia,' 'Jackpot,' 'Roma,' 'Brandywine,' 'Yellow pear,' 'Arkansas Traveler,' 'Costaluto,' 'Riesentraube,' 'Black Krin,' 'Pineapple,' 'Supersonic,' and 'President.'

Notes: Avoid the really large fruited northern varieties. They do not like our climate. Fall tomatoes taste better but are harder to find. Faster production comes from the use of water walls or floating row cover around the cages. Another increased production trick is to buy 2¼-inch transplants early and pot them in 4-inch pots. After they grow and the root system fills the pots, move them to 1-gallon pots. Move the plants out into the sun on warm days and back into protection on cold days and nights. When all danger of frost is gone, plant the gallon plants in the garden. You'll be amazed at how early and prolific the plants will be.

Another trick is to use the Japanese planting ring. It will maximize your tomato production in the garden. It is like a compost pile with tomatoes (or other vegetables) planted around the outside. See Chapter 2 for instructions for use.

Still another trick is to plant a cover crop such as hairy vetch *vicia villosa*, a hardy annual legume. See Chapter 2.

Set the tomato transplants through the mulch into the vetch's root system. Use manure, compost, or nitrogen fertilizer. The tomatoes will thrive until it's time to replant the vetch in fall.

This system has performed phenomenally in USDA tests in Beltsville, Maryland.

TOMATO TROUBLE SOLVER

SYMPTOMS	CAUSES	SOLUTIONS
Transplants fall over and die	Cutworms	Treat with DE, crushed red pepper, and spray with garlic-pepper tea
	Damping-off fungus	Work on improving soil health, treat soil with cornmeal, and spray foliage with Garrett Juice plus garlic and potassium bicarbonate
Plants grow slowly and lack vigor	Cold soil	Cover cages with floating row cover
	Wrong soil	Add granite and fireplace ashes and crushed limestone
	Low fertility	Add organic fertilizer
Blooms abort	Wrong variety	Use recommended tomato varieties
	Cold temperatures	Temperature below 55°, spray Garrett Juice
	Thrips	Spray Garrett Juice plus garlic and add citrus oil for heavy infestations
	Heat	Plant early maturing varieties; blooms will abort if daytime temperature exceeds 92° in combination with nighttime temperature above 75°
	Trace mineral deficiency	Apply organic fertilizer, soft rock phosphate, Texas Greensand and spray with Garrett Juice
Trails in leaves	Leaf miners	Spray Garrett Juice plus garlic and add citrus oil for heavy infestations
Yellow spots and mottling on leaves	Spider mites	Spray Garrett Juice plus garlic and add citrus oil for heavy infestations
Plants yellow from bottom up, dark spots form on leaves	Early blight fungus	Work on improving soil health, treat soil with cornmeal, and spray foliage with with Garrett Juice plus garlic and potassium bicarbonate
Leaves are curled and twisted, plants are stunted	Virus	Work on improving soil health, treat soil with cornmeal, and spray foliage with Garrett Juice plus garlic and potassium bicarbonate; cover with floating row cover until plants are large.
Leaves missing large holes in fruit, black droppings	Tomato hornworm	Hand pick or treat foliage with *Bacillus thuringiensis*
Small worms in fruit near stem end	Pinworms	Spray Garrett Juice plus garlic and add citrus oil for heavy infestations
Plants suddenly wilt and die	Southern blight fungus	Work on improving soil health, treat soil with cornmeal, and spray foliage with Garrett Juice plus garlic and potassium bicarbonate. Change varieties.*
Fruits crack around stem end	Heat, variety, uneven soil moisture	Mulch, water properly, and use large, flat fruited varieties

TOMATO TROUBLE SOLVER (Continued)

SYMPTOMS	CAUSES	SOLUTIONS
Bottom of tomatoes turn black	Blossom-end rot	Maintain even soil moisture and apply lava sand and soft rock phosphate
Fruits rough, "catfaced"	Cold temperatures during bloom	Fruit that set when temperatures are below 55° will often be misshapened, rough, but edible.
Jagged holes in fruit	Bird damage	Plant chili pequins, birds like the peppers better than tomatoes; use red Christmas ornaments
Whitish, water-soaked areas on the tomatoes	Sun scald	Cage the plants and spray regularly with Garrett Juice

*Example: Spring Giant is especially subject to southern blight north of San Antonio, but not south of San Antonio.

Ripe Tomatoes

Turnip/Rutabaga

Common Name: Turnip/Rutabaga

Botanical Name: Turnip—*Brassica rapa;* Rutabaga—*Brassica napus*

Family: *Cruciferae*

Type and Use: Bienniel, grown as an annual, with edible greens and roots.

Location: Sun to partial shade

Planting Dates: For spring, plant seed 4–8 weeks before frost. For fall, plant seed 6–8 weeks before first average frost. In general, February 7–March 10 and September 1–October 15.

Planting Method: Broadcast or plant seed in rows ¼–½ inch deep

Seed Emergence: 3–10 days at 60–105°

Harvest Time: For turnips, harvest greens in 30 days, roots in 45–60 days. For rutabagas, greens in 40 days and roots in 75–100 days after seeding.

Height: 8–15 inches

Spread: 8–10 inches

Final Spacing: 2 inches apart for greens and 4 inches apart for roots

Growth Habits: Turnips are a leafy vegetable with a swollen, edible root. They mature during cool temperatures. Rutabagas are similar, but have a longer growing season and do best when planted for fall harvest.

Culture: Prepare soil with the standard ingredients: compost, lava sand, organic fertilizer, and Texas Greensand in alkaline soils. Use high-calcium lime in sandy, acid soils. Fertilize twice per growing season and spray at least monthly with Garrett Juice. Maintain even soil moisture level, especially as the plants mature. Mulching the bare soil around the plants is very important.

Troubles and Solutions: Grubworms and wire worms are the most troublesome pests. They can be controlled with beneficial nematodes, citrus products, and sugar. Aphids and flea beetles can be controlled with Garrett Juice and the release of beneficial insects such as loopers; caterpillars can be controlled with trichogramma wasps and Bt products. Citrus-based sprays

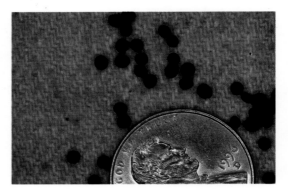

Turnip Seed

are also effective for these pests. Cracked or misshapen roots can be avoided by maintaining an even moisture level.

Harvest and Storage: Turnip greens, even the small ones removed during thinning, can be used in salads. Turnip greens can be harvested by the cut-and-come-again method or by removal of the whole plant.

Store the turnips at 32–40° for up to 12 weeks. The greens will only last a few days.

Varieties: 'Just Right,' 'Royal Globe,' 'Tokyo Cross,' 'White Lady,' 'All Top,' 'Purple Top' Turnip greens—'Top Seven,' 'Crawford,' 'Dr. Poindexter'. Rutabagas—'American Purple Top,' 'White Globe,' 'Shogun'

Notes: Rutabaga greens are not normally eaten due to toughness and an "off taste."

TURNIP/RUTABAGA TROUBLE SOLVER

SYMPTOMS	CAUSES	SOLUTIONS
Seedlings don't emerge	Old seed	Always use fresh seed
	Seed planted too deep	Don't plant deeper than ¼", ½" in heavy soils
	Dry soil	Maintain even soil moisture
Seedlings die quickly	Damping-off fungus	Work on improving soil health, treat soil with cornmeal, and spray foliage with Garrett Juice plus garlic and potassium bicarbonate
Sluggish growth and poor color	Acid soil	Apply high-calcium lime, fireplace ashes, granite sand
	Wet soil	Avoid overwatering, use raised beds
	Low fertility	Add organic fertilizer
Shot holes in leaves	Flea beetles	Spray Garrett Juice plus garlic and add citrus oil for heavy infestations
Small football-shaped insects on leaves	Aphids	Spray plants with Garrett Juice and release lady beetles
Spindly, weak plants	Crowded plants	Use the correct in-row spacing
Roots don't enlarge	Wrong variety	Use root forming variety
	Crowded plants	Thin to proper spacing
Plants flower prematurely	Cold weather followed by hot weather	Plant at the correct time to avoid temperatures below 45°
Roots cracked and misshapened	High levels of barnyard manure	If manure is used, it should be worked into the soil several months prior to planting or composted first
	Low soil moisture	Maintain soil moisture as roots near maturity
Bitter taste	Overmature	Harvest earlier
	Heat	Best for plants to mature at temperatures between 40 and 80°
White pustules under leaves	White rust fungus	Work on improving soil health, treat soil with cornmeal, and spray foliage with Garrett Juice plus garlic and potassium bicarbonate
Yellow spots on upper leaf surface, downy growth on lower surface	Downy mildew fungus	Work on improving soil health, treat soil with cornmeal, and spray foliage with Garrett Juice plus garlic and potassium bicarbonate
Worms on foliage	Cabbage loopers or greenworms	Release trichogramma wasps; control with *Bacillus thuringiensis* as a last resort

Viburnum, Rusty Blackhaw

Common Names: Rusty Blackhaw Viburnum
Botanical Name: *Viburnum rufidulum*
Family: *Caprifoliaceae*
Type and Use: Ornamental deciduous tree with edible berries
Location: Full sun to shade
Planting Dates: Year-round
Planting Method: Seed or cuttings
Harvest Time: Pick the blue-black berries in late summer when they are ripe—if you can get them before the birds do.
Height: 20 feet
Spread: 20 feet
Final Spacing: 10–20 feet

Growth Habits: Small-growing deciduous tree with white flower clusters in the spring, glossy leaves, and beautiful red fall color. Can grow to 40 feet, but that's rare.
Culture: Easy to grow in any well-drained soil. The plant is drought-tolerant and has few problems. Grows in a range of light locations from full sun to rather heavy shade.
Troubles and Solutions: Few problems other than poor drainage or overwatering.
Harvest and Storage Instructions: Pick and eat the berries in the late summer to early fall—but do it before the birds get there first.

Notes: Excellent native tree that should be used much more in Texas gardens.

Walnut, Black

Common Name: Walnut, Black
Botanical Name: *Juglans nigra*
Family: *Juglanaceae*
Type & Use: Deciduous shade tree with edible nuts
Location: full sun
Planting Dates: Year-round
Planting Method: Transplants. Walnut trees can be planted bare-rooted or from containers. They can also be planted from seed.
Seed Emergence: Seeds will germinate from a fall planting or a 60–120 day cooling at 34–41° and spring planting.
Height: 50–60'
Spread: 40–50'
Final Spacing: 20'–50'
Growth Habits: Walnut trees have an open-branching character, large common leaves, dark bark, and yellow fall color. Moderate to slow growth.
Culture: Walnut trees like deep soil but can grow in various kinds of soil. Fertilize once a year and keep the root system mulched. Spray the foliage with the fruit tree and pecan program. (See Pecan on page 153.)
Troubles and Solutions: Roots and leaves produce a harmful toxin that hurts other plants especially garden plants like tomatoes. The solution is to keep the walnut tree away by themselves.
Harvest and Storage: Gather the nuts in the fall when they release from the tree. Store the nuts in a dry, cool place prior to use. Our native black walnut, which is the only one that grows here, has an extremely hard shell that has to be broken with a hammer. The meat is delicious if you can get it out.

Watermelon Female Flower

Watermelon

Common Name: Watermelon

Botanical Name: *Citrullus vulgaris*

Family: *Cucurbitaecea*

Type and Use: Annual vining plant with edible fruit

Location: Full sun

Planting Dates: Spring after all danger of frost is over and soil temperature is at least 70°. In general, April 1–30 and July 10–31.

Planting Method: Directly plant the seed ¾–1 inch deep. Use 3–4 seeds per spot, hill, or hole. Thin down to the two strongest and most vigorous seedlings. Pinch the unwanted ones off at the ground so the remaining roots won't be damaged.

Seed Emergence: 4–14 days at 68–90°

Harvest Time: Harvest in 75–100 days, when the melons are ripe. Using transplants instead of seeds can shorten the development time by about 10 days.

Height/Spread: They have large-growing vines that will climb and spread to over 20 feet. Watermelon vines need lots of room.

Final Spacing: 4–10 feet, rows 6 feet apart. Hills can take up as much as 25 square feet.

Growth Habits: Watermelon has small yellow flowers and large stems and leaves. The fruit is either yellow or red. It is deep-rooted and drought-tolerant.

Culture: Watermelon loves sandy soil but will grow in any soil, especially if well-prepared with compost, lava sand, rock phosphate, and organic fertilizer. Add Texas Greensand to alkaline soils and high-calci-

Watermelon

Moon and Stars Seed

Watermelon Yellow Seed

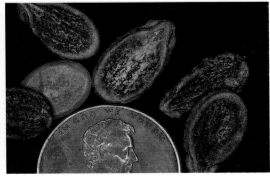

Big Red Watermelon Seed

um lime to the sandy, acid soils. Apply a second application of organic fertilizer at 20 pounds per 1,000 square feet as the plants begin to vine.

Troubles and Solutions: Aphids are controlled with soil health, molasses and water spray, and release of lady beetles. Poor pollination can be prevented by encouraging biodiversity with a basic organic program. Blossom-end rot is controlled with even soil moisture and high calcium in sandy soils, soft rock phosphate, or alfalfa meal for the alkaline soils. The condition called white heart can be prevented by avoiding overfertilization. Treat powdery mildew outbreaks with Garrett Juice plus garlic and potassium bicarbonate. Treat damping-off and nematodes with cornmeal.

Harvest and Storage: Watermelons are ripe and ready for harvest when the tendril nearest the fruit has completely turned dry and brown or the second one out is brown. The other method to tell whether the fruit is ready is to thump it; mature fruit has a deep, dull sound. The ground spot should be an off-yellow and rough to the touch. Will store for 2 to 4 weeks.

Varieties: 'Crimson Sweet,' 'Sugar Baby,' 'Royal Sweet,' 'Charleston Gary,' 'Jubilee' Seedless will do well in black soil but needs a pollinator such as 'Sugar Baby.'

Notes: Some gardeners like to use black plastic to warm the soil faster. Holes are cut in the plastic for the seeds. We like the natural way better.

Zucchini. *See Squash.*

WATERMELON TROUBLE SOLVER

SYMPTOMS	CAUSES	SOLUTIONS
Poor germination	Old seed	Always use fresh seed
	Cold soil	Wait to plant seed until soil temperature is above 70°
	Seed planted too deep	Plant seed 1–1½″ deep; use deeper depth in lighter soils
	Lack of soil moisture	Water
Seedlings or transplants die suddenly	Damping-off fungus	Work on improving soil health, treat soil with cornmeal, and spray foliage with Garrett Juice plus garlic and potassium bicarbonate
	Cutworms	Treat with DE, crushed red pepper, and spray with garlic-pepper tea
Slow growth and lack of good color	Cold soil	Plant when soil temperature is above 70°
	Cold air	Plant after night temperatures remain above 60°
	Wet soil	Avoid overwatering and improve drainage
	Low fertility	Add organic fertilizer
	Wrong soil	Add high-calcium lime
	Nematodes	Drench soil with citrus oil or till citrus pulp into soil
Older leaves wither and die	Downy mildew fungus	Work on improving soil health, treat soil with cornmeal, and spray foliage with Garrett Juice plus garlic and potassium bicarbonate
Crown leaves die and bleeding on stems	Gummy stem blight fungus	Work on improving soil health, treat soil with cornmeal and spray foliage with Garrett Juice plus garlic and potassium bicarbonate
Flowers abort	Lack of pollination	Plant lots of flowering plants and encourage beneficial insects
Misshapen and gourdy fruit	Moisture stress	Prepare soil properly; avoid crowded growing conditions; water careful and keep soil mulched
Stunted plant with mottled leaves	Virus	Work on improving soil health, treat soil with cornmeal, and spray foliage with Garrett Juice plus garlic and potassium bicarbonate
Sudden wilt and death	Fusarium wilt	Work on improving soil health, treat soil with cornmeal, and spray foliage with Garrett Juice plus garlic and potassium bicarbonate
Good color but poor flavor	Cold air	Fruits that mature in cool weather will lack sugar and taste; avoid planting late
	Excess soil moisture	Use raised beds or hills and avoid overwatering
Large, white, tasteless area in fruit	White heart	Too much fertilizer
End of fruit shriveled, often black	Blossom-end rot	Uneven soil moisture and lack of available calcium; apply high-calcium lime in acidic soils and soft rock phosphorus in alkaline soils.

APPENDIX

RECOMMENDED VEGETABLE VARIETIES FOR TEXAS

Note: These are good varieties; however, they may not be the best in your environment.

Asparagus—UC 157, Jersey Giant, Jersey Gem

Beans (Lima)—Jackson Wonder, Florida Butter, Henderson Bush

Beans (Pinto)—UI-114, Dwarf Horticultural, Luna

Beans (Snap)—Topcrop, Tendercrop, Tendergreen, Kentucky Wonder, Greencrop

Beets—Pacemaker, Detroit Dark Red

Broccoli—Galaxy, Packman, Crusier, Baccus, Green Comet

Cabbage—Bravo, Rio Verde, Red Rookie

Carrots—Texas Gold Spike, Orlando Gold

Cauliflower—Snow Crown, Snow King

Chinese Cabbage—Jade Pagoda, Monument, Napa, China Pride

Cucumbers (Pickling)—Calypso, Carolina

Cucumbers (Slicers)—Poinsett 76, Sweet Success, Dasher II, Sweet Clice

Eggplant—Florida Market, Florida High Bush

Eggplant (Oriental)—Tycoon

Garlic—Texas White

Greens (Collards)—Blue Max, Georgia Southern

Greens (Chard)—Lucullus, Ruby

Kale—Vates, Blue Knight

Lettuce (Crips Head)—Mission

Lettuce (Loose Leaf)—Prizehead, Red Sails, Black-Seeded Simpson

Lettuce (Butter Head)—Buttercrunch

Melons (Cantaloupe)—Mission, Primo, Caravelle

Melons (Honey Dew)—TAM Dew, Honey Star

Mustard—Green Wave, Tendergreen, Southern Giant Curl

Okra—Clemson Spineless, Lee, Emerald, Beck's Big

Onion (Bulb)—Texas 1015Y, Early Grano 502, Granex 33

Onion (Green)—Evergreen Bunching, Crystal Wax

Pepper (Bell)—Shamrock, Jupiter, Valencia—orange, Lilac, Big Bertha, Pimento

Pepper (Hot)—Habañero, Cruz, Long Red Cayenne, Serrano

Potatoes (Irish)—Red: Red LaSoda, Norland

Potatoes (White)—Kennebec

Potatoes (Sweet)—Beauregard, TAMU Corder, Centennial, Jewel

Pumpkin (Large)—Connecticut Field, Big Max

Pumpkin (Medium)—Jack O'Lantern, Funny Face

Pumpkin (Small)—Jack-Be-Little

Radish—Cherry Belle, Sparkler, White Icicle

Southern Peas (Purple Hulls)—Purple Hulls: Texas Pink Eye

Southern Peas (Cream)—Cream 40, Champion

Southern Peas (Black-Eyed)—California #5

Southern Peas (Crowder)—Mississippi Silver, Zipper

Spinach—Savoy: Green Valley II, Ozarka II, Fall Green, Coho (semi-savoy)

Squash (Summer)—Goldie, Gold Bar, Multipik

Squash (Zucchini)—President, Senator

Squash (Butternut)—Waltham, Early Butternut

Sweet Corn—Summer Sweet 7800, Sweet G-90, Kandy Korn, Silver Queen

Tomato—Bingo VF, Carnival Super Fantastic, Heatwave, Celebrity Presto, President, Merced, Sunny VF, Reisentraube

Tomato (Cherry)—Small Fry, Cherry Grande

Turnips—All Top, White Lady, Royal Globe II

Watermelon (Standard)—Jubilee, Royal Charleston, Royal Jubilee, Royal Sweet, Sangria. Sweet Seedless: Tri-X 313, King of Hearts.

Fruit and Nut Varieties for Texas

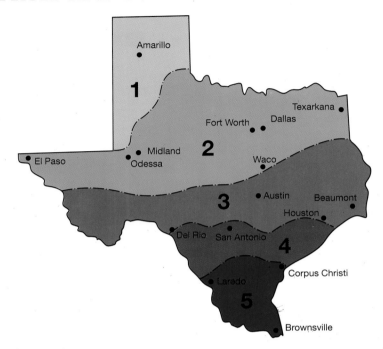

Zone 1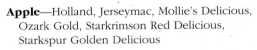

Apple—Granny Smith, Holland, Jerseymac, Prime Gold, Red Chief, Smoothee, Starkrimson Red Delicious, Starkspur Golden Delicious, Top Red, Gala

Apricot—Bryan, Hungarian, Moorpark, Manchurian, Wilson

Blackberry—Brazos, Rosborough, Womack

Cherry, Sour—Montmorency

Figs—Celeste, Texas Everbearing

Peach—Bicentennial, Denman, Jefferson, Milam, Ranger, Redglobe, Sentinel, Springold, Surecrop

Pear—Ayers, Kieffer, LeConte, Magness, Maxine, Moonglow, Orient, Surecrop

Plum—Allred, Bruce, Methley, Morris, Ozark Premier

Strawberry—Cardinal, Sunrise

Zone 2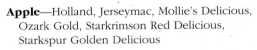

Apple—Holland, Jerseymac, Mollie's Delicious, Prime Gold, Red Chief, Smoothee, Starkrimson Red Delicious, Starkspur Golden Delicious, Top Red

Apricot—Bryan, Hungarian, Moorpark, Manchurian, Wilson

Blackberry—Brazos, Rosborough

Figs—Celeste, Texas Everbearing

Peach—Bicentennial, Denman, Dixiland, Frank, Harvester, Jefferson, Loring, Milam, Range, Redglobe, Redskin, Sentinel, Springold

Pear—Ayers, Garber, Kieffer, LeConte, Maxine, Moonglow, Orient, Zyers, Asian

Persimmon—Eureka, Hachiya, Izu

Plum—Allred, Bruce, Methley, Morris, Ozark Premier

Strawberry—Cardinal, Sunrise

Zone 3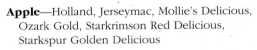

Apple—Holland, Jerseymac, Mollie's Delicious, Ozark Gold, Starkrimson Red Delicious, Starkspur Golden Delicious

Apricot—Bryan, Hungarian, Moorpark, Wilson

Blackberry—Brazos, Rosborough

Figs—Celeste, Texas Everbearing

Peach—Bicentennial, Dixiland, Frank, Harvester, Jefferson, June Gold, Loring, Milam, Redglobe, Redskin, Sentinel, Springold, Summergold

Pear—Ayers, Garber, Kieffer, LeConte, Maxine, Moonglow, Orient, Monterrey, Asian

Persimmon—Fuyu

Plum—Allred, Bruce, Methley, Morris, Ozark Premier

Strawberry—Cardinal, Sequoia, Sunrise, Tangi

Zone 4 ▪▪▪

Apple—Anna, Dorsett Golden, Ein Shemer, Mollie's Delicious

Apricot—Blenheim, Royal

Blackberry—Brazos, Rosborough

Cold Hardy Citrus—Changsha Tangarine, Eustic Limequat, Kumquat, Meyer Lemon, Satsuma

Figs—Alma, Celeste, Texas Everbearing

Peach—Bicentennial, Dixiland, Harvester June Gold, La Feliciana, Loring, Redskin, Rio Grande, Sam Houston, Sentinel, Springold

Pear—Moonglow, Kieffer, LeConte, Orient, Monterrey

Persimmon—Fuyu

Plum—Allred, Bruce, Methley, Santa Rosa

Strawberry—Douglas, Sequoia, Tangi, Tioga

Zone 5 ▪▪▪

Apple—Anna, Dorsett Golden, Ein Shemer

Apricot—Blenheim, Royal

Blackberry—Brazos, Brison, Rosborough

Cold-Tolerant Citrus—(Acid Citrus): Calamondin, Eustis Limequat, Kumquat, Meyer Lemon; (Mandarin Types): Changsha Tangerine, Clemtine, Orlando, Satsuma; (Oranges): Hamlin, Marrs, Navel

Figs—Alma, Celeste

Peach—EarliGrande, Early Amber, Floridabelle, McRed, Rio Grande, Sam Houston, Sun Red

Pear—Fanstil, Kieffer, LeConte, Orient, Pineapple, Monterrey

Persimmon—Tanerashi, Tamopan

Plum—Bruce, Methley, Santa Rosa

Strawberry—Douglas, Sequoia, Tangi, Tioga

GRAPE AND PECAN VARIETIES FOR TEXAS

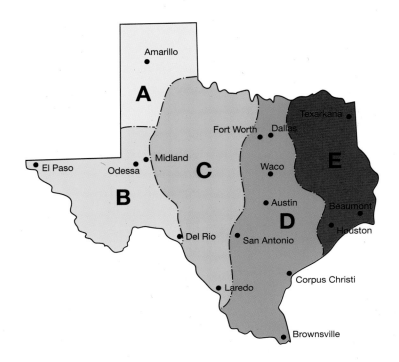

Region A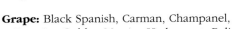

Grape: Black Spanish, Carman, Champanel, Favorite, Golden Muscat, Herbemont

Pecan: Cheyenne, Mohawk, Shawnee, Shoshoni, Pawnee

Region B

Grape: Black Spanish, Carman, Champanel, Favorite, Golden Muscat, Herbemont; Vinifera: Barbera, Chenin Blanc, Emerald Riesling, Ruby Cabernet, Thompson Seedless

Pecan: Cheyenne, Mohawk, Tejas, Western, Wichita

Region C

Grape: Black Spanish, Carman, Champanel, Favorite, Golden Muscat, Herbemont

Pecan: Caddo, Cheyenne, Choctaw, Kiowa, Mohawk, Shawnee, Sioux, Western, Wichita

Region D

Grape: Black Spanish, Carman, Champanel, Favorite, Golden Muscat, Herbemont, Reliance, Flame

Pecan: Caddo, Cape Fear, Cheyenne, Choctaw, Desirable, Kiowa, Shawnee, Kanza, Osage

Region E

Blueberry: Briteblue, Delite, Garden blue, Tifblue, Woodard

Grape: Black Spanish, Carman, Champanel, Favorite, Golden Muscat, Herbemont; Muscadine: Carlos, Cowart, Fry, Higgings, Jumbo, Magnolia, Regal

Pecan: Caddo, Cape Fear, Cheyenne, Choctaw, Desirable, Kiowa, Shawnee

EDIBLE AND MEDICINAL LANDSCAPING PLANTS

Shade Trees

Ginkgo—tea from leaves
Jujube—edible fruit
Linden—tea from flowers
Mulberry—fruit
Pecan—edible nuts
Persimmon—edible fruit
Walnut—edible nuts

Shrubs

Agarita—fruit for wine
Althea—edible flowers
Bay—tea and food seasoning from leaves
Germander—freshens air indoors
Pomegranate—fruit
Turk's cap—flowers and fruit for tea

Annuals

Begonias—edible flowers
Daylilies—edible flowers
Dianthus—edible flowers
Ginger—food, seasoning and tea from roots
Hibiscus—edible flowers
Johnny jump-ups—edible flowers
Nasturtium—edible leaves
Pansies—edible flowers
Peanuts—food
Purslane—edible leaves
Sunflower—edible seeds and flower petals

Vines

Beans and Peas—food
Gourds—dippers and bird houses
Grapes—food (fruit and leaves)
Luffa—sponges from the fruit, edible flowers
Malabar spinach—edible foliage
Passion flower—edible fruit, tea from leaves

Ornamental Trees

Apple—fruit and edible flower petals
Apricot—fruit and edible flower petals
Citrus—food
Crabapple—fruit and edible flower petals
Fig—fruit and edible flower petals
Mexican plum—fruit
Peach—fruit and edible flower petals
Pear—fruit and edible flower petals
Persimmon—fruit
Plum—fruit and edible flower petals
Redbud—edible flowers
Rusty blackhaw viburnum—edible berries
Witchhazel—tea from leaves

Perennials

Anise hyssop—edible flowers, foliage for tea
Blackberries—edible berries, foliage for tea
Chives—edible foliage and flowers
Garlic—edible flowers, greens and cloves
Hibiscus—edible flowers
Hoja santa—leaves for cooking with meats
Horsemint—insect repellent
Jerusalem artichoke—roots for food
Lavender—teas and insect repellent
Monarda—edible flowers and leaves for teas
Peppers—edible fruit
Purple coneflower—all plant parts for teas
Rosemary—food and tea from leaves
Roses—petals and hips for tea
Salvia—edible flowers, foliage for teas
Sweet marigold—food, flavoring and tea from leaves and flowers
Tansy—chopped and crushed foliage repels ants
Turk's cap—flowers and fruit for tea

Ground Covers

Clover—tea from leaves and flowers
Creeping thyme—teas and food flavoring
Gotu kola—tea from leaves
Mints—food and teas from flowers and leaves
Oregano—teas and food flavoring
Violets—leaves in salads and tea from flowers and leaves

Note: Pregnant women should avoid all strong herbs, and no plant should be ingested in excess by anyone. None of these should be eaten unless they are grown organically.

EDIBLE FLOWERS

Aloe vera
Althea
Apple
Arugula
Basil
Begonia
Borage
Broccoli
Calendula
Chicory
Chives—onion and garlic
Clover
Coriander
Dandelion
Dill
Elderberry
English daisy
Fennel
Hyssop
Lavender
Lemon
Lilac

Mint
Monarda—red flowered *M. didyma*
Mum (base of petal is bitter)
Mustard
Okra
Orange
Oregano
Pea (except for sweet peas)
Pineapple sage
Radish
Redbud
Rosemary
Scented geranium
Society garlic
Sweet woodruff
Squash blossoms
Thyme
Violet
Winter savory
Yucca (petals only)

EIGHT RULES FOR EDIBLE FLOWERS

1. Not all flowers are edible. Some are poisonous. Learn the difference.
2. Eat flowers only when you are positive they are edible and nontoxic.
3. Eat only flowers that have been grown organically.
4. Do not eat flowers from florists, nurseries, or garden centers unless you know they've been maintained organically.
5. Do not eat flowers if you have hay fever, asthma, or allergies.
6. Do not eat flowers growing on the side of the road.
7. Remove pistils and stamens from flowers before eating. Eat only the petals, especially of large flowers.
8. Introduce flowers into your diet the way you would new foods to a baby—one at a time in small quantities.

COMMON GREEN MANURE CROPS

Alfalfa. Deep-rooted legume grown throughout the United States. This crop does well in all but very sandy, clay, acid, or poorly drained soils. Apply lime if the pH is 6 or below, and add phosphate rock. Inoculate the seed with rhizobia bacteria when growing alfalfa for the first time. Sow seed in the spring to the north and east and in late summer elsewhere at 20–30 pounds of seed per acre or 1–2 pounds per 1,000 square feet. Alfalfa has high protein and high nitrogen content. It also contains calcium, magnesium, potassium, and many trace minerals. If cotton root rot appears, take the alfalfa out and use other annual winter legumes.

Alsike clover. Legume grown mostly in the northern states. This clover prefers fairly heavy, fertile loams, but does better on wet, acid soil than most clovers. Sow 6 to 10 pounds of seed per acre in the spring, or in the early fall in the south. Use ½–1 pounds per 1,000 square feet.

Alyce clover. Legume grown in the extreme southern regions. It prefers sandy or clay loams with good drainage. Sow in late spring, 15 to 20 pounds of scarified seed per acre. It is a summer-growing clover.

Austrian peas. Legume and winter crop for warmer climates. It prefers well-drained soils. Sow at 15 pounds per acre or 2–5 ounces per 1,000 square feet.

Barley. Non-legume grown in the north. It requires rich, loamy soil and does not perform well in acidic or sandy soil. In colder climates, sow winter varieties; elsewhere, sow spring varieties, 1½ bushels per acre.

Black medic. Legume grown throughout United States. Very closely related to alfalfa, black medic is a vigorous grower on reasonably fertile non-acidic soils. Sow 7 to 15 pounds of scarified, inoculated seed. In the north, sow seed in spring; in the south, plant in the fall. It needs ample calcium in the soil.

Buckwheat. Non-legume grown mostly in the northeast. It is one of the best choices for rebuilding poor or acid soils. It has an enormous, vigorous root system and is a good bee plant. Plant seed when the ground has warmed in late spring or early summer. Sow 2 bushels per acre or 2–3 pounds per 1,000 square feet.

Cowpea. Legume and a good soil builder because its powerful roots crack hardpans. Inoculate the seed when planting it the first time. Sow seed as soon as the soil is well warmed, broadcasting 80–100 pounds or sowing 20 pounds in 3 foot rows. Grows very quickly.

Crimson clover. Winter legume that does well on almost any fairly good soil but likes sandy soil best. On poor soil, grow cowpeas first for a preliminary buildup. Sow 30–40 pounds of unhulled seed or 15–20 pounds of hulled in fall. Hard-seeded strains volunteer from year to year in the south.

Hairy indigo. Summer legume grown in the south. Will tolerate a moderately poor sandy soil and will make a very tall, thick stand. Sow in early spring, 6–10 pounds broadcast, 3–5 if drilled.

Hubam. Winter legume for Austin and the south for fall planting only, at 10–30 pounds per acre. It will grow to 8 feet tall in calcium-rich soils.

Lasi clover. Lowest-growing white clover that is available.

Lespedeza. Legume grown in the south and as far north as Michigan in all types of soil. The northern species *L. cuneata* is particularly good for poor, sour soils. In the spring, sow 30–40 pounds of seed per acre. Fertilize with phosphate rock. Many varieties are available.

Millet. Non-legume grown in arid regions of the south and southwest. Does better on poor soil than many other forage or green manure crops. It is usually planted thickly at about 35 pounds of seed per acre. Many varieties are available.

Oats. Non-legume widely grown throughout North America. Oats can be grown on almost any soil provided the climate is cool and moist. Winter oats are only suited to very mild winters. In the spring, sow 2 to 3 bushels of seed per acre.

Persian clover. Winter legume grown in southern and Pacific states. This clover prefers heavy, moist soils. Sow 5 to 8 pounds of seed per acre in the fall.

Rape. Non-legume that is a good cover for short growing periods in summer. Sow at 5 to 8 ounces per 1,000 square feet. Excellent for grazing. Should be used more.

Red clover. Legume grown in most areas, but is most useful in the north. This clover will thrive in any well-drained soil rich in phosphorus. Its decay is of exceptional benefit to crops that succeed it. Sow seed early in the spring; 15 pounds of seed per acre is adequate, 4 to 8 ounces per 1,000 square feet.

Rye (cereal or elbon rye). Non-legume widely grown in the northeast. Rye tolerates many soil types, even very poor ones. It is easily cultivated and adaptable to any cool, dry climate. Recommended for nematode control when planted as a cover crop in gardens.

Ryegrass. Non-legume planted in the late summer or fall. Good plant for soil building and for crowding out nutgrass. Plant at 7–10 pounds per 1,000 square feet. Primarily for use on lawn grasses.

Soybeans. Summer legume, grown throughout North America. Soybeans thrive in nearly all kinds of soil. They can stand considerable drought. Use late-maturing varieties for best green manure results. Sow 60–100 pounds per acre, spring to mid-summer. For best results, inoculate the seed. Use 2 to 3 pounds per 1,000 square feet.

Sudangrass. Non-legume grown in all parts of United States. Sudangrass tolerates any soil except wet. It is a very fast grower and therefore excellent for quick organic matter production. In late spring, broadcast 40–50 pounds of seed per acre, 2 to 3 pounds per 1,000 square feet.

Sweet clover. Legume grown in all parts of United States in just about any soil. Plants are especially adept at utilizing rock fertilizers and are excellent honey plants. Sow 15 pounds of scarified seed to the acre, ½ to 1 pound per 1,000 square feet in fall or early spring. A fast-growing annual, white sweet clover can be turned under in the fall. Other varieties have their biggest roots in the spring of the second year, so turn them under then. Also sold as Hubam and Madrid. A great soil builder. It is a tall-growing clover.

Velvet beans. Legume grown in the south. One of the best crops for sandy, poor soils. Plants produce roots 30 feet long, vines up to 50 feet long. Sow seed in warm spring at 100 pounds per acre broadcast, or 25 to 30 pounds in wide rows.

Vetches. Legumes with varieties for all areas. Grow in any reasonably fertile soil with ample moisture. Hairy vetch does well in any soil and is the most winter-hardy variety. Hungarian is good for wet soils in areas having mild winters. In the north, sow seed in spring, elsewhere in the fall. Depending on the variety, 30–60 pounds will plant one acre.

Weeds. Whenever weeds do not steal needed plant food and moisture, they can be used as green manures to produce humus as well as to help make minerals available and conserve nitrogen.

Wheat. Non-legume grown throughout North America. Wheat prefers a fairly fertile soil with a pH of about 6.4. Broadcast 1½ bushels per acre in the fall.

Winter cover crops. The best winter cover crops are rye, wheat, oats, ryegrass, hairy vetch, and other legumes. All may be sown from mid-August to mid-October, so they are well-established before the frosts begin. During winter they hold the soil in place and prevent erosion. Winter cover crops usually feature large fibrous root systems that add organic matter to garden soil when plowed or spaded under. Plowing or spading is done in the spring. They are mostly used as green manure. The seeds of grasses and legumes should be mixed together 50/50. Shallow rooted grasses take nitrogen and moisture from the shallow soil. Legumes have deep roots and take nutrients and moistures from deep in the soil.

'Yuchi,' arrowleaf clover. A winter annual legume native to the Mediterranean. It is one of the best forages and produces the most tonage of forage per acre.

DISEASES AND SYMPTOMS

DISEASE	DESCRIPTION	PLANTS ATTACKED	CONTROL
Bacterial blight	Small dead spots with yellow halos on leaves	Beans	Practice crop rotation; don't work in a wet garden
Bacterial wilt	Leaves wilt and plant dies	Cucumbers, melons	Control cucumber beetle, which spreads the disease
Damping-off	Base of the stem near the soil pinched and bent over	Seeds and seedlings of most plants	Plant in well-drained soil; use sterile soil mix for indoor plants
Downy mildew	Irregular brown or yellow spots on upper leaf surface; purple or white hairy mold covering lower leaf surface	Brassicas, cucumbers, muskmelons	Plant resistant varieties; avoid wetting the top of plants when watering
Fusarium wilt	Yellowed, curled, and wilted lower leaves	Cucumbers, peppers potatoes, tomatoes	Plant resistant varieties; solarize the soil; destroy infected plants
Powdery mildew	Powdery white growth on the tops of leaves	Beans, cucumbers lettuce, peas	Plant resistant varieties; avoid overhead watering; water early in the day
Septoria leaf spot	On older leaves, yellow spots that later turn dark brown with tiny black spots in the middle	Blackberries, celery, parsley, tomatoes	Plant resistant varieties; solarize the soil; control weeds that can carry the fungus

RECOMMENDED READINGS

Acres USA Primer by Fred and Charles Walters is one of the best overall guides on organics and *Acres U.S.A.,* a monthly publication, is one of the best on eco-agriculture. The new name of the revised book is *Eco-Farm.* P.O. Box 8800, Metairie, LA 70011.

Ag Access is a catalog for books on alternative agriculture and horticulture methods. P.O. Box 2008, David, CA 95617, 916-756-7177.

Agriculture Testament and *Soil Health* by Sir Albert Howard are state-of-the-art guides to organics and the use of compost to bring soil back to health. They were written in the 1940s, but are still two of the best publications on the market. Oxford and Rodale Press.

The Albrecht Papers by William Albrecht is a compilation of papers by the late Dr. Albrecht and is considered the bible for managing soil health. Acres U.S.A.

Bread from Stones by Julius Hensel is a classic explaining the role of earth minerals in the production of wholesome food crops. Acres U.S.A.

Common Sense Pest Control by William Olkowski, Sheila Daar, and Helga Olkowski is an excellent reference for low-toxicity pest control. The Taunton Press.

The Dirt Doctor's Guide to Organic Gardening by J. Howard Garrett is a compilation of essays covering all aspects of organic gardening from bed preparation to making herb tea. University of Texas Press.

Establishment and Maintenance of Landscape Plants by Dr. Carl Whitcomb provides excellent research and backup for the practical approach to horticulture. Lacebark Publications.

The Garden-Ville Method (Lessons in Nature) is written by the king of compost, Malcolm Beck, one of the most knowledgeable people on organics in the country. Malcolm Beck, 7561 E. Evans Road, San Antonio, TX 78266, 210-651-6115.

Growing Great Garlic by Ron Engeland is the best book about garlic on the market. Acres USA, 800-355-5313.

Holistic Resource Management by Alan Savory is a book for anyone involved in the management of land. This book teaches you how to think and to treat people and their environments as one whole. Island Press, Washington, D.C.

Howard Garrett's Texas Organic Gardening provides organic information specifically for Texas, including plant varieties, planting instructions, and maintenance techniques. Houston: Gulf Publishing Company, 1993.

How to Have a Green Thumb Without an Aching Back, Exposition Press; *Gardening Without Work,* Devin-Adair; and *The No Work Gardening Book,* Rodale Press; by Ruth Stout, are great. She was a humorous writer, a philosopher, and an advocate of mulching.

J. Howard Garrett's Organic Manual offers easy-to-follow, money-saving advice on the proper selection, installation, and maintenance of organic landscaping and gardening. The Summit Group.

Nature's Silent Music by Dr. Phil Callahan explains how to preserve the health of the land by avoiding toxic chemicals and

The Organic Method Primer by Bargyla and Gylver Rateaver, San Diego, California

The One-Straw Revolution by Masanobu Fukuoka is an introduction to natural farming and an excellent book on the philosophy and practicality of organic gardening from one of Japan's living legends.

Passion Flowers by John Vanderplank is the ultimate book on the fascinating passion flower. Just ignore the chemical recommendations. MIT Press.

Plants of the Metroplex by Howard Garrett is totally revised and covers the trees, shrubs, ground covers, vines, and flowers that do well and those that don't do well. University of Texas Press.

Seaweed and Plant Growth by Dr. T. L. Senn explains in detail the wonderful powers of seaweed as a fertilizer, growth stimulator, and pest repellent.

The Secret Life of Compost by Malcolm Beck is a "how-to" and "why" guide to composting. Acres U.S.A.

Science in Agriculture by Dr. Arden Anderson is a "must-have" and "must-study" book for anyone interested in eco-agriculture. Acres U.S.A.

Silent Spring by Rachel Carson is a must-read. If you don't convert to organics after reading this classic, you never will. The Riverside Press, Cambridge.

The Three Sisters: Exploring an Iroquois Garden is a Cornell Cooperative Extension publication. Requests should be sent to Cornell University, Media Services Resource Center, 7 BTP, Ithaca, NY 14850.

Weeds by Charles Walters is a thorough review and explanation of how to control weeds through soil management. Acres U.S.A.

INDEX

Note: Numbers in boldface type indicate photos.

J. Howard Garrett is the host of the Dallas gardening show "The Natural Way," a columnist for the *Dallas Morning News,* and the author of several gardening books, including Gulf's *Texas Organic Gardening.*

Long-time organic farmer **C. Malcolm Beck** is the founder of Garden-Ville Fertilizer Company. Garden-Ville was founded in 1957 by Malcolm and Delphine Beck as a family firm successfully operating without using any toxic pesticides or chemicals. In 1980, Garden-Ville Fertilizer Company was incorporated and is a leader in composting and recycling, and has created and produced many new products for the horticulture industry.